Gangster's Moll

My life has been like a red tap that pours cold water and a blue tap that pours hot water!

Marilyn Wisbey
8th August 2000,
Acton Court Hotel, Stockport

Gangster's Moll

MARILYN WISBEY

LITTLE, BROWN AND COMPANY

A *Little, Brown* Book

First published in Great Britain in 2001
by Little, Brown and Company

Copyright © Marilyn Wisbey and Rosanne Gilbert 2001
All pictures copyright © Marilyn Wisbey 2001

Every reasonable effort has been made to acknowledge the ownership of
copyrighted photographs included in this book. Any errors that have
inadvertently occurred will be corrected in subsequent editions provided
notification is sent to the publisher.

The moral right of the authors has been asserted

A CIP catalogue record for this book
is available from the British Library

ISBN 0 316 85208 2

Typeset in Centaur by M Rules
Printed and bound in Great Britain by
Clays Ltd, St Ives plc

Little, Brown and Company (UK)
Brettenham House
Lancaster Place
London WC2E 7EN

For the men in my life:
My darling son Jonathan, my courageous
father Tommy, my kind friend Frank, my
funny ex-Valentines, plus my beloved four-
legged friend Danny, R.I.P.

Most of all to my amazing mother,
Renée (so sorry I've let you down), and to my
grandchildren (I hope you never follow in my
footsteps! Or if you do, you make a better
success of your life than me!).

Also in memory of my darling sister Lorraine –
I miss you so much – and my dear friend
Michael Corbett. Tragically lost but never
forgotten – the good die young! And to my
friend Terry Sansom, Junior – simply the best.
You suffered your guilt greatly. And Rita
Howell who tragically died aged 45, R. I. P.

Acknowledgements

My thanks go out to all those people who have come on our Gangland Tour, and listened to these stories straight from the horse's mouth (though not in bed!). We aim to give a truthful insight into the South London community we were part of, without all the fabrication, exaggeration and rumours you sometimes see in the media.

My thanks also to Anglia TV, the Indian Army Museum, Phil and the boys from Walthamstow, the boys from the Two Pups in Wokingham, Tony Craze, the Stockbrokers from London Wall, Kenny from the Old Red Lion on the Scottish borders, Roger and Deggie from Chester, Michael Dalton and Chris from Cleethorpes, Tony Burns and Repton Boys' Boxing Club, Tony Lockwood and Philippa, Jack Trickett and Avril, Patrick Newley, the BBC's Frank Symonds, Tony (fruitcake) and all from Southend, Boo-Boo from Stockport, Becky, Mark and Jan, Vincent Haynes from the music hall, Shoreditch, The Jermyn Street Theatre, The Andrew Lane Theatre, Dublin and RTE.

Special thanks to Barbara Boote, Linda Silverman and all at Little, Brown, and to James Morton, for having faith in me.

Contents

Introduction

When you come home after a visit to the abortion clinic, you don't need a raid from the Drugs Squad. But that's exactly what I got on 8 June 1988. It was a really beautiful day outside our flat; the sun was shining and everybody on the streets was eating ice-cream. I felt so hot and very tired. I said to my Mum, 'I think I'll have a lie-down.' And she said, 'I think I'll have one too.' We're like that. Just like sisters.

The front buzzer went fifteen minutes later. We were all living in Duncan Street, Islington, in a little two-bedroom flat I had on the fourth floor. Mum and I were sharing a room and my boy Jonathan had his own. Tom, my father, slept on the sofa when he was there. Mum and Dad had just come back from America and were waiting for their tenants to move out from their place.

My mother didn't hear anyone but I heard a tremendous

bang on the door. 'Who is it?' I shouted. 'Police, open up!' I quickly jumped up, saying to Mum, 'What the hell are they here for? Have we got anything here?' – meaning like tom.[1] Mum was always buying bits and pieces and wasn't always too careful of their pedigree but she said, 'Not that I know of, so let them in.' I opened the door carefully and quickly said, 'Wait a minute – I hope you've got a search warrant.' Then up came a piece of paper which was shoved in my face and in walked about eight plain-clothes police with all the usual rabbit that they always have. They never gave us a chance. My mother asked them what they were looking for and they said, 'The usual – stolen jewellery.' She asked them if they wanted a cup of tea and I suddenly realised that I had half a gram of coke in my handbag from the previous night. I always bought a bit when I was going to a club. I thought, 'Oh my God, no', and started shaking. I couldn't stop. It's funny when you're innocent, you always feel guilty, it's as if your mind says to you, 'You're guilty!' Everything seems worse than it really is at the time.

In all the confusion I just had time to take the wrap of coke out of my bag and then I heard Mum say to the police, 'There's only my handbags and all my husband's suits in the bedroom.' I asked if I could go to the toilet and I had to have a policeman wait outside. Thank God there was no police-woman or she'd have made me keep the door open. I got rid of the wrap down the pan and felt like a schoolkid when you have taken the top layer off a box of chocolates and eaten all the nice ones.

Then I was followed into the living room. It's such a humili-ation watching complete strangers ransacking your home. I

[1] 'Tom' is the cockney slang word for Tom Foolery – Jewellery.

suppose as police go, they weren't that bad. I think nine times out of ten they are more frightened of you if the truth be known. Then, after they had drunk their tea, the bombshell was dropped.

'Martin, we've found it!' Now there's me thinking they wouldn't make that big a fuss over a small bit of white Charlie and I wondered if I had left a gram or two in some old handbag. Surely not all this fuss, Marilyn, I thought. I knew I should have let that Ange the Gannet have the last few lines the previous night. As I stood next to Mum, there it was: one kilo of the stuff wrapped in brown paper. 'You know you're in very serious trouble,' said DS Martin Gill. 'You'll get fifteen years for this,' and with that we were asked to wait. Him and his colleagues had smiles on their faces as if they had backed a 100-1 winner at Epsom on Derby Day, 'Where's your father?' they asked and as I went to dial a number my hand was pushed away.

They took some articles in see-through sacks and I shouted to them, 'I hope you're not going to show the whole world and its mother – can't you cover them up, please?' We were then taken away in a white police van to pick up another suspect, Chris Scarfe, who was a lovely man of about sixty. He was a sort of partner in our flower shop – My Fair Lady in Exmouth Market. They'd found a whole lot of powder and he was crying his eyes out. He was telling the police, 'Look, it's only flower food!' So I said to him, 'Don't worry, Chris, just keep your mouth shut. They know you're only an assistant that works in the shop.' He just kept on crying. Nothing like this had ever happened to him before.

I got Kathy Dudley to look after Jonathan. Kathy's dad and mine had been close friends. At the time Reggie Dudley was away along with 'Fat Bobby' Maynard over the Epping Torso murder[2]. She was also a friend of a friend, Harry Hicks, who must be just about the only person I know who's never been in prison.

We got taken to Barking police station, where we were put in separate cells. After they tried to question us a bit they knew it was a waste of time and then all I did was sleep. I was asleep on the hard bench in the cell when finally the jailer said that I had someone here to see me. It was a solicitor sent in to me, Jerry Coffey. At first I was unwilling to talk to him because I thought he was the police 'duty' solicitor, but then I remembered meeting him once socially. I knew then he must have been sent to represent us.

He tried to get us bail the next day at Redbridge Magistrates' Court, but they remanded Mum and me in custody. They had arrested Jimmy Hussey who was also on the Great Train Robbery with Dad. They'd been watching Dad and Jimmy in a park and they'd seen Dad hand him a parcel. They'd followed Jimmy who'd taken a cab to Streatham and nicked him there, but Tommy was long gone. I suppose they were holding us as a sort of hostage for Dad. Well, I thought me and my Mum were going to a women's prison, but it was in the days when prisons were overcrowded and they were using police cells for remand prisoners. After a night at Barking they took us to the dispersal centre at Lambeth and I said to one policeman, 'Well, where are we going now?' and he said, 'Oh

---

[2] Dudley and Maynard were convicted in 1977 of the murders of Billy Moseley and his friend Mickey Cornwall. Moseley's body was cut up and his head was later found thawing in an Islington public lavatory. Despite the fact that the evidence was not strong and a principal witness against them, Tony Wild, withdrew his statement, they served over 20 years before Dudley was released. Maynard at the time of writing was still in prison.

you're going to a real posh gaff, you'll have your own television and all that. It's in Hyde Park.' I said to Mum, 'That's handy, at least we can watch the racing from Royal Ascot on the television.' Little did we know it was a small tuppenny-ha'penny police station right in the centre of the park.

Dogs were barking non-stop. There were a number of us and we were all put in these tiny filthy cells, two in each as there was six of us. As we went and sat down I said to my Mum, 'Ah, they even have pink toilet paper, that's unusual.' All you could see was all pink toilet paper sticking out of what was now air vents, but I thought it was good of them to supply such nice toilet paper. My Mum said, 'No, it's to keep the cold out, dopey.' I laughed.

As I looked through the sliding opening there was an officer putting names and charges up on a blackboard; three of us was for drugs, two for armed robbery and one for attempted murder. I was gobsmacked. After that I rang the bell and eventually an officer's face peered straight into mine. 'Yes, what's the problem?' I said, 'Can you tell them to shut them barking dogs up, please, they've not stopped since we have been here.' He gave me quite a stern look. Then I said, 'Better still, can you take us back to Barking police station, it's much quieter there?' He laughed and he shut the sliding door in my face.

One of the others in the cells, a poor Moroccan girl, was crying as she was cold from coming off heroin. I kept ringing the bell to ask the officer but no one came for what seemed like hours. Eventually an officer did come and I said, 'Please give the Moroccan girl this cotton vest of mine as she is very cold, plus she needs to see a doctor.' For once he was one of those humane officers and I gave him my vest. She shouted with a quiver in her voice, 'Thank you.' That night was broken up with the police dogs barking and phones ringing, but at least Mum and me were together. I thought of my Jonathan aged fifteen; what must he think of us? He hated it even when the Train Robbery was mentioned in any newspapers or books, he was just getting to like running his own business as he had a market stall. Then I started to worry about my Mum.

We were there overnight. Next day there's room in Holloway and we're transferred. We were all in a coach with me handcuffed to Mum. It took sixteen uniformed coppers to look after us six females. As I sat near the coach window, my Mum was chatting to another young blonde girl who had been crying on the coach the previous day. 'Oh,' Mum said, 'Cindy, to think one of us six is here for attempted murder. I wonder if it's that quiet girl with long black hair.' Cindy said, 'No, Renée, it's me.' 'What?' my Mum gulped. 'What in the hell happened?' 'Me and another girl with a black guy mugged a woman in her forties over in South London – Woolwich. It was the way she fell, we didn't mean to hit her that hard.' And she started crying again. We'd wondered why she kept crying earlier on the coach. You can never tell if people are telling the truth. For all I know she'd stabbed the woman and couldn't bring herself to admit it.

My Mum said, 'For heaven's sake, how much did you get out of it?' She snivelled and said, 'Only twenty each.' Mum and I chorused in and said, 'Twenty pounds!' My Mum turned round to her and said, 'Why didn't you go to Harrods and nick a fur coat if you needed money that bad, or go on the game?'

There was a radio in the coach and it was playing that Kylie Minogue song, 'I Should be so Lucky'. Every time I hear it I think of Mum and me that day. On the way down Oxford Street as we passed Selfridges, Mum said, 'Just to think we were there a couple of days ago having ice-cream sundaes. I knew I should have bought that new garden furniture for two and a half grand.' In all the bad situations in life the best thing to do is keep your head together and always try and keep your sense of humour. I think if you have no sense of humour in your soul you might as well take 100 paracetamol and die. But this time Mum and I just looked at each other with tears in our eyes.

Looking back, I knew we were right in it. We'd planned to go to Royal Ascot the following day. We'd really been looking forward to meeting all the ex-shoplifters — Olive Cornell, Shirley Pitts and the others that met up in Tatts enclosure for a reunion every year. As usual we'd bought new hats, handbags and shoes from Harrods. Mum and I weren't ever good-class hoisters, but we did buy a bit of gear in those days and, of course, we knew them all.

And so there we were the next thing in Holloway prison. My mum was down on one end of the landing and me on the other — on our hands and knees scrubbing. All I could hear was Mum saying over and over again, 'That fucking Tommy Wisbey — wait till I see him!'

I

Growing Up

My parents named me Marilyn after Marilyn Monroe who was my Mum's screen idol. Late while she was carrying me she craved the cockney dish of jellied eels and she made my father, Tommy, trek all the way down the Walworth Road in a December blizzard to get two cartons. On his way back, he noticed a large brown satchel. He had a look in what he thought was going to be an empty bag and there were two packets each with £50 in them, so Christmas was extra special that year. My Mum said he looked like a smiling snowman by the time he come back. Mum and I missed out on the family's New Year's Eve knees-up party. My due date was 31 December, but I came late on 3 January 1954 – weighing in at 7 pounds 8 oz, with loads of black hair and blue eyes, and making me the sign of Capricorn, the frolicking goat, and so a climber. And I think I've climbed and climbed and climbed! They're also meant to be nimble-footed and obstinate. Obstinate, yes, but I'm not so sure about the nimble-footed.

In those days Mum and Dad had two rooms on the top

floor of a big Victorian house in Sharstead Street, Kennington, in South London. The toilet and bathroom had to be shared with the landlady and her family and all the others in the house. My Dad worked for his dad, also Thomas Wisbey, who had a small bottle recycling business in Occupation Road, Walworth. My Mum, Renée Margaret, was a seamstress, born on the same day as Princess Margaret – which, I suppose, is why they gave her that second name.

My grandad was strict with the boys in his family. He was a quiet man, grumpy-looking when he got older, but he did have a very quick wit and was never lost for a sharp answer. Looking back on him now I think he had more brains than any man I knew, but I never did really get to know him as a person and now I wish I had. He was from the Victorian era and to express affection was unmasculine for his generation.

Then, after Dad went away, the family got separated. Grandad's wife – my nan, Florence, who was always known as Flo – was an excellent cook and mother and hard worker. She worked for Unilever as a cleaner and she was the typical mum indoors doing what her husband asked of her. She bore five children, three boys and two girls, and when I was born my aunts and uncles spoiled me rotten.

My grandmother on my mother's side was a real strong hard-working character, a lovely lady, Jane Elizabeth Hill. Her husband, George Albert, was some sort of cousin to Billy Hill, who ran Soho in the 1950s. George died when he was 44. He came back from the war with TB and he never recovered. Jane was left to bring up six kids under the age of 14. She was a moneylender, a staunch Conservative voter and, like many of her generation, she would have terrific piano parties.

My Mum would tell me about the first time she took my Dad back to Nan's home in Camberwell Road. They were kissing and cuddling in the passageway and suddenly there's a thunderclap. Jane's always had a bit of wind trouble and now she's on her way to the lavatory and has heard something downstairs. She calls out, 'Is that you, Renée?' and comes down with her winceyette nightdress tucked in the drawers she wore in bed. 'Oh, Mum,' says my mother, 'this is Tommy.' Dad loved her straight away.

When Mum was courting my Dad, her gang of friends included Maureen Foreman and her cousin Joanie. Mum was Maureen's bridesmaid at her wedding to Freddie Foreman, who did ten years for helping clean up after the Jack 'the Hat' McVitie murder, and he became my godfather when I was christened.

Poor Jane got knocked down in 1962 by a 66-year-old woman when she was crossing the lights at Camberwell Green. I don't know why my sister and I didn't go to the funeral but we regularly went visiting her gravestone in South London; we went nearly every Sunday. Once, coming out of the cemetery when my sister and I were standing on the kerb, our black poodle Perry ran out in the traffic and got knocked down himself. I was screaming my eyes out. But luckily he was just slightly injured.

Dad was an astute ducker and diver, which means that he was always on the look-out to make a bit of money and he'd try his hand at anything that would bring in something extra. He needed to be because his father kept him on tight wages. Well, there wasn't much of it to go round, and after six months Mum fell pregnant again, this time with Lorraine who was born a year and a bit after me on 7 April 1955. There was no such thing as betting shops in those days and street booking was illegal. If you were caught then it was up in front of the beaks at Lambeth and a fine. It was almost always the runners who was caught and, so Dad says, the coppers worked on a rota basis. They'd be told to have a sweep and they'd round up anyone about, whether they was working or not. Other times the bookies would post a look-out for the coppers. Most of Dad's ducking and diving at the time was running bets for his uncle and his friends or being a look-out, but he picked up a good bit of money.

As for my uncle and aunts and the older generation, Great-Uncle Tommy and Aunt Jessie Shaw were both really outgoing personalities. Most families had an old piano and at Christmas, weddings and for any other excuse there was nothing like having a party and a sing-song. They were all good workers except Uncle Lights, whose real name was John Hurndall and who was a bit work-shy. He was known as Lights because of his glasses – they were double lensed like light bulbs. His love was betting on horses or playing cards in the local spieler. Cards were a magnet for him. Other times you could find him in my Aunt Jane's little yellow kiosk in the Camberwell Road near where Bloomfield's, the petrol station, used to be. She sold tobacco, newspapers and chocolates, and Lights could be found sitting there with his cap on, with an untipped John Player cigarette dangling from his mouth, reading the *Sporting Life* and studying the form of slow horses. Any money they had came from her; she was the grafter.

Once Harry the market trader and Lights had a chance of collecting scrap-metal from a yard in the East End, in an old Bedford van with no tax or insurance. The van crashed and Lights had two cracked ribs and was taken to Plaistow Hospital. The police came and said who did the van belong to, so my uncle said some old gipsy guy who had just died. Lights soon had it away; he ran off from the hospital to go to his local one, King's College. As Lights was coming home my Aunt Jane was opening the kiosk.

It was freezing cold at about 5 a.m. when Lights appeared. Jane said, 'Where the hell have you been? You're supposed to be opening up. It's your turn, and I've got loads of washing to do at the baths today!' He replied, 'Jane, love, let me explain. I've been in the hospital all night with cracked ribs!' As he was saying this a Number 12 bus went past the kiosk, and Jane said to John, 'I wish you'd get under that Number 12 bus.' John said, 'I can't, love, I'm not a mechanic.'

It was nothing unusual for Lights to have a sense of humour. One day he went to get a mid-day *Standard* in his slippers and he came back four months later. He ended up doing time in Oxford prison. Being a wheeler and dealer with a great passion for gambling, he was the unluckiest man. Many times my sister and I would pass him in the kiosk, and he would always give us a couple of bars of chocolate.

Another time my Mum took us down to see Jane, who was saying that she hadn't seen John or received any housekeeping money for weeks. I think I was only about twelve at the time and I was earwigging. I piped up and said, 'Perhaps, Aunt Jane, he's met another lady and she has got your housekeeping money.' My Aunt Jane, with her Minnie Caldwell rollers in and her scarf done up like a turban, gave me such a stern look. My Mum went, 'Tut, tut, tut' and said, 'Go and play on the piano with Lorraine.' With that the phone rang, and it was my Uncle Lights who said to Jane, 'Go to the Lord Clyde, there's three G's waiting for you there.' She screams, 'What? Where have you been?' With that she undone her rollers and asked my Mum to go round to the pub with her; us two girls had to wait – the usual thing, with a packet of crisps and lemonade. Aunt Jane was walking around saying to my Mum, 'I hope he's had it off on the horses, Renée. I'll be able to pay my electric and phone bill, buy some new carpet for the stairs and curtains.' When they walked in the barman said, 'Hello, Jane.' She said (thinking to herself it was £3,000), 'Has my John left three "G" here?' 'Yes, Jane.' He pulled up three bottles of Guinness. No new carpet and no new curtains. The names he got called!

As much as my Uncle Lights was a gambler, he had some special qualities. When he used to visit my Dad in prison with us, on the long journeys much to his annoyance my sister and I would be jumping over his bad ulcerated leg to occupy the time but he never complained. Little did we know that this illness of his was to lead up to his bad chest complaint, emphysema.

When Uncle Lights was dying, after visiting him in hospital Jane went to the Peckham bingo, where she met all her friends who had lost their husbands. When she got home there was a rat-a-tat on their door. It was Lights with a hospital blanket around him. 'What are you doing here?' Jane asked. 'Oh,' he said, 'if I'm dying, I wanna die in my own bed; make me a mug of tea, Jane.' My Mum and I were amusing ourselves; Jane went up to make him comfortable and as she was puckering his pillows, she remarked how comfortable her friends had been, since their husbands had left an insurance policy. Lights remarked, 'Well, love, you'll be comfortable when I die.' She said, 'Oh yeah?' He said, 'You'll have two extra feather pillows, Jane!'

My Mum and Dad managed to save hard and when I was five we moved from two rooms to a brown brick, small ground-floor two-bedded flat with its own toilet and bathroom on the Vassall Road Estate, Brixton. Dad continued wheeling and dealing. Sometimes he was successful and as often not so. Once he had what he thought was a touch with a lorry.

That night he kept jumping out of bed, going to the window and pulling the edge of the curtain back to look into the street. Mum was used to his doing odd things but this was a new one. He knew what he was doing. In the flats was a 50-foot container lorry parked up. Dad was one of the hi-jackers and he was keeping an eye not for the coppers but in case another team hi-jacked it from him. I think Mum was a bit shocked. After all, this was a bit of a step up in class. The next day his mates came round and they put it in a slaughter where it was unloaded. Dad was usually reasonably cool about the potential value of any booty, but he was unusually bullish about this one. Mum and Lorraine and me were all asked what presents we wanted.

It was a case of counting your chickens. When they got the container open to get a sample to take to the fence, all they found was rolls and rolls of muslin sacking material. Needless to say the fence refused the load.

We didn't always see a lot of Dad. Every evening he went out to work and by the time he was back Lorraine and me and often Mum would be asleep. He'd let himself in quietly and we'd never hear him. There would be weeks when we'd be eating cheap dinners and then all of a sudden he'd have a touch and money would be available for better food and new curtains and carpets. Then it would be back to chips for a bit longer. Hi-jacking lorries was the name of the game then, and Mum would sell any booty which she fancied direct to her workmates and the neighbours. Everyone knew things had fallen off the backs of lorries, but it was an opportunity to save scarce money and everyone bought.

One Christmas Lorraine opened a present and it was a big white doll. She didn't fancy it at all, and neither did I when I opened mine and it was another cheap doll. Dad must have done a toyshop, because every kid on the estate had the same doll that year.

Whenever he had a really good tickle we would all be taken off for a holiday. The days of hop-picking when people joined the line of broken-down cars, lorries and horses and carts going down the Old Kent Road were over. Then MoT didn't mean a certificate of roadworthiness; it meant More on Top of the lorry. People even walked. Now it was Leysdown on the Isle of Sheppey where South London, and East London for that matter, went.

Primary school was fun. *West Side Story* was the hot musical and when the school decided to put on a show of it, I was dying to be Maria. When they asked for candidates I had my arm out first for the teacher and my face was bright red with determination, but perhaps I was too keen. The part went to a girl I didn't get on with, Susan Edwards. Maybe the reason I didn't get on with her was that her father was a policeman at Peckham police station. I didn't know then that our dads knew each other. When Tommy got nicked for handling stolen LPs and was given four months he was taken to Peckham. I don't remember missing him whilst he was away. Mum certainly didn't take us to see him because it was such a short time. I think she told us he'd had to go away on business and we just accepted it.

Anyway, I ended up playing one of the Jets. At least I was glad I didn't end up as a Shark. I joined the school choir and I started to learn the violin. I'd proudly walk home with my violin case and damage everyone's ears by practising for hours.

Even though there was fifteen months' difference between us, Lorraine and me were very alike and we were often mistaken for twins, but she was better looking, more refined. She was slim and had long blonde hair, large blue eyes and a lovely smile. She was so pretty she could have been the sister of that Miss World, Eva Reuben-Staur, instead of mine.

15

She would always stick up for me if I got in fights with some of the other girls at school. I knew I could rely on her to back me up. I remember one day just outside Ayton House on the Elmington Estate I had a fight with Carole Cooper's older sister Pauline who was also older and taller than me. Now I've no idea what it was about, but I know I was steaming into her. I tore her top and pulled her long red hair and got her to the ground. Then Carole jumped in on me and of course Lorraine piled in as well. There were the four of us scrabbling about. We did the pair of them, and they went off crying and calling us names and the neighbours were shouting at us, 'Leave them alone.' Even though the others were bigger we got the blame as usual. It all got sorted out and we made it up between us. 'Make up, make up; never do it again' was what we was told.

We used to go to the Saturday morning pictures at the local cinema, the Regal at Camberwell Green. Mum would give us 2/6d each and afterwards we'd walk down Westmoreland Road to the pie-and-mash and eel shop for lunch. Then we'd go and buy a 45 rpm record from the AI Stores at the bottom of East Street Market opposite the Walworth Road. Nine times out of ten it would be a Beatles or a Small Faces. We were both more Mods than Rockers. If you were a Rolling Stones fan then you were a Rocker, but we were die-hard Beatles. My favourite was John Lennon and Lorraine's was Paul.

When we got older I used to take her tights straight out of the packet and then forget to pay her for them. If she was going out with her boyfriend Terry Sansom she'd be hunting high and low. 'Where's my Mary Quant tights?' she'd yell and even though she was the quieter one she had a temper like me. That's when the rows would start. I remember how she loved her job as a manicurist in Beckenham and how her nails were always so well polished.

When I was eight the council moved us to a much bigger maisonette in Ayton House on the Elmington Estate, Camberwell. The flats were all on top of one another. It was very trendy then to have one of these rabbit hutches in a high-rise block that had its own lift and our flat had a little private balcony. Mum liked them but I thought they were concrete jungles. Looking back I think both Mum and Dad must have been having their own private brainstorms when they allowed themselves to be sweet-talked by 'caring' council officers into moving from friendly Vassall Road into this de-personalised concrete matchbox on stilts. Those architects of the time must have been the worst designers of residential buildings in the world. They should have been nicked for false pretences, and the council officials for aiding and abetting them.

Parties around our flat in Ayton House would be nothing for my Mum and Dad. When our parents came back from the pub, Lorraine and I would sit on the top of the stairs listening to the laughter and the sing-songs; the sound of glasses clinking and Mum going out to put more ice in a glass bowl with a large splosh; and the smell of tins of salmon for the sandwiches to soak up the booze. Once you could smell the salmon that's when we knew the party was to fold up.

We would host the Christmas parties sometimes, but they were mainly held in my Auntie Jane and Uncle Lights' house in No. 104. Aunt Joan and Uncle Sam Oesterman, my second cousins, plus many of my Mum's brothers and sisters would be there. You would hear them talking about the War and hopping days. I loved to listen to them. Their friends Patsy and Orry Keeling and Bertie Cochrane (who was known as Bert the Bread Bandit) who owned the Charlie Chaplin pub at the Elephant and Castle would arrive; and after them my Mum's uncle, Tommy Shaw and his wife Jessie with their son David. We would have to take turns to sing. It would always start off with the older generation and work down to us kids. I always knew when it was me and my sister Lorraine's turn because my cousin Johnny would sing 'Don't you Kick a Man while he's Down'. Our song would be 'Me and my Shadow'. We'd both learnt it from a Reprise label sung by Sinatra, Dean Martin and Sammy Davis.

Sometimes me and Lorraine would roller-skate back to welcoming Vassall Road to see our friends, but however much we disliked the flat we took care to boast how lovely it was. We'd tell them it was a French design and we could sunbathe on our private balcony. We didn't tell them we couldn't get on it for the washing.

Once a week a paraffin tanker lorry would come round. It used to fascinate me to see that liquid pour out of the tap like pink lemonade. I used to feel sorry for the people queuing because I thought that was all they were going to have to drink. I didn't realise that it was for heating. At home we had an electric fire, which was a bit grand because many still had the old coal fires. I felt a bit of a snob. It was silly really because I'd nothing to be snobbish about.

Sundays always had a certain air about them. I could see all the men in the neighbourhood in their suits standing about on pavements waiting to go into the pubs on street corners. Then there was the smell of Sunday roast cooking along all the landings. You couldn't beat that, and at tea-time it was the smell of all the salad and a bottle of Heinz Salad Cream on the table. Cockles and winkles and the smell of celery, and everybody was getting ready to go out somewhere. It used to fascinate me watching my Dad getting ready and polishing his shoes using a can of wax. In between the polishing he used to get up and put on a Sinatra record on the record player and sing to it; he used the long handle of the Hoover as a microphone. I used to copy him after he'd gone out with his mates and put on a record of Doris Day or Eydie Gorme and pretend I was one of them. I suppose that's how my singing started off. I always wanted to be in show business.

I remember one of the first times that I ever got up and sang in public was at a party given by Charlie and Eddie Richardson.[1] I must have been about eight at the time. They had a warehouse in Addington Square and they used to do bits of charity work like arranging coach trips for the pensioners to go for days out to Southend. That day I sang 'If I Knew You Were Coming, I'd Have Baked a Cake'.

One particular time during the school holidays when I was about the same age I saw a kids' programme about kids who were really poor. We weren't rich, but we weren't poor like them. By comparison we were very fortunate. So I said to Lorraine and five of our friends that we should put on a show and raise money for Dr Barnardo's. We put a rope across the landing by the rubbish chute and put a blanket over it as the stage curtain. Then we put out postcards advertising the concert, dropping them in the letter-boxes over the estate. Everyone was very good about turning up. We all took turns singing and tap dancing to the record player. I couldn't resist trying to hog the limelight and I sang as if I was Doris Day. The climax was when Lorraine and I mimed to Sammy Davis and Sinatra. The neighbours put money in the tin we'd left at

[1] In 1967 Charles and Eddie Richardson, along with Frankie Fraser, were convicted in the so-called Torture Trial at the Central Criminal Court. It was alleged they had beaten minor criminals who had deceived them. Charles Richardson received 25 years in prison, his brother and Fraser got 10 years each.

the top of the stairs and we were so excited when we counted about £6. We sent it off to Dr Barnardo's and when we got the letter back thanking us, we used Sellotape to stick it and the receipt to the lift door to show everyone where their money had gone.

My parents also used to take Lorraine and I with Billy Hart and his wife and two girls on camping holidays down to Cornwall during the school holidays, stopping at various campsites along the way. Unbeknown to us, these holidays used to be a convenient way of offloading electrical goods at every port of call.

2

The Train Robbery

In fact Lorraine and me were very ordinary children. I love
watching old films on the telly. I was watching *The Railway
Children* at Christmas and I remember Jenny Agutter saying
how they were ordinary children and then it all changed. It was
the same with us. We were very ordinary children and then
things were never the same again.

In the summer of 1963 lots of Dad's friends began to
come round and sit drinking tea. I remember seeing them on
Saturday afternoons watching the horse-racing on the telly.
We'd say hello quietly to some of them and then go to our
toy cupboard to get something and then leave the room
quickly and go upstairs to our room or out to play. I suppose
on the whole Lorraine and me were good, well-behaved children. Well, that's what people used to say to Mum and Dad
anyway. We were always told off if we banged a door; we
had to close it quietly. And that summer we always seemed
to be sent out of the room to play as soon as Dad's friends
came.

During the school holidays I practised my violin and one particular day Mum got the right hump with me scratching away and she made me stop. Mum was sewing on her machine and when I asked her what she was doing she told me she had to make some coats for Christmas. I remember it was raining and so Lorraine and me started to play hide-and-seek. We had a big airing cupboard under the stairs and that was a good place to hide. I started looking under a pile of sheets and there was a green woolly balaclava with holes for the eyes so I put it on to frighten Lorraine. We didn't dare tell Mum what we'd found. Years later Mum told me that what she'd really been sewing was a whole series of sixteen balaclavas ready for the 8th August.[1]

Dad didn't tell her it was the Train as such – I don't suppose she'd have known what he meant even if he had – but when he said he had to disappear for the weekend, Mum knew something was up. Apparently he'd been telling her he was going on 'a big one'. Now Lorraine and I were told not to go to our toy cupboard, which was behind an armchair in the living room.

In those days the Bank Holiday was the first Monday in August and on the Friday Mum took me and Lorraine down to a place called Vanity Farm at Leysdown on the Isle of Sheppey where she'd got Nan's chalet. We went in an old Ford Consul with George Liffin's wife, Jeannie, and their kids. By now Leysdown had replaced hop-picking as the summer holidays for the South London working class, just as a few years later Butlin's and Pontin's would eventually replace it in

---

[1] At 3 a.m. on 8 August 1963 the Royal Mail train was halted by robbers at Bridego Bridge in Buckinghamshire. The train driver Jack Mills was coshed and £2.6 million (£25 million in today's terms) was stolen.

turn. You have to drive across a bridge to get there, and I knew when we got to the bridge we'd nearly arrived. There was a famous robbery of a security van that took place just there.

On the other side was a beautiful bungalow with a ship's wheel in the garden. It belonged to Rita Downes' mum and dad. Rita married Wally, who got 18 years after doing the tie-up of a magistrate in Manchester. He got it with Ronnie Scrutton, who died in prison. Sadly Wally died in January 1998.

We'd been down before, but it was just as exciting as it always was. We were about ten minutes from the beach and when we got there we were so excited we wouldn't unpack, but we grabbed our buckets and spades from the beach bag and ran along the beach towards the donkey rides and the amusement arcades. As we walked past a novelty shop there was a nurse's uniform and I asked if I could have one. Lorraine wanted a donkey ride but we both got a blank. Then we asked if we could go on the helter-skelter and got the same answer. I cried a bit. I didn't understand it because Mum loved giving us treats, but she was absolutely skint at the time. All she had was a £20 note that Dad had given her and she had to make it last for us and for Horsey George's family until the following Wednesday. Lunch was sausage, beans and chips and dinner was the same. Every time I went past that shop I begged Mum for the uniform until at last she bent down and whispered, 'Wait until Tuesday', but I had no idea what she meant.

I never heard my Dad's voice when he came in the middle of the night. Mum tells me it would have been the Tuesday. What he did was come down to her with a Player's cigarette packet stuffed with £500 and say, 'Can't stop, darling, I'm going away but I'll be in touch.' I don't know that he ever came in and kissed me and Lorraine goodbye, but then I don't suppose he thought he'd be gone as long.

The next day it was treats all round. We was in a café restaurant and there was a mixed grill and steaks for us. Mum would just load up the trolley in the supermarket. We had all the rides and money to play the fruit machines we wanted, and I think I got three nurses uniforms. I was a bit chubby and I kept ripping them.

Horsey George's wife said to Mum, 'I thought you didn't have no money', and she made out she'd found another twenty quid which she'd taken off Dad when he was drunk. That's what she used to do, go through his pockets when he come home of a night and went to sleep on the sofa.

Much later my Dad told me that as he and some friends who hadn't been on the job went from one resort to another in the northern part of Spain, the English tourists would be sitting eating ice-cream, sunbathing and reading the English papers with the headlines like '£100,000 Mail Train Robbery – Where Are The Robbers?' Then they would go to another resort and the papers would read '£500,000 Train Robbery' and two days later it was up to a million.

As they all booked into a hotel my Dad and his friends gave their names, got their room keys, had a shower and made their way to a local bar. They got chatting to some pretty girls from Liverpool and a friend of my Dad's, Billy, said to the girls, 'Wanna drink?' The girls said, 'Yes, please', and, of course, the birds wanted to know who they were. As the drinks were flowing they were all shocked when Billy said, 'Don't worry, loves, we're the Train Robbers!' It was a joke, though a joke in the worst possible taste, but everybody burst out laughing, more so my Dad because even his friends didn't know he was actually involved in 'the big one'. Months later, when they found out the truth, they were really surprised. Silence is definitely golden.

My Dad also told me a story about a friend of his called Spud. The two of them were in our flat in Ayton House and Dad said, 'Spud, have you had a bet today?' Spud said he had but Dad said, 'Well, go down to William Hill and have a thousand pounds to win that the Train Robbers' money reaches two and a half million', and Spud said, 'Tom, that will smell if I do that, won't it?' Dad replied with his dirty laugh, 'Not much!' Maybe silence wasn't always golden.

As for Mum and me, a month or two later Mum, my little sister and me were all shopping regularly in Harrods in Knightsbridge. What a beautiful shop it was! Lorraine and I tried on loads and loads of dresses, patent leather red shoes, scarves, hats, in fact everything we could lay our hands on. Mum bought loads of things and we filled up carrier-bags galore. From Harrods we would go out for a meal somewhere and it was none of your egg and chips either. I felt like a princess as we rode around in taxis with all the bags and all dressed up, and then Mum would say we should go to Selfridges next and it really did seem like it was Christmas every day. It seemed to have come early. There were more and more bags in the taxi – some of them nearly as big as me. Then it was time to go home and sometimes Mum would have the parcels delivered to one of her brothers. Otherwise as the taxi approached New Church Road, Mum would tell the driver to stop and we would have to get out and walk round into the Elmington Estate. We'd pass Charlie Richardson's scrap-metal yard and sometimes George Cornell, who was later killed by Ronnie Kray, used to be standing outside. Often he would whistle at my Mum, as she was very attractive. He didn't know then that she was Tommy's wife. Later, I married George's wife Olive's second husband.

Bear in mind that in those days women weren't supposed to go out without their husbands. It was on a Saturday night they went out, all dressed up with them. Mostly the 'Chaps'[2] would all meet up on Friday night and the wives would be left at home. That was the men's night where some of them would meet up with their bit on the side – their mistresses, or they'd pick up one of the girls from the Astor or one of the other clubs in the West End.

I remember that on the weekend of the Train my Mum and Jeannie had gone dancing at the Island Hotel at Leysdown. Away from the dance floor there was a bit for kids and from it I could see my Mum with another man, a stranger. I ran across and got hold of her dress, crying and saying, 'That man's not my Daddy.'

As the years went by and before Lorraine had her accident, I knew from the way she dressed up that Mum was seeing other men. It didn't upset me. After all, she couldn't be expected to be a nun and she never brought them home. When she had gone out I used to try on her mink jacket and I'd smell her expensive perfume. Later, one of her boyfriends was Jimmy Moody who tried to help Frank get away after the shooting at Mr Smith's Club in Catford. He was nice. A bit after Mum had finished seeing him I met him in a club in Streatham. Mum had told me how nice and what good company he was and I thought, 'I'll have a bit of that for myself.' We used to meet in a little flat off Streatham Common. Unfortunately he was seeing someone else and we broke up after about four months.

[2] See Chapter 16.

Poor Jimmy was shot dead a few years ago at a pub in East London. No one was ever done for it. After he died the papers said he had an enormous sexual appetite and was very well hung – and they were right.[3]

Gill Hussey – who at the time of the Train was the girl-friend of Jimmy Hussey, and who later married him – came to stay with us. She used to drive all the way over to a dry-cleaner's in Mayfair so that the Camberwell cleaners wouldn't get suspicious of all her designer suits by Jean Varon, Chanel, Dior and the like. The snotty-nosed Mayfair assistant said, 'That will be £25 please, madam,' and Gill gave her three old £10 brown notes. The assistant took them and put them to her nose and said, 'My, these notes smell all musty; they're not from the Train Robbery, are they?' Gill went bright red and said, 'Do you mind! If they had come from the Train Robbery I certainly wouldn't have put my clothes in here to be dry-cleaned. I would be out shopping for a whole new wardrobe', and with that she turned on her heels and walked out.

Our flat was newly decorated. We had purple paint on the walls and one of them was done in orange, which was very modern then and very sixties. The old fireplace was pulled out and a new imitation coal fire one was put in, and we had a new up-to-date stereo with a smoky black lid, which was very expensive.

Of course the cozzers knew almost from the start who they were looking for. Once they picked up Billy Boal and Roger

---

[3] On 16 December 1980, Jimmy Moody escaped from Brixton prison where he was on remand waiting trial for a series of armed robberies. He completely disappeared until he was killed on 1 June 1993 in the Royal Hotel, Hackney. His death was almost certainly the result of a quarrel with a South London family.

Cordery down in Bournemouth they knew who was on it. Bill should never have been involved by Roger; he wasn't any sort of calibre at all. But there's so many different stories depending on whose side you are on.

Whatever happened, the raids started. Ron, my father's youngest brother, was a compositor in the print and he was saving to get married. He was still living at home and he kept his money in the chimney. It wasn't that unusual a thing to do in those days – only in the summer of course. When Tommy Butler (who appointed himself the scourge of the robbers) raided my Grandad's, he took the money and Ron was calling out it was his savings. My grandfather made a joke of it with Butler, saying, 'You must be a good cozzer to find that. I've been looking for it for months.' Uncle Ron was never arrested or nothing, but it took him months to get it back. I think Butler raided them three times but he never found the Train money. The reason was my Grandad had the money in the panels in the doors of his home. I feel quite proud of him putting it there and covering it so no one could tell. He was a handy carpenter. Men were handier in those days.

I don't remember the police coming round, but I know Mum was upset after one of the visits. What she'd done was she'd left a postcard from Dad on the mantelpiece which he'd sent from Callafel. And of course when Butler came he saw it, so he knew they were still in touch. Mum told him she was finished with Dad and he'd gone off with a younger woman, but they never believed her. The coppers behaved in a funny gentle-manly sort of way. They could easily have taken Mum down the station and given her a good questioning, and in those days there'd have been nobody to complain to, but funnily enough they didn't. Of course, they came round a few times unannounced but I was never there when they did so. Really, when it came to it, I was in the dark as to where Dad was.

Then the bombshell was dropped. One day I went into the local sweetshop (which was called Tatnalls) to buy my sweets, and I looked down at the evening papers which were always kept at the front of the shop like a fan. I paid for my sherbet dabs and liquorice and suddenly I saw my Dad's photo along with all these others on the front page of the old *Evening News*. I felt my face going completely red and I panicked. I left all my sweets on the counter and ran out into the street where my sister was playing hopscotch. I shouted, 'Lorraine, Lorraine, let's go home now!' She said, 'It's only five-thirty, Sis. Mummy's not back till later.' I said, 'No, let's go now – I've got something to tell you, it's very important.'

The lift ride up to the third floor in Ayton House was the longest that I've ever had. I just couldn't wait to see Mum and as I opened our front door, the one next to it opened and it was our neighbour Sheila. She said, 'Hello, girls, are you OK?' and we said, 'Yes.' But I wasn't. Sheila was a typical mother and was a godsend as a neighbour. Neighbours in those days were very different; they were helpful and always ready to do you a good turn. Not like today when an old person can be dead from the cold for a week in the next flat before anyone notices.

When we got in, Lorraine said, 'Well, go on then, what is it? Tell me.' But then I changed my mind and, well, I couldn't tell her, not until Mum came. That hour waiting for Mum seemed more like days. Then the phone started to ring non-stop. It would ring a few times, I'd answer it and then it would just go dead. Then Lorraine would answer it and exactly the same thing happened. You can imagine how frightening it was for both of us. Lorraine would shout down the line, 'For fuck's sake, just answer me, please!' but it just clicked and whoever it was hung up. So this went on and on until Mum came back.

'Sorry, darlings, I got caught up,' she said. I shouted at her, 'The phone's not stopped ringing, I'm frightened.' The phone rang again and Mum shut the living-room door and told us to go and watch TV. I said to my sister, 'I wonder where Daddy is? We haven't seen him lately, have we?' Lorraine went off to the bathroom and I went into the kitchen and there on the table was the *Evening News* with the Train Robbers' pictures on the front page. 'What's Daddy's picture doing in the paper, Mum, and where is he?' Mum said, 'He's joined the army', and quickly snatched the paper out of my way. So I said, 'How long for?' and she replied, 'I don't know really.' It's strange because, looking back, for a few months I really did believe that he was away in the army. But I could never work out why he had his picture in the paper for joining up.

Things began to change quite quickly in our everyday lives. When Lorraine and I went out neighbours would peer through their curtains as we walked down the street. Women on street corners would natter about us and stop and stare and point at us, but still it never clicked. I didn't understand why. Nobody explained. When the actual trial came up, Mum had to go off to Aylesbury Crown Court for the proceedings and then Sheila told us a bit about what had happened. And then finally Mum did too.

Sheila would often look after us while Mum was away at the trial and make us tea, or have our door-key so that we could let ourselves in when we came back from school. Gradually Mum would give us a list of things to do and a timetable of how to cook a roast dinner as she didn't get back from the trial until half-past seven. When she opened the door there I'd be at the age of nine stirring the Bisto, with a leg of lamb on the table just ready to be cut and dished up.

On the actual day of the sentencing Dad didn't want Mum to go to court. She and Gill Hussey were at home. Mum was hoovering the stairs and suddenly Gill, who was listening to the radio, shouted out, 'They've got thirty years!' Mum called back, 'Thirty! That's not bad between them, they've had a result.' 'No, thirty years each,' says Gill and with that Mum fainted with shock.

Dad would say later that they were all waiting to go up and be sentenced individually, a bit like the Christians waiting to be sent out to face the lions one by one. When they got their sentences and came down to say what they'd got as the next one went up, they all halved them to try and shield the ones waiting for a bit longer.

You can imagine what happened next. The press were ringing and ringing and the phone never stopped. My sister and I were round at my cousins and that shielded us a bit. Years later Mum told me about her first visit to Dad in prison. She looked at him through the glass and said, 'Well, what am I supposed to do then?' and he said, 'Never mind about you, what am I supposed to do?' So then she said, 'Don't worry Tom, I'll wait for you', and he said, 'Thirty years, don't be silly. You'll have to make a new life for yourself and the kids, Renée.' What a man to say that. I have to say that whenever we used to visit Dad we never once heard him moan. But she did wait. In fact I can hardly think of a wife or girlfriend amongst them all who didn't.

3

After the Train

I didn't go and see my father after he was charged and before he was sent down. Mum wouldn't let us. She just told Lorraine and me he was going to be a long time away and we took it in our stride. I shall never forget my first visit to see him in Oxford prison. Oxford with its dismal grey steel doors to this old fortress and quite a small wall all around the prison; the officer with his shiny button uniform, polished black boots, white starched shirt and peaked hat, looking down at our Visiting Orders as all of the families queued to see their loved ones. Then the small door cut into the main one would open. There was always a big step to get over and we made a crocodile queue to the waiting room. The officers would be stern looking, as if we were the convicts and not just visiting them. I was frightened then. Funnily enough the walls at Oxford were very low and Dad, he could just about have stepped over them. He should have done because he never really got any better chance. Certainly not after the attempt at Leicester.

Dad would tell me that Leicester wasn't very secure in those days and in 1968 he was in the escape attempt with Joey Martin, who got life for the murder of a milkman in a wages snatch, and Bobby Welch who was on the Train as well. In fact there was a couple of others with them too, including an older man who'd tried to get out of Dartmoor. They chose a Saturday in August when Ipswich was playing Leicester at the beginning of the football season. The idea was that people left getaway cars with sets of clothing in the boot for them, and what with the supporters parking they thought no one would notice. I've never been sure what was planned after that, but obviously Dad was going to have to go abroad. What he always said was he put his heart and soul into it. They all did.

They needed two ladders to get over the walls. Joey was a craftsman and he made them in the security wing on the landing which they used as a sort of a gym. He did them in parts so they fitted into one another to make one big one. The screws must have been daft not to see what was going on. Dad said the major problem was that things had to be done by guesswork; they didn't know exactly how long the ladders had to be. Sometimes they'd say to the screws, 'We're having a bet. How long is it from here to that building?' The screws might even pace it out for them, but even so they were left guessing.

They tied up a couple of screws and the first ladder worked a dream. First one went up then another and so on and they hauled the second ladder up with them. They balanced on the wall and they had to get the ladder over so it could form a bridge to the second one. And then the second was just a few inches short. All fitted together it was too heavy for them to pull up easily, and by then the alarms had gone off. Joey and Dad and the others were stranded. Dad didn't half get some punishment for that. They all did. Theirs was the last of the attempts by the Train Robbers to escape. Charlie Wilson had gone from Birmingham and Ronnie Biggs got clean away from Wandsworth. Funnily, although I never knew, Frank was involved in that one. One of the men who got out with Biggs made his way to Frank's gaming-machine firm off the Tottenham Court Road and Frank hid him out and then got him up to Scotland to stay with Arthur Thompson in Glasgow. I'm pleased to say Joey Martin's out now, but he had a hard time inside. He did over thirty years. I saw him at Charlie Kray's funeral and he was looking well.

Mum and me and Lorraine were in Majorca when Dad tried to escape. Mum and Uncle George, one of Mum's brothers, had taken us for a holiday to this posh five-star place. Mum knew he was trying to get out, but she didn't know the details. There was me and Lorraine – a couple of cockney kids in this grand place. The first night we couldn't sit still through all those courses at dinner. We wanted to go swimming again at 8 in the evening. We knew Mum wouldn't let us do that, but eventually she said we could go to our room. Of course straight away we were in our costumes and in the pool. The next thing we knew the *maître d'* was hammering on the window of the restaurant telling us not to make so much noise as we were interrupting a string quartet which had come to play.

Mum heard about the failure whilst we were in Majorca. She was in the hairdresser's when George heard about it. 'Take the kids and go back home,' said George. But Mum wasn't having any of it. 'Leave off,' she said. 'I've been waiting for this holiday for years.'

I think that was the last holiday we had abroad, although sometimes Mum would take us to Butlin's and I won a talent competition at Barry one year. I liked going in for them.

Some of the screws were decent but a lot of them, they

used to make up their own rules. Prison governors have a lot to put up with because the men that are underneath them are the ones who really run the prisons and the POs make their own rules to suit themselves.

Over the years Mum took me and Lorraine visiting to see Dad and we had to take time off school. I remember meeting Violet and Charlie Kray Senior and Harry Roberts' mum, Dolly. She was a lovely woman. Harry got life for shooting some police in Shepherd's Bush and he's done over thirty years now. I think that's more than long enough and he should be released. For the first few years we had to sit at one end of a table with a board in the middle like a wooden table-tennis net. One screw would be behind us and the other behind Dad. Then there were the times when we could only see him through glass with a little vent at the side like bank tellers have to talk through. We were never allowed to sit on his knee or kiss him when we left. Mum used to get very upset after those visits.

Then things got better after a couple of years and there were open visits. The majority of the time we went on our own, but sometimes we went with Dad's brothers or his Mum and Dad, usually by train. We'd get up early in the morning, six, and leave to go to Durham, Hull, wherever. The visits would be over by four and then we'd get the train or drive back. We'd get home eleven, twelve o'clock at night. It was a long day. Mum only missed two visits in twelve and a half years.

Sometimes there was time for a quick bite to eat at a restaurant in the main high street before the actual visit which started at 1.30. The visiting rooms would be filled with people all smoking. The women had all these hairdos with black roots, and badly stained nicotine fingers. Some of them would have white high-heeled shoes with no stockings on, black pleated skirts, red jumpers and thin coats, black patent handbags and loads of cheap jewellery on. The kids and the screws all used to stare at me and my sister as we were wearing Harrods clothes. When it was cold those kids had thin anoraks, and we had fur-lined sheepskin overcoats. Lorraine and I felt a bit sorry for them and at times a bit guilty, and I sometimes felt like saying, 'Look, I'm sorry, but we can't help looking nice. It's my Mum's fault, she wants us to look extra special for Dad.' Saying goodbye to him always ended in tears for me and Lorraine.

Once we went up to Durham in the snow. I'd been given a jigsaw from Harrods and in the hurry changing trains I dropped it on the platform and Mum wouldn't let me pick it up in case we missed the connection. When we got to Durham we were ten minutes early for the visit and it was snowing heavily. Mum knocked on the gate and when a screw opened it he said we was early and we had to wait outside. Mum knew there would be a fire in the waiting room, but we just stood there with her coat pulled round us huddled together in a blizzard till the time come and they let us in.

It was my Dad's birthday on 27 April, and one year when I was still quite young I wanted him to have a toy casino game to play with. My poor Mum was telling me he wouldn't be allowed to have it, but I still carried the large box the game was in. When it got too heavy Lorraine and I took it in turns to carry it from home to Hull prison. As we approached the reception desk only to be told 'No!', I felt my lip sort of quiver and I screwed up my eyes when they went all watery so they wouldn't see me cry. The screws said I would have to write in and get written permission, but we never bothered. Years later I said, 'Maybe I should have brought in a Monopoly or a train set'.

It was when Dad was in Leicester that I first met Frank. Things had relaxed a bit by then and we was able to have tea and some biscuits. Frank was in the visiting room at the time and Dad had asked him if he would pour the tea out as 'Renée's coming up with the two girls.' Frank said to me, 'You know you've got the best Dad in the world.' I said, 'You don't need to tell me. I know I have.' Mum always said I'd end up with one of Daddy's friends. I told her I wish you'd said I'd end up with a rich solicitor.

What Mum and Lorraine and me hated is what still goes on today. A woman maybe has two kids and has to go on public transport, and she travels all the way to see her husband or son, and she's not been notified they've been moved. There's no reason for it, specially now when there's all these computers inside the prison service. They could easily let the people know. Sometimes we would go to a certain prison only to be told that he'd been moved, say to Leicester. Nobody ever phoned Mum to tell her, so we'd make the whole trek for nothing. No wonder children of certain criminals grow up with such a chip on their shoulders. I mean unless something's really happened they don't decide to shift someone on less than 24 hours' notice.

During the twelve years when Dad was away I would think it happened about six times. You wouldn't know until you got there that they'd moved him in the early hours of the morning. They wouldn't tell him where they was going either. After Ronnie Biggs escaped they locked them all up for twenty-three hours a day, and Daddy got on the roof at Leicester to protest about the conditions which were already bad but were even worse after Ronnie escaped. That's when Dad lost some of his remission and he got bread and water for his trouble.

One cold night in November, just before Guy Fawkes night,

I wanted to go round to the paper shop to get some sparklers. The lifts to our flats in Ayton House weren't working and when my sister and I made the trudge up the six flights of stairs, a man followed us up and decided to help carry me for some reason. He put his hands down my woollen tights and touched me underneath. When we got home I was very sullen and quiet; then all of a sudden I cried out about what had happened. With that my Mum went banging on all the doors starting from the top floor screaming, 'Where is the bastard?' All I can remember is that he was tall and had left his bike down by the stairway. Mum was armed with a hammer and she would definitely have killed him if she had found him. After that, for about eighteen months I used to wet the bed sometimes and have bad dreams. Mum used to get so cross with me. My poor sister, I would often tell my Mum it was her. Lorraine would say nothing and take the blame for me, so I would not get told off.

But generally, as the elder, more often than not I was the one who would always get smacked. If my sister and I were naughty I would take it. My Mum always used to say sorry afterwards and say the eldest always got hit. But I don't agree with hitting kids; a smack on the back of the legs or backside now and again, but kicking or hitting around the face is not at all right. I think the only time I ever lost my temper with my son Jonathan was when he let our Lhasa Apso dog off the lead and Danny sped down City Road, Islington, back to our old pub the Trafalgar.

The two wives who were close to my Mum were June Edwards and Jim Hussey's girlfriend Gill. June Edwards was a diamond while Buster was away, and when Lorraine died. Gill was a redhead, Mum was blonde and June was a brunette, and they were three stunning-looking women.

June was always saying, 'I won't speak to the press', but once Buster came out she sort of drifted away. Later I asked her, 'What's it like having Buster home?' but she didn't seem enthralled. I often wonder whether he'd turned gay over those years.

I really truly feel that when these men decide to take the criminal road they shouldn't have children and families. It's not fair to the kids. I don't think Dad was fair to us. I love him, of course, but I'd still say it's not fair to the wives and children when they do something which is going to bring them a long sentence. Four months, six months, that's one thing but five years is different. It's a terribly long time to lock a man up for.

We never got much help after the Train. Neighbours would draw back the curtains and there'd be whispering. It was always in the back of my mind that Dad was away. Because of the high media attention I used to say 'Wisbey' in a soft tone if I had to give my name to anybody. If I put my hand up in class I would never be picked. I wanted to be a prefect, but my impression was that I wasn't made one because of the stigma. Mum always kept Lorraine and me looking nice and the other girls used to chant, 'Your Dad's a Train Robber' at us.

I just never got picked for anything any more, except by one teacher who was Polish and she taught us English at Westwood School for Girls in Upper Norwood. She had a lot of sympathy for me. Before Westwood we went to a private school because Dad had put a bit of his money away, and we had a year there. Neither of us liked it there. I used to play up and be a bit of a comedienne, making the other kids laugh, pulling funny faces and imitating the teachers behind their backs. But I did love the private school drama class.

I was smacked across the hands with a blackboard ruler by the maths teacher for the mimicking. Me and Ronnie Oliffe's daughter, Christine, were sitting in the back row, repeating everything he said after him. When the teacher said the children repeating him were to stand up, no one answered, and then the kids in front of us turned round and gave the game away. We had to come to the front and got five strokes on each hand. I suppose that was the first time I ever met a grass.

Funnily enough quite a few people in the private school were the children of 'faces'. There was the odd remark made in the playground, but we weren't isolated. Once my sister was in a group playing in a ring with the usual questioning. 'What does your Dad do?' And the answers came: postman, painter and so on. When it got to Lorraine she said, 'He's a Train Robber and he's fucking handsome.' And Dad was.

One of the most bizarre things that happened to us was that after one long trek home we found that we'd been burgled. I suppose some people will obviously find this very funny, happening to us, and say it couldn't happen to nicer people, but I know for sure that it wasn't the local petty thieves. It was more likely the insurance company or Special Branch looking for the train money. It happened to us three times over the years while my Dad was in prison. I remember once they left Mum's mink coat and Dad's prison letters all over the bed. No one would insure her even though she was going by her maiden name. She used to forget, and when the next-door neighbour said 'Mrs Hill' she would ignore her. She liked the best, did Mum, and when we had the house wallpapered she went to that grand wallpaper shop Sanderson's and the same thing happened. When the salesman called 'Mrs Hill' she ignored him.

Only recently, a lovely old lady named Peggy came on one of Frank's 'Gangland' tours. She told me she'd been a cleaner for Mum while Dad was away. The other cleaners used to say to her, 'You know who you work for, don't you?' 'Yes,' she'd said, 'and mind your own business. I get paid good and that's why I'm working for her. I don't have to wait for my wages.'

Mum used to take us down to Brighton sometimes for a day out at the seaside, and I can remember the Mods and Rockers there in the 1960s. One Bank Holiday weekend we happened to be there, and when we parked up outside the Queen's Hotel on the front there were mobs of them fighting. I wanted to go over and watch, but Mum wouldn't have it and she said, 'You're not going over there with them Rods and Mockers!' and Lorraine and I burst into laughter. There were police everywhere and TV cameras filming it all, and it was headlines in all the evening papers. Looking back to then, it was a bit like when the rave scene first started and police would raid a club or a do; it was the same kind of bust-up.

Once when we were on the Isle of Wight Mum took us on a coach tour right round the island and there was this guide who started giving us a commentary. He said as we passed Parkhurst Prison, 'And over to our left we have the world-famous Parkhurst Prison which houses some of the most notorious criminals in Britain, the Krays and the Great Train Robbers and . . .' I shouted out to Mum, 'Oh look! That's where Daddy lives', at the top of my voice; and my Mum slapped her hand over my mouth so quickly and she went red with embarrassment as everybody in the coach all turned round and stared at us.

It was a great day when Dad came out. His brothers went and picked him up from Maidstone and they brought him back to the house we had in Norwood. There was champagne and photos all round. In a funny way I remember Dad's coming out more because of a bender I went on with Jacqui Kramer's friend, Bobby Dixey. Bobby had been shot in the shoulder and done 12 years over a job in Hampshire. He came out the same day as Dad and he took me and Jacqui out. It lasted two days. We started off in a club off the Marylebone Road he'd heard about in the nick. Sometimes I think inside you hear more about what's going on than out.

But prison doesn't make a man come out normal, not at any rate anyone who's served any length of time. They all have their problems, mentally. Some are just worse than others, and Frank's the best of them I've known. For example, a lot of them don't like the door closed in the bathroom and they make a big thing of anything they have to do. It's like they're asking you to give them permission. 'I'm going to have a haircut' they say, but what they really want is for you to agree they should go, and tell them it's all right. It's like they're putting an application in to the Governor.

For years after he came out the first time, Dad had everything in order on the bathroom shelf. Mum would say, 'Why are you doing that? You're not in prison now.' But they've been trained to be tidy over all those years and they can't break the habit.

They often come out with a quick temper as well, and as though the world owes them a living. Dad was like that, though maybe Mum tormented him a bit. He had a short fuse and was very, very moody. When he was happy he was happy and when he had the hump he had the hump – and there was nothing much in between. I remember one day Dad picked up a whole load of plates in the Trafalgar and he made as though he was going to throw them at Mum and me. We was cowering in the kitchen, but then he just threw them on the floor and called us a pair of cows. I don't even know what we'd done wrong. It was after that I went up the Council and got a flat nearby for me and Jonathan.

As for Mum, she changed. By the time Dad came out she was much more assertive in herself, much tougher, much more independent. I remember before the Train she'd told my Dad she was going to learn to drive, and he'd laughed at her and said, 'You're silly as arseholes, you'll never learn.' He'd never have said that to her after he come out.

4

Boys

My Dad was seven years into his thirty-year sentence when I had my first real boyfriend, Teddy Warner – a brother to a very good shoplifter, Colleen. At the time she was married to a handsome man called Gordon who was also away. I went out with Teddy for about a year. Poor Ted really went through it from me. I remember the things he offered me – a choice of diamond rings or 18-carat gold rings, and maybe a dress or two. He got them from his sister, of course. I wasn't really into the jewellery, but the dresses were worth £800 each. I would quickly put one on and wear it very revealingly, little realising that this was the big build up to me losing my cherry one night when we was babysitting Colleen's daughter Simone in Page's Walk. I shall never forget; I turned around to him afterwards and said, 'Is that it? I don't know what all the fuss is about.' Which I suppose wasn't very nice of me. I was just 16 and he was about ten years older than me. We went out for a few months after that and then I gave him up and started to enjoy myself. I suppose he really loved me in his own way. He reminded me of the American actor Don Johnson.

Colleen ended up marrying her best friend's husband Mickey Toomey. She later died of cancer, having never smoked a cigarette in her life. She was a lovely girl. We often used to meet up at the Embassy Club when Jerry Callaghan,[1] a friend of my godfather, Freddie Foreman, had it. The club in Bond Street used to have hostesses, the music was great and the cabaret was very good. There was also a guy who used to play like Jerry Lee Lewis. The tables were full of handsome, suited men and you could always tell when some of the Chaps had had it off with a security van or something. Champagne, bottles of scotch, gin and vodka were handed around. Purple hearts and puff were around then, but it was never in your face. In fact I didn't really start taking drugs until the late 1970s.

There was a hostess at the club whose sugar-daddy was a top QC who later became a judge. She used to give him hoisted clothes, cashmere jackets, silk ties and shirts that had come from Jermyn Street. One night Colleen and I were sitting at a table and in walks the judge with a diamond-patterned cashmere and a V-necked maroon sweater; and we laughed out loud because Colleen had nicked the jacket for her the night before – 'Late-night shopping,' she said. I said to her, 'More like late-night shoplifting.'

Before that, when I was fifteen I left private school. Mum

---

[1] Jerry Callaghan, one of a number of brothers from South London, was involved in the shooting in February 1960 at the Pen Club when Selwyn Cooney died. A great friend of Alfie Gerard, he was later suspected of being involved in the killing of Frank Mitchell but was never charged. At the trial Freddie Foreman was acquitted of the killing. Callaghan died in 1999 after a long illness.

couldn't afford it any longer; and besides, it was too strict and I'd have asked Mum to take me away sooner or later. As I said before, most of the kids were children of certain 'faces' of one kind or another. Even the kid of Sir David Frost — a famous face on television, not the other kind — went to Oakfield. I asked my Mum if we could go to a nearer school which my two cousins — Aunt Joan's daughters Julie and Sharon — went to. Their dad, Sam, would pick them up in his red Jaguar, and he would often take the four of us off horse-riding at Streatham Riding School. Then there came what seemed like a bonus when a girl at school told me she had a Saturday job at a hairdresser's over in Sutton and they needed juniors. I had got up at 7 o'clock this Saturday morning, and went all the way over there, and to my dismay the owner did not know anything about it. But she could see my eyes were watering up and she said, 'Don't worry, love, I can fit you in.' The girl had told me complete lies. I was furious with her, I really thought that she was my friend and then to set me up like that.

Lorraine and me used to hang out with Pauline and Doreen Bailey who were two lovely Jamaican sisters. They would come to tea or stay at our house as my Mum would allow us to have friends over. Linda Brett was a good friend and Mum liked her mum, Pat. I loved to stay at her house because we could go dancing at the Crystal Palace Hotel and Pat didn't mind us not getting home until eleven-thirty. Plus, Linda had a big bust size and used to pull all the boys. It was good experience watching her. I was very slow at that age, but I've tried to make up for it since. Lorraine and I and Jean and Sally Guest from Walworth, Patsy Wallis and Jacqui Brown — who was a stepsister to Gary, the father of my boy Jonathan — we would all meet up and go to the Locarno, Saturday afternoon dancing where sometimes there would be live bands. I used to be mesmerised by the girl singers and wanted to be on stage, either singing, acting or dancing. Later on as we got into the mid-teens we would try and get into the Bali Hi club at Streatham where all the Chelsea footballers used to go — we were Chelsea supporters at the time. I used to like Peter Osgood and Lorraine liked David Webb. It always reminds me that when Chelsea won the league my Dad, who was a Chelsea supporter at the time, had Mum send the Chelsea football team a case of champagne. He got a lovely letter back from David himself. Poor David, a couple of years ago he tragically lost a son.

At 15 my first real job was at Boots the Chemist in Croydon selling make-up and perfume, and my fortnightly wage was twelve pounds. I then got accepted for a job at Selfridges, working for Gala cosmetics, which sold Mary Quant stuff. It was funny, my dancing partners used to be outside selling the 'back of a lorry' perfume on a United Dairies milk-crate, and I used to be selling the expensive overpriced straight perfume inside. Sometimes in my lunch break I would rick for a guy called 'Brains'. Ricking was pretending to go in with a £5 note, and act like you realise it's a bargain. The public would be like sheep and follow suit; it was a bargain all right. It's amazing how many law-abiding people will buy stuff they think is stolen if no one is watching them. Of course the stuff the men were selling outside wasn't off a lorry, it was straightforward fake. Lorraine and I often worked on a Saturday ricking. The wages was good, about £15 a day working up and down Oxford Street.

But I was a good saleswoman. I had only worked in Selfridges for about a week when I ended up having my photograph in one of the evening newspapers with Charles Clore, the owner. He had been given some business award and he was pictured with us girls clustered round him. A week later, my father's name was in the same paper saying that he was on a hunger strike over the prison conditions.

After I was at Selfridges, my sister Lorraine and me both worked for the media. Lorraine was a junior secretary to the editor of the *Daily Express* in Fleet Street, and I worked for David Hill, editor of *Weekend* magazine which was similar to *OK* magazine. It was a great job being a junior secretary answering the letters. David was a good boss to work for and when Marion, his personal secretary, was engaged in other work, he would often ask me to pour out the drinks when he had important appointments in his private office. More often than not my serving would be gin rather than tonic.

One evening, my sister and I went to a club called the 'Sloop John D' which was on a boat in the middle of the Thames. Terry Sansom, from the big South London family, who was just a bit older than me, was a wheeler-dealer in American Express cards. We would have the works and meet up with all the Australian conmen who were working over here. I thought they were sheep farmers. They *looked* like sheep farmers, but I was told they were Chaps. They were all handsome, tough guys, suited and booted with names like Bruce and Ralph. The next day when I had to get up for work, I had a terrible hangover from a mixture of Dom Perignon and vodka. I've learned since then never to mix the two. I staggered in to work that day and asked Marion what time Mr Hill was going out for lunch and whether it would be a liquid one or a full lunch at the Wig and Pen, a lunching club in Fleet Street. She said he was going for lunch at the Wig and Pen, so I thought great. That sort of lunch meant he would be gone for at least three hours, and that meant I could have a long sleep on his sofa. Marion and Caroline, my colleagues, went to have their lunch. Mr Hill went out, and I took my shoes off and lay down on his sofa. Later, I woke up to find my boss looking down and prodding me, saying, 'Marilyn, young lady, are we keeping you up?' Apparently I had been snoring. 'Oh dear, I'm so sorry, Mr Hill, what time is it?' 'It's 3.30 p.m.' 'Oh, I'm so sorry, I had quite a late night.' He was amazingly good-natured about it and said, 'I suggest you go home now and don't let it happen again, my dear.' The girls all laughed as I shamefacedly made my way out of the office.

But it was a great job and they was good to me. I got to meet Bubbles Rothermere, as well as Caroline's mum, Ann, who was a well-known journalist; she was a lovely lady. Caroline and her brother-in-law got me my first work with a photographic magazine *Young Love*. With the increased salary and the money I got for being the girl in a photo-story, I was able to take my Mum on holiday to Tunisia. There was no 'young love' for me there. I ended up with prickly heat rash all through the holiday.

It was Terry Sansom who introduced me to Michael Corbett who was playing for Charlton Reserves at the time. Terry was going out with Lorraine and the four of us would go down to the Londoner Club in Leicester Square where Mike McKenzie, a black guy who had no legs, used to play the piano. Strangely enough the song he liked to sing a lot was Frank Fraser's favourite — Erroll Garner's 'Misty'. Michael would get up and sing 'Paper Doll' to me, and then maybe a Mills Brothers or a Nat King Cole number. Terry would get up too, then me and my sister would follow. John and Colin Bewick would be there and they'd sing 'Don't Worry About Me'. Mike used to love it when we all came in because it would give him a break from singing, plus he would have all his drinks lined up waiting for him. You would be surrounded by the gay gangsters and the straight ones, but I was naïve about all this. I think the odd joint would be smoked, but in the years we ventured into Soho you would not ever see the anti-social behaviour that you see today. If someone did play up, they were soon marched out politely by discreet bouncers who otherwise would be enjoying themselves and mingling. The club is now a gay bar, Jonathan's, owned by Colin Bewick, an ex-boyfriend of mine who was also a friend of Terry Sansom and who was very funny, generous and gay. In the days when I knew him, at the very worst he was bi-sexual. He was the one who first introduced me to Ronnie Knight and Barbara Windsor all them years ago. I think we all went to the Talk of the Town, which was a big place for dinner and dancing, and always had a top cabaret like Shirley Bassey. It was where the Hippodrome is on the corner of Charing Cross Road. Frank goes back with her to the time when she and Danny La Rue used to do the cabaret for Bruce Bracewell who ran a club in Clifford Street.

Then, after that our favourite pub was the Rock in Walworth Road. Sylvie and Charlie owned it and Terry Stevens, a good girl singer, would sing there. Of course, I always used to ask her first if I could sing when she was having a break. She would actually encourage me to sing. It was her that helped me – unlike most singers today who don't like competition; they think you're going to nick their spot. I believe she was as good as Shirley Bassey. She even went over to America and worked there. I think her manager messed it up for her – Ginger was his name; he died a couple of years ago.

I shall never forget being introduced to a guy, Jimmy Gate[2], one night at Kojak's in Regent Street. It was a place used by actors and actresses and the usual Chaps. I was talking to Ginger Del when this guy Jimmy Gate asked me if I would like a ride home in his white Jensen as he was going my way.

[2] A pseudonym.

I felt a bit tipsy and I had to get up early for work at the pub, so I said, 'Yes.' I thought he looked OK and like an idiot I went along. I saw Regent's Park coming up in front of us and he pulled into some private flats behind some garages. I was in the back and his mate was in the front. He got out and suddenly Gate pulled back the front seat and I could see that he had a knife and he started to try and rape me. I pissed myself with fright and I could see his mate looking in through the steamed-up windows. I shouted at him, 'Have you got a mother or a sister or a daughter?' My fist was clenched between my legs trying to stop him, but he was leaning very heavily on me, still trying to get into me. I shouted again and said, 'Do you know who you're messing with? How could you do this to me? My father's in prison.' Then gradually Gate calmed down and he drove me home.

Some years later I was having a drink with Bryan Turner from the Wembley bank robberies, who was grassed up by Bertie Smalls,[3] and who was my boyfriend at the time, in the Little Jerry pub in Maida Vale and who walks in but this Jimmy Gate with a tall slim brunette! Before I could say anything the landlady of the pub, Sheila, could see something was going down and she begged me not to cause trouble, but I carried on nevertheless. Saying, 'Excuse me one moment' to my friend Bryan, I went towards the door where Jimmy Gate was standing. He saw me coming and moved away, so I went outside and shouted to him, 'Oi, do you remember me?' He looked a bit sheepish and said, 'Uh, no.' I said, 'Yes you do, you bastard, you

[3] In March 1973 Bertie Smalls, who had been the leader of a team of bank robbers in North London, became Britain's first modern supergrass, giving evidence against his former colleagues of whom Turner was one. Turner received a sentence of 21 years, reduced by the Court of Appeal to 18 years.

were the person who tried to rape me in the back of your white Jensen.' Then I said to the brunette girl, 'If I was you, love, I would have nothing to do with this pervert.' They both left immediately. It turned out to be common knowledge that Gate had done this many times, but to this day nothing was ever done about it. If I had pressed charges the police would have said to me, 'How long have you known this man? Why did you accept a lift from someone you hardly knew?' Back then the police force was not taught how to cope with attempted rape. And then again it would have all come out that I was the daughter of Tommy Wisbey, Train Robber. So what could I do? Plus my father had just come out on parole, so I kept quiet. I didn't want to get him into any trouble or publicity. In fact it's only recently I told him. That's how men get away with these things.

Back in the seventies there was a drinking club called the Log Cabin in Wardour Street, owned by Tommy McCarthy, where you would get barmaids playing records behind the bar – usually Frank Sinatra, Brook Benton and Dinah Washington. You could guarantee to buy a cashmere overcoat or a Burberry raincoat for at least a third of the price. Some afternoons there it was like the January Harrods' sale. Michael Corbett would shout out, 'Old Joe's got some Hermès silk scarves over there, Harry.' 'How much?' would come the reply and he'd say, 'A hundred quid the lot.' The scarves would be marked up for sale at £45 each. Then everybody would have a glass of gin and tonic and they all crowded round a table while the dealing went on.

If a fight started it was sorted out quickly. The guy who started it would have his arm behind his back and be marched or thrown out into the street. Sometimes I used to feel sorry for the guys who 'accidentally' slipped down the stairs, but really fights in most drinking clubs then were few and far between. Most of the rows in clubs would be over women.

In fact, I was once one of these women when I ended up in Charing Cross Hospital while drinking in Jerry Callaghan's brother's club just off Leicester Square. I had been going out with my godfather Freddie Foreman's nephew, Michael Irons, who was also from South London. I was 16 at the time. Now there was a handsome man. Mum was pretty strict with Lorraine and me. There was no question of us taking boys to our rooms whenever we liked as far as she was concerned. Nothing like today when kids come down to breakfast with a different boy twice a week. If we had a regular boyfriend that was all right. Anyone else just saw us to the door.

Michael Irons and I talked about living together, but I had broken the relationship off because I thought he was getting too possessive. He was bang in love with me so what did I do? I went to Valencia in Spain with some mates from where I was working as a silver service waitress in the City. One of them had heard about a job as a barmaid, and I went along with them.

I remember I said to Mum and Lorraine, 'I can't wait, I'm going away for six months!', and my Mum said, 'I'll give you six weeks and you'll be straight back home.' We had a nice clean room in a *pension* for about 350 pesetas a day. That would have been about £3 then, so it seemed all right.

I thought I was dead clever by working behind this Spanish bar, but I was so naïve. It took me a couple of weeks for the reality to sink in, but it was really great at the time and at least I picked up a bit of the Spanish language. What it was, the place turned out to be a brothel. Customers would get hand relief or a blow job behind a curtain, and then us English girls would have to serve them up tapas. At least they didn't expect us to do the blowing. Mum was right though, and it wasn't long before I decided to come home. I had trouble getting my fare together so I had to go the British Consulate for help and they got me a ticket for the train. It must have been the slow one because it seemed like it was going on for ever.

When I got back, my cousin Janice told me that there was a new club that Jerry's brother, Michael Callaghan, had just opened, and we should try it out. I was dolled up in my leather boots, red hot pants and a red tee-shirt, and dancing away there, when Janice and I started being chatted up by these two fellows. All of a sudden Janice spotted my ex and I saw him as well, just out of the corner of my eye, but I carried on talking to this guy. I looked over to sort of shout or say hello to Michael when he came bowling over and said to me, 'You fucking cow! I've spent all that money doing a flat up and then you fuck off and leave me!' I said, 'I'm sorry, but I can't stand your possessiveness.' 'I love you,' he said, and as he was about to continue there was this guy behind his back winking at me and I thought to myself, 'Oh no, don't you start.' Then I sort of giggled as I tried to take the situation in and my ex gave me one big punch and it knocked me across a table and I landed on the floor. All I can remember is half waking up outside Charing Cross Hospital.

The next morning when I was back home my Mum brought me a cup of tea and when she saw me she was really shocked. She wanted to know what had happened and I said that I'd fallen over drunk, but of course she didn't believe a word. Eventually, I had to tell her the truth. I suppose you could say the rest is history. My poor ex ended up with not one black eye but two, because my Dad's brother soon sorted him out. It's strange how someone can declare mad passionate love for you one minute and then within a month be a completely different person. I suppose that's what makes most men different to women. I have to say though that I've seen Michael since over the years and we've laughed about what happened and let bygones be bygones.

The Spanish thing didn't stop me going abroad. Nor did it teach me any lessons either. A few years later when we had the Trafalgar pub there was an ad in the *Evening Standard* about girls working as waitresses in Germany, and the spiel was that they could earn about £300 a week. So Anna (a friend of mine) and I went for the interview in a poky little office in Marylebone, somewhere off the Edgware Road. I suppose I should have realised then that it wasn't on the up. We were given a few quid for expenses and told to meet with our suitcases at London Airport a couple of days later. I think there were twelve of us, and once we flew to Frankfurt we were herded into two houses – half a dozen in each, and then we were taken to where we were going to work. It was a bar showing porno flicks. The next thing we were told we had to hand over our passports for registration. I said to Anna, 'For Christ's sake, don't give them your passport', and so we made out they were back in our suitcases.

What the guys made clear was that there wasn't going to be any wages if we didn't accommodate the punters, and some of the girls were prepared to graft. I wasn't having it and we got chatting to some Italian guys who said they'd help us. They said they'd meet us on a spur road to the autobahn at one o'clock in the morning. When we got back to the house we got locked in our rooms, but Anna and me were on the ground floor. We'd nicked a supermarket trolley to wheel our luggage in and we broke out that night. I was half afraid it was a set-up but the Italians were genuine; they were there waiting and they drove us to Heiga and got us a job in a pizzeria until we could get enough money together to come back home. I don't know what happened to the other girls, but I did see that the people who'd interviewed us in London got done later for controlling prostitutes.

5

Michael

Michael Corbett and I went out together for about a year. And he was the only man I've loved that I never went to bed with. I still miss him dearly. Terry Sansom Junior and my sister were very much in love and whilst Michael was away with Charlton FC they'd invite me out with them, but nine times out of ten I wouldn't go out and I'd let them be together. Terry spoiled Lorraine something rotten. He often took her down the King's Road and spent a lot of money on clothes for her.

What I wanted to do more than anything else in the world was to get my singing career off the ground. Roger Cordery was the first one of the Train Robbers to get out and he recommended a couple of guys to come along to a pub in Grove Park, the Chinbrook, where you could get up and sing. One of them was meant to be that Jonathan King who had such a big hit with 'Everyone's Gone to the Moon'. And the idea was that if it all went well I might get a contract. Roger had been an old friend of my Dad, and in fact they'd done a few

London-to-Brighton trains together before they got caught on the big one. What they did was to distract the guard and get his van by some trick or another. Once Bobby Welch, who worked with them, pretended to have an epileptic fit which got the guard's attention lively. Then sometimes they'd just do straight tie-ups.

Anyway, Roger thought that if these guys he knew heard me they might be able to do something for me. Michael was back from Ireland where he'd been playing and that night he said he would meet me down at the pub as he was going to Catford dogs with Harry the market trader, Johnny Crozier and Alan Cosson, a nephew of Gill Hussey. He said that after the dogs was finished they'd all come down to hear me sing. My cousin Johnny came down with his brother Alan and quite a few relations were there as well. It was my great talent-spotting night.

When it was over my Uncle George and Aunt Dot invited us all back to their house in Bromley for coffee and sandwiches. For the journey home there was not enough room for my two cousins, myself, Michael, Terry and Lorraine in one car and, as we were saying goodnight, my sister and I were both grabbing the front passenger door to get in. My mother wasn't having so many of us get in the same car, and she shouted over, 'Oi! One of you girls come with me.'

I said to my sister Lorraine, 'You go with Mummy' and we started arguing, so Michael said, 'Marilyn, go home with your Mum and we'll drop Johnny off.' I remember being upset because we would usually sing a song on the way home, but anyway it left Michael driving Terry, Lorraine and my two cousins. My last words to Terry and Lorraine were, 'I'll see you back at 116', meaning our home in Upper Norwood. 'Don't be going to any clubs now, without me. I'll have the coffee on.'

Mum and I got home and were waiting for Lorraine. Then about 1.30 a.m. she went up to bed saying, 'Don't be up too late. You girls have work tomorrow.' I put the coffee percolator on and went into our lounge, where we had a beautiful white upright piano. I had the curtains open and I was playing it, looking at every car light that came round our street.

It was then the telephone call came. It was Michael's dad, 'Blind' Tom, saying, 'There's been a terrible accident.' With that my Mum and I were in her car driving to King's College Hospital.

When we entered the hospital all I remember is my mother asking about our Lorraine. A nurse quietly put us in a room, but we could not sit still. We were waiting, pacing up and down, in the corridor – I don't remember who else was there – until I saw my cousin Alan wheeled out on a bed. I know Tom Corbett and his family were there crying. No one would or could speak. There were no answers from the doctors or nurses. Unbeknown to us, my sister was in the intensive care unit while we were down in the emergency unit. I remember asking, 'What about Lorraine? When can we see her? What about Michael? How's Michael? How's Terry? How are my two cousins?' and that's about all. I don't think I ever got any answers. That night to me was a complete blur and a total nightmare in slow motion, full of the most evil pain God could have put into all of us. It had been such a happy evening but, in the end, it turned everybody's life around.

Finally, as we were still sitting there in oblivion, all I could hear was someone crying as if in pain. Then eventually a senior doctor asked my mother and me to go to the private room to tell us that my lovely Michael had died instantly and that my sister Lorraine was undergoing emergency treatment. I was so numbed. We were allowed to see her hours later; she just lay there with her eyes closed and all those tubes and instruments. All I can remember was the sound of 'Beep, Beep'. I held her hand and said, 'Lorraine, it's your sister here, please, please God.' Her lovely angelic face was puffed up; her hair still had blood on it. We were allowed to stay in the side room. The sound of crying was coming from Terry Sansom. Everyone was in deep shock. My boyfriend was dead and my sister was fighting for her life. My cousins were alive but badly injured.

Until then I really thought that hospitals, with doctors and nurses, were just like *Emergency-Ward 10*. They were places where people didn't die, and Lorraine would pull through. At 16 life was just beginning for her. We had no idea what would happen. No one seemed to be able to tell us and so we continued, my mother and I, to support one another.

One of the first things we did was go round to Michael's mum, Lil, to pay our respects. Poor Lil was sedated upstairs. One of Michael's sisters opened the door. He was lying to rest in the living room. He was the first dead person I had seen lying in a coffin; he was eighteen years of age and had the world at his feet; all it seemed, down to me. Terry's mum Elsie was there. Freddie, her husband, was in prison up in Hull, doing time with Mark Owens from Liverpool. My Dad was doing his time in Parkhurst. We all had our crosses to bear. I will never forget the reception Mum and I received from one of Michael's sisters. I was not the driver that night and yet I was accused of his death, shouted at while Michael lay in his coffin. Coming as it did after we'd been visiting my sister Lorraine it was unbelievable. To this day I don't know why I was blamed. I suppose it was one of those chain things: 'If they hadn't come to hear me sing and then gone back to my uncle's . . .' Things like that.

Harry the market trader got a phone call the following day when 'Blind' Tom asked him to go with him to Peckham police station. Years later I investigated the matter and found out that the car was as smashed up as Princess Diana's car, that awful night she died with Dodi Fayed.

In fact it was Terry who was driving that fatal night. 'Blind' Tom was told by the police officer that there was no way Michael was the driver and the two people who bore the brunt of the car crash were my sister and Michael. Terry came out with no injuries and in fact he was likely to be held on a manslaughter charge. The part of the car he'd been in was not badly damaged. But 'Blind' Tom protected Terry and said to them, 'A dead man tells no lies.'

Michael's funeral was at St George's Cathedral at Waterloo. My Mum and I went to the house before the service with our wreath, but we were left standing on the street as everyone got in the cars until Johnny and Patsy Collins offered us a lift. Michael was buried at Streatham Cemetery.

After Michael's funeral, my sister was still fighting for her life. Day in day out we spent sitting with her, holding her hand, talking to her, trying to coax her out of the coma she was in. The Home Secretary at that time was Reginald Maudling, and my father was allowed out for one hospital visit to King's College Hospital, handcuffed and led into the intensive care unit. The whole area was full of armed police and prison officers. We never saw my father that night of the hospital visit. In fact we never knew he was coming. The only person who accidentally met him was my Uncle Lights.

Of course the family spent the whole time at the hospital, but Lorraine never recognised us. Then on 19 November we got a telephone call at midday asking us to come in and talk to one of the top consultants. He was very kind but he told us to prepare ourselves. He said, 'We need a miracle, Mrs Wisbey, I am so sorry.' We were all there. Tom and Flo, my grandparents, my mother, my Uncle Ron (my Dad's brother) and myself were told by the consultant, 'We have tried, there is nothing more that we can do. It's a matter of time.'

Mum and I had gone back home to get some rest after being at the hospital all afternoon; when that phone call came from my Uncle Ron to say that Lorraine had died peacefully in her sleep, my mother let out a howling noise and cried out about there being no God above. I couldn't bear it and I ran out into the street screaming and crying. Junie Edwards, Buster's wife who had been staying with us, came out looking for me. I don't remember much for some time after that; I only knew I had to have some strength, and support my mother who was upstairs in her bedroom crying and calling God names. Our doctor was called in to prescribe some green and black Valium capsules for us both. The telephone rang constantly and most of the time it seemed to be the press wanting to know how we felt. In the end we just took the phone off the hook. Our relations came round and for days afterwards I was worried about my father. Could I run to him to put my head on his shoulder, and could he do the same for my mother? The answer was no.

In fact my father begged Mr Maudling to be allowed home for the funeral and to comfort my mother at this critical time, but he was refused on the grounds that he was a security risk. He'd had his favour by being allowed to see Lorraine while she was in a coma. However, Mr Maudling did write to the prison authorities regarding my father's case, and they allowed him a few extra hours' visits. In the letter to Mr Maudling my father recalled that Maudling's daughter had given birth over in Kenya and Mr and Mrs Maudling had both flown out there to be at their daughter's side – quite rightly so when a loved one was being brought into the world. Here my father's daughter had been taken away, but he still refused to let him attend my sister's funeral.

Little did we know at the time that Mr Maudling was to become part of one of the biggest financial scandals that Britain has ever known. My father Tom was no angel but here was a man, Reginald Maudling, who was at the time about as big a crook as could be, involved with the architect John Poulson. He resigned in 1972, a year after my sister died, but he'd been involved in deals as early as 1966. He'd helped a company of Poulson's to obtain a contract from the Maltese to build a hospital. It turned out to be a white elephant costing the British taxpayer £1.6 million.

Maudling was also caught up in the collapse of the offshore Real Estate Fund of America, of which he was president during 1968–69. It took years of litigation though no one was arrested, but he was never allowed to return to the USA. Maudling was investigated by the police, but was cleared of corruption by a parliamentary select committee. But I still do not know who was more of a risk to society.

Through all this Junie Edwards looked after us. I don't think we would have managed to cope without her and I'll always be grateful to her. The funeral people came and she was the one who did so much of the organising. Lorraine had three hundred wreaths. What will always stick in my memory is that the only two old friends from Westwood School who sent wreaths were the two black girls, the Bailey sisters. I thought the world of them on that day, 24 November 1971.

Our lives carried on but the sadness of it all never stopped there, because of course poor Freddie Sansom and my Dad were away in prison. What was so uncanny was they both had the same photograph of my sister Lorraine and Terry taken at the Beachcomber restaurant at the Hilton Hotel; each had the same photograph in different prisons.

Poor Freddie Sansom never came out of prison. Over the years he'd had some bad beatings, and when he was in Hull in March 1972 he came back from a football game and just keeled over and died.[1] Prior to this and after my sister's death my father kept asking the prison authorities for him to be moved nearer home, and so did I. Freddie came out to be buried and Mum and I went to the funeral in Streatham. Instead of Dad being moved nearer to us, he then got moved from Parkhurst to where? Yes, Hull prison. Officers said to my Dad, 'We're sorry, Tom, but you have to have Fred's old cell.' My Dad's reply to this was, 'He never did me no harm when he was alive. He was one of the best.'

The death of my beloved sister left me and my family absolutely shattered. I not only lost a sister, I had lost a very dear friend who I've never found in anyone since except Frank. Now in the eighth year of his sentence, my father Tommy was knocked for six. It seems like there was an evil spell on anyone connected to the Train Robbery, similar to the Kennedys over in the States.

---

[1] In March 1972 Freddie Sansom died in Hull prison at the age of 38. He was serving a sentence of 12 years for a series of armed robberies for which he had been convicted on 24 May 1965 together with Mark Owens. Sansom had appealed against the conviction on the grounds that the foreman of the jury had been seen talking to the officer in charge of the case. An inquiry showed that the discussion had been about rugby and the appeal was dismissed. Sansom received a handsome funeral with wreaths from the Train Robbers and the Parkhurst rioters for whom he had given evidence. The floral tributes were said to have cost the then very considerable sum of £1,000.

Michael

When Lorraine died, for my Mum's sake, I never gave out a lot of tears. I kept strong but then, about 18 months later, I started to go downhill. I gave up my job soon after Lorraine died so as to be with Mum, and after that I couldn't get a grip on what was going on. If I saw people laugh I was jealous they had something to laugh at. I couldn't be bothered to wash and then I couldn't be bothered to get out of bed. I missed my sister and the best friend that I ever had, all my happiness had gone away. Where I had been supportive of my mother, I just could not cope any more in myself; I did not want to live.

Mum finally persuaded me to go for counselling and I had some one-on-one sessions at the Maudesley in Denmark Hill, but it didn't really suit me. I had three visits with a psychiatrist at the age of 18; I felt the stuffing had been torn from within me. I just wanted the doctor to talk to me, but all he would do was listen. I think the mind is so powerful. Whether it is drink, drugs or bereavement, you have to get over it for yourself. It may be that the sessions did help focus me on what I had to do, and I did it. I started getting up, washing, and I went and got a job.

At the time I was depressed and trying to rebuild my life, I have to thank Arthur and Sheila Sutty and their daughter Kim who asked my Mum if I would like to spend a weekend away from London, which was ever so thoughtful of them. Arthur always reminded me of Michael Caine, the actor, but a darker version. They have a beautiful place in Epsom with a swimming pool and horses and, with Kim being a show-jumper who rode for the British team in Canada, they had a string of show-jumpers. Arthur used to let players from his favourite football team, Chelsea, keep their ponies there. It was a good place to unwind. In fact it was a very therapeutic way of helping me get over this nervous breakdown that I had been going through.

Having been riding with my sister when we were younger it was like having a small part of her back again — something which brought back happier memories. One of the string was Sacha, a small white 15-hands-high pony. Anyway this particular weekend I was feeling very subdued and quiet and Arthur told Kim to let me ride out Sacha. I said to Arthur, 'Don't be giving me any big horses to ride out. I'm not that good a rider and also I've lost my bottle.' He assured me that Sacha was as safe a ride as you could get. He was until we went onto Epsom Downs, and then he took off as if he was in the Derby himself. I was just hanging on. It wasn't as if I pulled him up, it was just that he ran out of breath. I got off and walked the two miles home. The next day I could hardly stand up straight.

Kim married and went abroad, but our family kept in touch with Sheila and Arthur. I was so sorry to see he went down in an arms deal with the Scotsman Paul Ferris in 1998. Paul had been acquitted of killing Frank's friend Arthur Thompson's son years ago. A bit earlier Frank and I had been down to visit Arthur Sutty with Mum and Dad and in fact when we had to do a broadcast that evening the station sent a cab down to Arthur's to collect us. We'd no idea what was going on, but if the police had raided him that day they'd have had a fine haul.

I'm glad to say Arthur's out now. It was wonderful of him and Sheila to have me. They say that animals are therapeutic for people in grief and Sacha certainly was, even though he ran away with me. Back before Arthur went away I went down to see them and Sacha was still alive. He gave a sort of whinny and came to me as if he recognised me, but I expect he thought he was just going to get some sugar.

For a time my Mum went into a sort of decline. She badly wanted another child to replace Lorraine and she knew she'd be too old by the time Daddy came out. She even went and wrote to the Home Secretary to ask if she could have a conjugal visit. Of course she got knocked back. Another prisoner's wife, not from the Train, had been knocked back a couple of years earlier and they weren't going to do my Mum and Dad no favours. All through their sentences the Train Robbers were of media interest, and after Lorraine died we were of human interest as well. A reporter from the *News of the World* approached Mum and, in a way, words were really put a bit into her mouth. But there again it helped to publicise the outrageous sentences of thirty years because the visit wasn't permitted.

One day Terry came round with a friend of his, Gary, who I happened to notice, very smartly dressed, green eyes, blond hair, a bit like Robert Redford. Terry introduced me to him and now and again he would take me out.

Later when I was 19 I fell pregnant. I didn't want to get married at that time, but I wanted to have a baby and I said to my Mum, 'The baby I'm having will be for you and Daddy.' My Jonathan was wanted. His dad, Gary, was the first man I truly fell in love with. Jonathan was wanted for all of us. I had him when I was twenty and that's what he was, a much-wanted baby. When he was born all the screw did was put a bit of paper under Dad's cell door which read, 'By the way, your daughter's had a little boy at 6.30 this morning.'

Young Terry Sansom was so full of guilt; we loved him and we never blamed him. My Dad being the man that he is never blamed him. 'Blind' Tommy Corbett never blamed him. In fact we saved him from a prison sentence; he had suffered enough over that night.

Terry would often visit me and my Mum. We told him he had to carry on with his life and be strong, he was such a lovely good-looking, happy-go-lucky person – just like his dad, from what certain people had told me.

Eventually, not long afterwards, Terry — with his father Freddie, Lorraine and Michael all gone — went into a depression too and flipped high on drugs. Our darling Terry drowned in the River Thames, after seeing a rock concert. We were never sure if he killed himself or if he slipped and fell. I like to think he slipped, but whichever it was it won't bring him back. So within a space of two years, all our lives had been shattered — the Corbetts, the Wisbeys, the Sansoms. As had been written on my sister's gravestone: 'The times we shared together will never be the same, Lorraine, God bless, Your sister Marilyn.' Eventually Michael was reburied next to her.

In 1974 Myra Hindley was allowed out for a walk across Hampstead Heath. I was pregnant at the time and I wrote a letter to the *Evening News* for their readers' column complaining of the unfairness of such an evil person as Myra Hindley — a woman who allowed her lover Ian Brady to torture children while she watched those perverted acts being done — having a walk over Hampstead Heath. My father, who only robbed a train full of money on its way to be burned, was not allowed out to his daughter's funeral. They printed it and Eamonn Andrews, the Irish television presenter who was really big in those days, asked me to go on this show and put my point across. The solicitor Victor Lissack, who looked like the actor Robert Morley when he was being pompous, was on the other side. 'Your father is top security,' was his answer and I said, 'Well, it just goes to show that our government thinks more of money than people's lives.'

6

The Pubs

Towards the end of Dad's sentence Mum and me got a pub, the Alliance in Sumner Road, Peckham. It was in Uncle Ron's name, but we bought the lease with the last bit of money Mum had left from the Train. This was just about the last of Dad's money altogether and we had to do something with it. It had all gone. In that book *The Train Robbers*, Piers Paul Read sets out how everyone's money went. He reckoned everybody had about £150,000 each, and Tommy's money went:

Legal fees	28,000
Burnt money	5,000
Changing money	7,500
Norbury House	6,000
Minders	10,000
Speculation	20,000
House for relatives	6,500
Living exes	20,000

| Betting shops | 15,000 |
| Relatives' exes | 20,000 |

And he was just about right.

We'd been comfortable at the beginning, but Mum did like shopping at Harrods and it came to a point where she couldn't make ends meet. Grandad gave her £25 a week and that had to pay for food, the house expenses, sending me and Lorraine to private school, going to see Dad and getting him the things he needed. Plus he'd quite often send a note to Mum to get her to send some money to some other prisoner's wife who was having a hard time of it. Once when Chelsea won the cup he had his brother George send a case of champagne to them. So by the time I was 20 and pregnant with Jonathan there wasn't much left. Mum had to go back to work as a representative for the Sunblest Bread Company. I thought it was unfair when others had Dad's money and so Lorraine and I became latch-key children. Eventually Grandad bought us a little house in Upper Norwood and we lived there – two bedrooms and a boxroom, and a little garden.

It was just a young girl's impression, but it's remained with me all my life that maybe some members of my parents' families had more dealings with the money from the Train than was ever realised. Some people will say why haven't we settled this, but then I'm not the person to judge. God will be the person to do that.

What we did have was enough to put down for the fixtures and fittings of a small pub. It wasn't such a daft scheme as you might think because over the years I'd done more than my share of working behind the bar, including a stint for my god-father Freddie and Maureen Foreman in their place, the Prince of Wales in Lant Street in the Borough. What was good was the people who helped. Even others who'd got interests in pubs themselves would come in and drink and put a bit of cash our way when they never needed to — not at all like when I had Pal Joey's in Islington many years later.

At the time we took the Alliance I was madly in love with Gary Howlett, who's my boy Jonathan's father. As I say, I'd met him through Terry Sansom — he was a friend of young Terry. The trouble with the Sansoms is that every generation has the same name as the next, so the son has the same name as his father or uncle and it gets so confusing. Gary had a stepsister, Jacqui Brown, who I grew up with. She married my childhood sweetheart from the Elmington Estate, Charlie Rumble. When I was ten we used to play kiss-chase, and his Dad would say we'd end up together. I was sorry to see his boy, also named Charlie, and a boxer, got a seven over a manslaughter in a fight not long ago. Charlie's brother Fred used to wash Mum's car at 10 shillings a time. If he'd known about the Train then he'd have charged a lot more.

The trouble with Gary was that he kept disappearing. He was a ducker and a diver and I'd only see him when he had had a touch. I was quite happy counting the money and spending his earnings, singing as we did so, but when I fell pregnant I couldn't stand the idea of him being like Tommy, away all the time my boy was growing up. I hadn't seen Gary much of the time I was pregnant. The grief at losing my sister was overwhelming, but the delight of carrying a much-wanted baby did ease it slightly. It gave me something to cling to, but by the time I was well pregnant Gary was off again. I didn't know whether he was arrested or injured or what.

A bit before Jonathan was born Gary and I got back together for a time. What I wanted was for him to go straight and to run the pub with me so he wouldn't have to go out thieving.

But he said no; he wanted his own pub. Even so, he worked in the bar at the Alliance with me.

Then it all fell apart again. It happened one day when me and Mum had gone shopping in Peckham and the coppers came round. Some regulars had been in and noticed that we had an old-fashioned till, one of those where you had to press the keys down and it rang up little flags. So they asked Mum if she wanted a more modern electric one. She bought it off them and put it down in the basement; she didn't even have time to wire it up. That afternoon the coppers came looking for Gary over some snatches in Knightsbridge – that was really his game at the time. While we were out they came and swagged him down to Peckham nick; and while they were lifting him they had a look over the place and found the till, which turned out to be stolen. They told Gary that he'd have to name some names about the snatches or we'd lose the licence. Naturally he told them to eff off and in retaliation they objected to our licence being renewed at the next Sessions and said the pub was a thieves' hangout.

And that, as far as Mum and I were concerned, was the end of the Alliance. Beryl Gibbons, the boxing promoter, took it over and she put in Paulie Hurley and his wife as managers. Funnily enough a bit later Paulie got nicked with Frank's nephew, Jimmy, over some puff in Belgium, but thankfully there was nothing in it. As for Gary, he got 12 years for a robbery in Sheffield or Manchester, some place like that. Then much later he got done under the new three strikes and picked up 9 years over a miserable ten grand's worth of clothing. He came out last year and we still keep in touch.

So now we were minus a pub. Dad was on the last part of his sentence and he didn't half tell Mum off, saying there was no need to buy something hookey.

It was about this time that gambling became legal and people could open casinos. I started work at the Knightsbridge Sporting Club dealing blackjack. I was about the youngest to be trained up. I got my licence and everything and it was just then that Hugh Hefner decided to open the Playboy Club. There was talk amongst the girls about how they wanted to go there and wear rabbit costumes with ears and a tail, and I went along with them. I applied and they said yes, if I had a licence. I was all set to go and then I got a knock-back: they wouldn't have me. Whether it was because of Dad I don't know. It might have been because once when I was at the Knightsbridge Sporting Club I was dealing and I badly needed to go to the toilet. I tried signalling to the pit boss, but he wasn't looking. I was standing there with my legs crossed waving away at him but he took no notice. Eventually it got so bad that I just left the chips on the table and went downstairs to the Ladies. I know it was a thing you should never do, but I just had to. Anyway, whatever the reason that was the end of my career as a Bunny girl. Over before it started — although I did, at least, get to try on a uniform.

We had some money to come from the tenancy and Mum and me had a discussion. She wanted to buy a big pub in another area, but I said that if we had a little one we'd have littler troubles with it, so we took a tenancy of the Trafalgar in Remington Street off the City Road. It was tiny, just one small bar.

We had a grand opening of the Traf; everyone came and the next morning seemed a bit flat. Helen, a Scots girl who now works in a solicitors' firm, was in and so were Mum and me. Mum said she'd make some ham-off-the-bone and cheese sandwiches. No one came until eventually an old boy, wearing a cravat as they used to in those days, with a dog-end in the corner of his mouth and a mongrel on a lead, shuffled in. He must have been about 80. He comes up to the bar and says, 'A pint of bitter and a half of Boar's Head.' Mum says, 'We've only got ham and cheese.' He says, 'No, love, it's tobacco.'

When I first took over the Trafalgar it always reminded me of the Queen Vic in *EastEnders* way back in the seventies and eighties, although I reckon our pub had more characters. The Queen Vic could have originated from our pub. Like most South London and East End pubs it was full of characters. Once the word went round, it didn't take long before my Mum and I had the faces pop in from all over London. One night we would have the Adams brothers from North London come in, another night Patrick O'Nione (who was known as Paddy Onions) and Paddy Junior, his son from over the water.

You always knew the Adams sisters were in because they had very loud voices, but it was their brothers who to me were perfect gentlemen: very quiet, laid back and good-looking. There was a new club Ra-Ra's I went to up at the Angel; Tommy Adams and his brother, Terry, owned it, and they would always send me over a drink. In those days, nine times out of ten a girl wasn't allowed to buy a drink. One night we got chatting. For some reason the mini-cab drivers had the night off and it was raining hard, so Tommy offered to take me home. It was about 3 a.m. and he parked behind the garages where I lived and started to kiss and cuddle me. I said, 'Leave off, Tommy, you're married', and he stopped right away. Once you've said that, a man's urges soon change – although I might have had second thoughts if he hadn't been married with children. At the end of the day we, as women, have to stand by our principles when we know a man's married. I have had a couple of affairs with married men, but I've never really felt comfortable with the situation. I think men should be honest and tell a girl first. Years later when I read about the Adams family and Tommy went away, I was shocked.

There was one married man I had a long run with, but that was strictly on a cash basis. It was when I come back from America and I needed some money. I'd never done hostessing, but I thought I'd give it a go and so I applied for a job at the Burlesque off Berkeley Square. There was no uniform like in a Bunny Club, you just turned up in sexy clothes, seamed stockings, a mini-skirt and a halter top. There were no wages but it was £20 commission for every bottle of champagne you sold the punters. I was the oldest girl and also the one with what they used to call the 'fullest figure'. I thought I'd never pull anyone, but within the first week there was a man from Norfolk who owned big estates up there and he was throwing money about like crazy. He must have bought half a dozen bottles of Crystal champagne that night and, of course, he wanted to meet me afterwards. The rules were that you couldn't leave the premises with the punters so the management couldn't be done for controlling prostitutes, so I told him to go and wait by my car in Berkeley Square. I don't know how I drove home with him that night to my flat in Langdon Court which was just near the Traf. That was the last time I set foot in the Burlesque. I nicked a punter, which is what I wanted, and I never went back.

The first time he came to see me after that I'd sent Jonathan to my Mum's and suddenly there was a knock on the door. I thought it was Jonathan back for some toys, and it was. I was trying to shoo him out quick but then there was the second knock. I thought it might be one of Jonathan's friends and he opened the door. There was Geoffrey wearing a deerstalker. 'Mum,' Jonathan called, 'it's Sherlock Holmes.'

Geoffrey and I had a wild time. I had my cocaine habit under control by then but I introduced him to it and we had a high old time. It must have gone on for six months. Did he mind I had other boyfriends? Well, he was married so he didn't have much choice, did he?

Poor Paddy Onions Senior got shot dead near Patrick's wine bar, Caley's, in Tower Bridge Road in November 1982. There were all sorts of theories about it, but most probably it was in revenge for the stabbing of Mickey Hennessey who I grew up with. Mickey was stabbed to death at a charity boxing evening. He'd been drinking and was making a bit of a nuisance of himself. Paddy'd got arrested but he was acquitted.

Then there was Winkle Kramer, Jacqui Kramer's son, Charlie Tozer[1], a kind-hearted man who was a boyfriend of mine for a bit, and the Kentish Town mob who would spend their last lot of money before their next tickle. Some of the Train Robbers who were now being released would occasionally come in. There'd also be the Fraser boys, Georgie Davis and his great friend Micky Ishmail; Terry Cox would be a regular as well as Mickey Morris, a friend of the Krays who was also a boyfriend of mine, very good-looking with blond hair. You'd think butter wouldn't melt in his mouth,

---

[1] On 22 May 2000 Charles Tozer from Kentish Town along with Francis Pope from Wapping, two of a team said to be known as the Wild Bunch, received sentences of 30 years each. They had been arrested in September 1997 after an operation involving some 60 officers from Scotland Yard. They had been convicted of the attempted robbery of a Safeway store in Bow in which a security guard, Stephen Sturgeon, had been shot and wounded. They were also convicted of a robbery at the Nationwide Building Society in Kentish Town committed whilst on police bail. Tozer had received 6 years for robbery in 1978 and a further 15 years in September 1988, this time for a series of robberies.

but he was completely wild. I liked all the robbers, although some of them changed once cocaine took hold of them. At the end of the day they weren't so bad – all they wanted was the money!

We used to have a whip system for the Chaps. They'd each stick a £20 note in a pint pot on the bar – stolen security money no doubt – and it would save a guy wasting valuable drinking time asking who wanted a drink and being the waiter. If you were in the whip you just asked the bar staff and ordered drinks for your friends.

It was never unusual for my Mum, who would be sweeping up after we'd officially closed while there was just a few people left having afters, to find a £20 note stuck to her slippers. She would shout out, 'Hey, you left this money!' and they'd say, 'Keep it, Renée, go and buy a dress.' That's how good they were. I can't tell you how many torn-up bank wrappers we swept up either.

Once we started having a Monday Club – the day the markets are closed – people would be in our pub and then go on to the A. and R., a drinker in the Charing Cross Road. One day a guy I knew as Johnny Bananas said to my Mum, 'Renée, I've got some lovely Jerseys.' 'Oh', she said, 'don't forget me and Marilyn, we like pink, mauve, all the pale colours, size 14.' In his drunken stupor he wasn't listening and in the early hours of the Sunday morning the pub doorbell rang and there was Johnny Bananas with a sackload of Jersey Royal potatoes. She roared with laughter. 'John, I thought they were knock-off jerseys as in jumpers!' she remarked.

I was there full-time and singing in other pubs and clubs when I could get the work. After he came out from the Train, Mum and Dad went for a holiday to America and they left me in charge. Dad had rung up his friend Alfie Gerard to make sure he'd help me out if there was any trouble . . . and there was. I let it go the first couple of nights, but there was a father and son causing trouble. I was going out with Jimmy Wooder's nephew, Eddie, at the time and they were digging him out from across the bar and winding him up, and they knocked him about a bit later on. The third night they were still being aggressive and I rang Alf who came straight over. Alfie just got hold of the younger one, held him up and said, 'Don't upset my pal's daughter when he's on holiday.' The boy just about wet himself. Alf looked like that American actor James Cagney, but far bigger. He had this restaurant, the Blue Plaice, over in Southwark Park Road, and his conger eel and mash with parsley sauce was blinding.

He also had the City Club in the City Road and often I'd go up there. Alfie owned it with Jerry Callaghan, and one of the regulars was that great thief and escaper Ruby Sparks who was then in his late seventies. I asked Alfie and Jerry if they could give me a job waitressing or any bar work when I had finished the pub hours, and Alfie said I could waitress in the afternoons, sharing the stint with another girl who worked there part-time. One particular morning I was there when the jukebox man appeared – he didn't seem to have been round for ages – to change the records on the jukebox. People were fed up with the old-style records, Elvis Presley's especially. Alfie was preparing conger eel for lunch and there were about six gigantic eels in the sink. I called to him that the jukebox man was here and he shouted back from the kitchen, 'Oh, about time, we've had the same records on for the last six months, everybody's sick to death of Bing Crosby's "White Christmas". Make sure you put some new Sinatras in, son!' As the guy had the top of the jukebox open with his head buried in it putting in the records, Alfie came out in his apron with the largest conger eel you could hope for with its skin all peeled back. He waved it and then placed it under the young guy's vest and said, 'Do you have Don McLean's new one "American Pie"?' Well, the poor guy nearly shit himself with fright to see this eel staring at him. I collapsed with laughter and Ruby did too. 'Don't get his vest dirty, Alf,' he said.

After that the jukebox man came once a fortnight with all the new sounds, and Alfie and Jerry always gave him a good tip and a bit of food, but he never would have the eel pie. I used to tell him he was lucky it hadn't been a live one.

Alf used to knock about with Freddie Foreman as well as Jerry, and for a time he was wanted for the murder of Frank Mitchell. But once Freddie was acquitted Alf was never charged. He died down in Brighton a good few years ago.

One Christmas a customer brought Jonathan a train set and by the Easter it was still in the wrapping paper. Mum turned on my Dad saying, 'You still ain't put the train set together. Poor little boy, you're all right at holding them up but you're certainly no good at putting them together.'

Mickey McAvoy, who got done on the Brinks-Mat, used to come and drink in the Traf, sometimes with his brother John and sometimes on his own. He could cause a bit of trouble, but John was much milder. Mickey glassed someone in the pub once. I don't even know what it was over. David Fraser, Frank's boy, cut John to ribbons once, but I don't know what that was over either. John was a proper businessman; he had a sweetshop and other things.

Years later when my Aunt Jessie died John lent me his Roller to drive Mum and Dad to the funeral. We felt ever so posh until we got just near the cemetery and the radiator ran dry. The engine started hissing, and boiling water was spraying out just when everyone could see us. I had to run and get some more.

It wasn't all work. Mary, Charlie Tozer's ex-wife, did a bit of barmaiding with us. There was a new club opened down the Balls Pond Road, and one evening after hours we went down there. There was a girl called Jackie Beer[2], a mixed-race girl whose husband was doing life, and she didn't half have a temper on her. I saw her waving her finger at Mary and I went over and told her to stop. 'Do you know who I am?' she asked. 'I'm Jackie Beer'. 'I don't care,' I said. 'I'm Marilyn Wisbey.' Mary was signalling to me to leave off. 'She fights men,' she told me. 'I don't care,' I said. 'Who the hell does she think she is?' A bit later the guy Jackie was with came over and started talking to me, and the next thing I know she's across the room and has knocked me down. She was pulling my hair and banging my head on the floor. The only thing to do was take a bite out of her tit, and that's what I did. Suddenly she's off me screaming. The police had been called and we went outside on to the pavement. Then when the coppers arrived she showed them her bleeding tit hanging out of her blouse and told them I'd done it. I wasn't waiting around; there was a black cab passing so I got in it and was away. But it wasn't right her going to the coppers. I was surprised at her.

Years later I'm in the Traf and in walks Mickey Head, who I used to go out with, along with this Jackie. I'm behind the bar serving afters and I asked him what he was doing with her. I told him about the fight, and with that he just give her the money for a cab and told her to sling it.

After Dad had been out about six months the brewery said we weren't selling enough beer and that if we wanted we could

[2] A pseudonym.

buy the freehold from them. Dad managed to get a bank to lend him £28,000 and that's what we did.

And then it all went wrong another time. Dad got banged up on remand for 15 months over about forty grand's worth of travellers' cheques, along with Billy Gentry and Jackie Mullins, old Dodger's son. Billy's girlfriend, Tina Meer, was the cause. She went and grassed them all. Billy had been doing parcels at King's Cross and she put his name and about thirty others to the Transport Police. You have to blame Billy really; you should never engage a woman in your doings, and certainly not just a girlfriend. She'd been having it off with a big man from South London before she took up with Billy. When we went to court Miss Tina was dressed down for the benefit of the judge, and she gave the jury and judge the forlorn look of a person who was swept into something she didn't understand. She was never a saint and she never said 'No' to Gentry's gifts of diamonds, Mercedes sports car, fine wines and dinners. She understood those things all right. She said she'd grassed because Billy'd been out with other women and given her a backhander or two. She was the first woman supergrass. She got given another identity and was off somewhere, but not before she wrote her story for the Sunday papers about how she feared for her life. In the end Tommy got a bender but not before he'd done those 15 months. The judge said he'd played a very minor part.

In the meantime, after being very busy in the pub our customers drifted away and we were nearly on the brink of having to sell. For our Monday Club we used to have a live band and on this particular Monday in walked two bailiffs. Mum and myself were behind the bar. At first I thought they were the Old Bill. I told them I was the landlady and they showed me a piece of paper and went behind the bar and started taking bottles of Smirnoff and Gordon's Gin down. All this was in front of about twenty customers half-pissed and playful.

'Oh,' I said. 'You can't do that.' 'Can't we?' was the reply. 'Please, please,' I said, taking one of the guy's arms. 'Let's talk about this upstairs.' 'Howard, I'll carry on taking stock, you go upstairs with the Missus.' He sat down in our personal sitting-room to discuss the situation and, as he was nosing around, he spotted our library of gangster books and videos. 'Oh,' he said. 'My sister used to be friends with one of those Train Robbers' daughters way back.' 'Which one?' 'Tommy Wisbey.' 'Well,' I said, 'that's my father, so what's your sister's name?' 'Susan Edwards.'

'Susan Edwards. I remember her. What a wonderful coincidence,' I said, thinking this might just be a way of gaining time. 'That's right, your father was a policeman at Peckham. Look, Mr Edwards, please give us six weeks and you will get the outstanding debt as soon as possible.'

With that he left me a form to fill in and said, 'Look, if only you could have told us earlier about your problems it would have saved you all this embarrassment.' Yes, I thought, in theory we should. What would have happened if we'd told the truth?

Dear Mr VAT Inspector,

Due to the misfortune of my father being nicked again – he was a Great Train robber and is a sort of celebrity – our customers have left our pub, our takings have dropped to zero, and we are behind as the case cost us six thousand pounds in solicitor's fees. What can we do?

I know what answer we would have had.

It does not work like that in the real world. Do the government know that small businesses have good days and bad days and do not run like big profit-making companies? That's why kids today who want to have their own businesses should think twice. There is no understanding in the real world, only the office pen-pushers, who think we all cheat the tax system of this country, and who set these unfair rules for small businesses.

Due to a brainwave I had (and with a great deal of difficulty) we managed to pay our debts. I had finished making a record a year before, so I said we will have a talent competition with a grand finale and for the first prize there'll be a record contract, second prize will be £250, and third prize a dinner for two somewhere.

I called up the magazine *The Stage*, and they sent someone along to make sure it was above board. We placed our advert for every Wednesday for eight weeks. People were calling in from all over England, Scotland and the Isle of Man. I told them no jugglers, magicians, opera singers or fire eaters were allowed, just vocalists, groups or comedians.

After that the phone never stopped ringing. The book that we used to list the contestants we kept at the back of the bar and one careless barmaid – who shall be nameless, but it might just have been me – left it under the dripping optic. Of course when I came to retrieve it the next afternoon, two pages had stuck together. That following week went well, so did the next, but when the fourth week of May arrived, I realised we had no contestants lined up. I called round to a few singers over in South London to do me a favour and come and sing, plus we were killing ourselves laughing as I had to go in for it just to make contestant No. 6.

The word got round, so people came along to watch. The

locals automatically thought it's a fix, the Mrs is going to win it. I could read it in their faces, but I couldn't tell them how we come to have made a bloomer. It wasn't a fix except that I couldn't win whatever happened. In the end, the judges voted for Jackie Hargreaves, a seamstress from Shoreditch. I think Jackie ended up getting plenty of work in Butlin's Holiday Camp.

The last night of the finals went with a swing until midnight when, due to a technical problem – instead of me drinking single vodkas that night the staff were giving me doubles – I forgot to call 'Time'. I would never have shouted out 'Time' anyway, only turned down the lights.

About half-past twelve in barged ten of the biggest uniformed policemen I have ever seen. The music stopped dead and there I was holding up the bar or the other way around. The white notepads all seemed to come out at the same time; all the police officers appeared to be really young, helmets too big with white little ears squeezing outwards. 'Yes, sir, can I help you?' 'Well, I'm sorry to say this but you are well over time, do you mind if we ask the customers some questions?' The senior constable approached some of the Chaps from South London with a young rookie. He spoke to Paddy O'Nione's son, Patrick. 'Excuse me, name please?' He answered, 'Ronald.' 'Surname?' Young Patrick said 'Biggs' and the young rookie wrote it down, then said, 'At what time did you last purchase a drink in these premises, sir?' Young Patrick; 'Half past eight.' So young Winkle piped up and said, 'You greedy bastard, you mean you've been here all fucking night and not bought a drink?' Well, we couldn't stop laughing and I had to turn away. The rookie then turned to young Winkle and said, 'Name?' Young Winkle said 'Reginald.' 'Surname?' 'Kray.' All the Chaps just gave the names of people who were either dead or in the nick. But my laughter soon turned to dismay when we were fined £500 for permitting drinking after hours.

I couldn't believe it; it was the dearest round of drinks I had bought in the pub. All my efforts to pay back the debts had just about gone to waste. I felt I just had enough with my father having been away in prison. I wanted out. When Dad finally came out we had a big welcome home party, but now I really had had enough of the pub. My part-time job working for the caterers at the races, travelling to either Sandown, Newbury, Kempton or Brighton every weekend and Boxing Day and New Year's Day as well, was getting me down too.

Then we had another bit of bother. A guy from the old days, Tommy Clarke, came in when my Dad was bottling up with his slippers on. Tommy Clarke wanted a lift somewhere, and Dad shouted, 'I won't be long.' He was gone so long that I looked out of the window and there was my Dad and his friend with arms behind their backs, across the bonnet of a motor, surrounded by plain-clothes police officers before being taken away. There was no problem for Dad but there was for Mum. The coppers searched the place and they found a tiny bit of puff in Mum's bed. Off she went to Highbury Court and it was in all the local papers: 'Train robber's wife fined – found with cannabis.'

All I wanted was to get into show business, but there didn't seem much chance. Then there seemed like an opportunity. A few of our regulars had been on a golfing holiday in Palm Springs, California, and they came back full of it – how they met George Peppard and what a beautiful place it was. They'd also met an English gipsy fellow called Kelly, and they were going on about what a good bloke he was as well. Then one night in the Traf I was up singing and Kelly came in. During a break he came over to me and said how he enjoyed my singing and would I like to sing in his restaurant in Palm Springs and manage it as well. Well, I jumped at it. 'No problem with the green card,' he said. 'I will take care of that.' And with that I started singing 'California, Here I Come!'

7

Cockney girl in America

The very first time I went to America had been when I was 22. In the Traf I'd met an American guy called Tom who was over here, and he'd told me about how he owned a Christmas tree farm near Carmel just south of San Francisco, where Clint Eastwood was later the mayor. When he went back to America he kept writing and then he invited me over. So I left Jonathan with my Mum and I went for six weeks. Tom met me at San Francisco airport and the idea was that we should tour the States together. I thought we'd be living in luxury hotels, but no such luck, what he had was a small camper van which looked like an ice-cream van without the 'Mr Whippy' on the side. And Tom didn't seem to have any money to go with it – or, if he did, he wasn't showing because I was spending for everything. I don't even know if he had a farm because we started travelling straight away.

I knew we'd be going to Las Vegas and so I'd taken two suitcases full of dresses and nice clothes. What I didn't realise was that we might be going to Las Vegas but we were to sleep in the camper. We stayed at Caesar's Palace on the Strip all right, but it wasn't in a room: it was in the camper car park. We got there and parked amidst dozens and dozens, possibly hundreds of homes. You could hook up to electricity and water just like on any camp site.

I said I wanted to go to a show and Tom said he wasn't paying $70 a head. For that you got a table and two drinks. I said I wasn't coming to Las Vegas and not seeing one of the top acts in the world – I think it was Sammy Davis Junior – and I was going anyway. I put on a cocktail dress and a fluffy little cape and eventually he came round and said he'd go too. The show finished about eleven and I said where were we going and he said, 'Back to the camper.' I told him no way was I doing that, and this time he wouldn't come with me so I ended up off on my own. I went to a club, the Brewery, and I was there dancing all night.

It was then that I met a Mexican who told me he was a record producer and he wanted to take me home. I said that I was staying in Caesar's Palace and so he took me back there. He wanted me to have him up to my room but I said I'd meet him at midday, which is when Americans start eating lunch, and I kissed him and legged it out to the car park. When I got there I couldn't remember which was our van. They all looked alike in the dawn and I thought I was going to have to start knocking on the doors until, when I was hunting through them, I came across one with bright orange and yellow curtains and I recognised it as ours.

Tom and I got as far as Fort Worth before I ditched him, or he ditched me is more like. It was freezing cold and we were quarrelling badly so I said, 'Just let me out.' And he did. It was just like one of those road movies. One minute I was in the camper with him and the next I was standing on the road with the suitcases either side of me watching his number-plate go off in the distance. I suppose I thought he might turn round and come back like they do in films, but he must have thought he was well out of it and he didn't.

I wanted to go on to Florida but I hadn't really got enough money to fly. A customer in the pub had an aunt who lived in Fort Lauderdale and I thought I'd try to go and see her. I thought since they were both Forts they'd be near each other, and it would be like going from London to Brighton.

I started to carry my cases and I found I couldn't. I hadn't any sensible shoes, everything was stiletto heels. Then a girl come along with a backpack and I asked her where I was and how near it was to the airport. She said there wasn't any airport; the best thing would be a Trailways, the rival to Greyhounds. I told her I'd buy her a hamburger if she'd help me with my cases.

So I went to the booking desk at the Trailways station and bought a ticket. It was then I asked how many hours it would take and the man said, 'Honey, it's four days. Change in New Orleans.' So I bought a 14-day pass. At least I saw the Southern States as I went. It's a brilliant way to travel. When the bus stops there's showers and a proper restaurant.

It was while I was on the bus that I was grateful for being brought up streetwise. The boy I was sitting next to was lovely and taught me to play draughts, but somewhere near El Paso a man got on and went and sat at the back. I could see him eyeing everyone up and I didn't think I fancied his look. Then, on a Trailways, they turned the centre lights off so people could sleep at night. I made sure my bag with my passport and money was fitted under the little pillow I had. Next morning I think I was the only person the man hadn't cleaned out – cameras, money, watches. People were saying, 'How come he's taken nothing of yours?' And the answer was that I grew up in South London, but I didn't rub it in.

When I got to Fort Lauderdale I rang my mother and asked the number of this girl's aunt, but she said she hadn't been in and she would ask her the next time she saw her, so that was a fat lot of good. I booked into a hotel for one night and then I started to try and find accommodation. I saw a house for rent and went and knocked on the door. The woman who answered was American-Irish, Nellie Monarco was her name, and she said the house was far too expensive for me on my own. When I asked where I could get something, she took pity on me and said she had a back room at the house next door where she actually lived, and I could have it at $100 a week.

The next day I'd gone to the launderette when I ran into these two older guys walking along the street towards me. I was wearing a smart cap and they offered to buy it for $25. Elmo Legge and Frank Reynolds they were. I told them I wasn't selling, so they said, 'Come and have a cocktail. It's Happy Hour.' I thought that with all I'd been through I needed to be made happy. They lived in some hotel apartment and they said I could use the facilities. Next day and the one after that I was there charging up my lunches to their suite and not even going to see them. But of course there was a price to pay. There's no such thing as a free lunch. I'd got to make a decision. Elmo was the one who fancied me, but when he said he had to go back to Marina Del Rey near Los Angeles and would I go with him, I said I wanted to stay in the warm. The next day he gave me an air ticket, so I sold the Trailways pass and a couple of days later I flew over to join him.

He was a rich man. He owned (or had concessions on) the roadside billboards as well as having a ranch near Palm Springs, and we used to tour round looking at them. I was begging him to take me there so that I could see my hero Frank Sinatra's house, and one morning we set off. At first I was entranced by

90

the cactuses which were everywhere just like in Westerns. But up close they just seemed like gigantic penises.

I've always liked my breakfast and I'd been a little pig with the pancakes and syrup. Although I've always been regular going to the toilet, once we were on the road I found I needed to go badly. I said, 'I've got to go. Like this minute.' 'Do you want a Texaco or a Shell?' he asked. Like he was wanting to know if I wanted my eggs well done or easy over. I think Americans can't do anything without having a choice. 'Elmo. Just hurry up,' I said, and when he finally got to a garage and was pulling in I was out of the car before he stopped. I was half afraid that he'd have gone by the time I came out, just like in that Jack Nicholson film *Five Easy Pieces*, but he waited.

Once I came home we kept in touch for some years – and then, you know how it is. Someone doesn't reply to a letter and that's it. I would love to see him again and have a few more pancakes.

8

America Again

The second time I went to America was just for a holiday, and it was Dad's connections which made it so great. It all goes back really to the singer Billy Daniels. He'd been a frequent visitor to London and, so Frank says, he'd known both Jack Spot and Billy Hill so he got to know a lot of other faces as well. When he was over here appearing in *Bubbling Brown Sugar* he and a couple of the Inkspots came down to play at the Traf. My uncle Ronnie Wisbey had been drinking in the pub all night and Fred, one of our locals, had been too. So Ronnie said, 'Fred, I bet you ten pounds that's Billy Daniels and the Inkspots singing.' Fred looked round. 'Leave off, Ronnie, the Inkspots wouldn't be singing in here, not at the Angel, Islington.' Then he stopped to listen. Billy was singing that old classic, 'That Old Black Magic'.

Fred looked round again after taking the bet and said, 'As it happens it does sound like him.' They all laughed. My Dad said it was unbelievable; I wish I had been there. Billy felt uneasy with a couple of fellows in the pub, so my Dad said,

'Don't worry, Bill, my brother and I will make sure you get safely to the White House' – the hotel up the top of Great Portland Street where he was staying. So with that Bill was safely taken home and as he was dropped off he said, 'Tom, any time you're over in the States call me.'

So when they went over they looked Billy up and later when I said I was going with my girlfriend Jackie Saintey – who was going out with Tony, Albert Falco's son – my Dad called Billy once again. While they'd been over there Billy had introduced them to David Goldstein who was the vice-president of the Dunes hotel in Vegas, and now Billy said I was to get in touch with him: 'He'll be waiting for Marilyn at the Dunes.' Dad said I had to take something over for David on his behalf.

Jackie and me rented a room and then did the usual things in Los Angeles, such as going to see Grauman's Chinese Theatre where the stars leave their handprints in cement, and then off to Disneyland. Then we flew out to Vegas and took a cab to the Dunes which was on the Strip. Now it's been pulled down and a newer hotel has been built, but it was very big in those days. I was really shy but Jackie said I had to do the talking. 'I can't.' She said, 'Go on', and more or less shoved me at the reception desk. We were shown up to David's secretary and then in to see him.

I said, 'Hello, Mr Goldstein, I'm Tommy Wisbey's daughter, he asked me to give you a call and bring you these.' I had about thirty silk ties to give him, hoisted by one of the Burberry Mac Mob and paid for by my Dad. Apparently the previous year when Tom had been over he'd said next time he'd bring him some ties and cashmere jackets. 'Well,' he said, 'thank your dad for me. Now, girls, what can I do for you?' Before I could say anything he had called down to arrange a room. I was so over-whelmed I really could not say anything. It was funny because my Dad had asked David to really look after me and my friend, while we were just wanting a room.

'Now, girls, wait for Alec and he will show you to your room.' And when Alec came it was, 'Alec, make sure these girls are OK.' We said thank you and went off down the corridor, behind Alec. The room was unbelievable. In fact it was a beautiful suite. After having had a shower and while we unpacked our suitcases there was a knock at the door and in walks a handsome young waiter with a trolley-load of drinks, every spirit, champagne on ice, even canapés. I said to Jackie, 'Did you order all these? This is going to cost an arm and a leg, I hope you've brought your American Express card.' She was giggling, 'No, you dopey cow, it's from him upstairs.'

Anyway, we'd just tipped the handsome waiter when all of a sudden the phone went. 'Are you OK, you two? My friend Romeo and I are coming down.' It was Mr Goldstein. We quickly got ready, and in came David and his friend Romeo, who must have been well over sixty. We thanked them for the drinks and poured them out. The drinks were now flowing, and when I went to the bathroom Jackie followed and I said, 'You can have the 65-year-old; I'll settle for the boss.' She started laughing then; we were making them laugh about London and Jackie told David that I sing in our pub back home in London. With that he said, 'I bet you don't know a Tony Bennett number.' Before he could finish his sentence I started to sing 'It's the Good Life'. He was gobsmacked. He couldn't believe that a girl in her early twenties would know that old ballad.

David told Romeo to take us anywhere we liked as he had to play golf, and we kissed him and thanked him. That evening Romeo took us to the Brewery night-club in his limo; he was a lovely little Italian man, you could just see his

94

silver-grey hair appearing over the steering-wheel in this great stretch limo.

Just about the last night we were there, David remarked on my singing again and took us down to the lounge showroom. It was then that he threw this great bombshell, saying, 'Marilyn, you can sing in this spot if you want.' I thought to myself, 'Wow!' But then cold feet set in and I thought, 'Who's going to look after the pub and take care of Jonathan?' Turning that down was probably the biggest mistake I ever made in my whole life – and I've made some really big ones.

Four years later Mum and Dad had a motel in Palm Springs. Just before they sold it and packed up and came back to England, I went out for a holiday. When they said they were going to Las Vegas for a couple of days, I immediately said I wanted to come too. It hadn't changed from the last time I'd been there.

We took with us two great Prince of Wales check cashmere (nicked) jackets. David could not believe that my Dad hadn't forgotten after all these years and he said, 'What's the bill, Tom?' He said, 'No, David, you looked after my daughter and her friend.' David asked us where we were going and we said we were going to the top of the Dunes because Keeley Smith was appearing.

That night we had dinner upstairs and the cabaret had started to get going. As I looked over there was David and another big young guy with him. I said, 'Dad, there's David.' He waved and started to come over to us, sat down and then ordered some food and drinks. All the staff were flapping as if some top film star had arrived and I suppose, since he was the boss, so they should have done. David then said to me, 'Marilyn, I hope you are going to sing here tonight.' I said, 'OK then, David.' He disappeared into the bathroom and I said to

Mum, 'Oh no, there will be murder if I sing on Keeley's bill.' 'Oh, she said, 'Take no notice, David will forget.'

As the night wore on Keeley was magic, her voice was still good as always. I remembered my Mum used to play her songs when my Dad was in prison, such deliciously romantic words and music. In the break, the word must have gone round that the vice-president himself was in the audience. The *maître d'* came up asking David if everything was all right. He replied, 'No.' 'What's wrong, Mr Goldstein?' David said, 'Well, you see this lovely lady sitting here, she's from dear old London town, Tommy Wisbey's daughter. I want her to sing for us all.' 'OK Mr Goldstein, I'll go and see the music director straight away.'

The music director came over to me and asked what I would like to sing. I thought I'd better stick to something old and said, '"You're Nobody Till Somebody Loves You", in B-flat with a swing beat.' 'OK, I will introduce you five minutes before Keeley's on again.' So the piano player introduced me and said, 'Now put your hands together, we have a special lady all the way from London, England. Ladies and Gentlemen – Miss Marilyn Wisbey.' I got up with ease; the sound system was just like nothing I had ever sung on; the piano player followed very well, I got huge applause in front of a packed audience of 350 people, and then I was asked to finish with a second one. So I sang 'Crazy' in B-flat.

The audience were great. I felt like Shirley Bassey. It was a terrific feeling; a buzz that I will never forget until I die; the best. It was a holiday with my Mum, Dad and my son that I will always treasure. Little did I know what would follow back in Palm Springs.

9

Palmy Springs

When Kelly made me the offer to go and sing and manage his restaurant in Palm Springs, at first I thought of taking Jonathan with me, but Mum and I decided that I would go out there first and find a place and then my best friend at the time, Jackie, would bring him over as she wanted to come for a holiday.

Two months after I met Kelly I was living in North Palms Canyon in Palm Springs at the Tikki Palms Hotel. Kelly and his wife, Lyn, had four children and I was taking care of them, cleaning the rooms and sometimes doing the odd bit of babysitting, while he was arranging the contracts for the restaurant with his lawyer. I couldn't wait. Kelly had won a liquor licence in a lottery and there was still some paperwork to be done. In the meantime Kelly and Lyn used to take me out and show me around and I soon got my bearings. The air was so clear and the streets were so clean (for any readers who can afford to go, and who suffer with asthma or chest problems, it's ideal), and I was staying where the best singer in the world lived – Mr Francis Albert Sinatra, who I actually got to meet a few months into my stay.

One night Kelly took me to Dollywood, a country and western bar partly owned by Dolly Parton, and introduced me to an English girl from Kent called Jenny Sivijer. What a stunner she was. A five-foot-nine blue-eyed brunette with legs up to the ceiling, and she became a friend. The first time I saw her I was flat on my arse and she was standing laughing at me; I'd fallen off one of those mechanical bulls which try to buck you off and quite often succeed. Some more customers came over and we all went off one night to a beautiful club, Cecil's, where everybody was good-looking and rich; you could smell the money. Jenny had a small studio flat in Palm Springs.

The first time I ever saw a Wiseguy to my knowledge was when I went to find Jenny one evening. She was staying in a small motel owned by Charley from a New Jersey family. It had windows from which you could only see out, and when I put my head through the reception area there were all the customers lined up against the bar with their hands in the air and Charley was saying, 'You lot are driving me nuts.' I got out as quickly as possible. Later Jenny told me that he was pissed off with them just sitting in the bar watching the baseball on television and not buying any drinks. Eventually I was introduced to him but, even though he was a small man no bigger than Frank, I was frightened of him and I'd say hello and goodbye and shake hands but I never went out of my way to talk to him.

Kelly had said he'd get me a work permit and green card, but when it came to it nothing materialised and so in fact I was an illegal immigrant. I learned about it in a funny way. A crowd of us had gone to Cecil's one night. I was sitting on a bar stool and overheard David Iser (who had been a customer at the Traf) say to Kelly, 'When's Marilyn going to start work?' He said, 'I've changed my mind!' When I swivelled my stool around and asked, 'What did you say?' he said, 'I've changed my mind because of the green card situation.' I said, 'Damn you, Kelly, you mean you've got me 3,000 miles over here for nothing. Well,' I told him, 'I hope you lose all your fucking money! I've got my arse out here and there's no work, thank you very much. You've taken a right liberty.' And I walked out.

Not that that helped me in any way. But I didn't want to go back to London, I was determined to stay on. And that's what I did. I stayed over there, green card or not, and I used to sing in restaurants and bars if I could get work. One of them was Pattie-z. Sometimes Frank Sinatra went there and that's where I met his valet-cum-housekeeper, 'Greek' Arturo, for whom Sinatra once bought a $3,000 hearing aid. I met Arturo through Rocky, the sort of gofer barman whose job it was to fill the shelves at Pattie-z and things like that, and we went out together for about six months. Actually Arturo looked a bit like Sinatra except he had brown eyes and not blue. He'd have been in his fifties then. He met my Mum and Dad and he gave Dad one of Frank Sinatra's cast-off hairpieces to try on. Dad looked like Barney Rubble from *The Flintstones*. 'Dad,' I said, 'you look better bald.'

Later Dad, Mum and I met Sinatra in Rancho Mirage just outside Palm Springs. They'd come over for a holiday and we'd gone to the restaurant with a car-hire owner Dad knew called Fat Willie. Suddenly in walks Frank and his wife and Roger Moore and his wife. Willie leans over to Dad and says, 'Your favourite singer's come in.' Dad thought he was kidding because there were more Frank Sinatra sightings in Palm Springs than there were of Lord Lucan in Europe.

Anyway Sinatra goes to the men's room and Willie follows him and when he comes out he marches him over to introduce him to us. He really did know him. I should think that was one of the happiest days of my Dad's life – apart from taking the money off the Train, that is. Dad had got me to give Frank a copy of Piers Paul Read's book *The Train Robbers* when he appeared at the Festival Hall. At the end all the other girls rushed up with flowers and I took up the book.

I had an old car which Kelly had helped me get by providing a reference, but I wasn't going to stay with him and his family after what he'd done and sneakily kept it from me, so now I had to get an apartment. I managed it thanks to an Italian guy I had met, Danny Magano, a friend from Buffalo. He found it for me, helped me move in and got me some beautiful Italian furniture. One of his friends was Keeley Smith who used to be married to Louis Prima. Now she was married to Bobby Milano and Danny used to take me to their house. They would sing around a piano and I would join in.

But there was still the question of work, so one night I paid a visit to Jenny from Kent at Dollywood to see if there were any jobs about. She had the shoe-shine concession there. I was feeling really fed up that night, but she soon livened me up and I started to mess around with her customers. You had to use different cloths for different types of leather while shoe-shining. What did I do? A cowboy type of guy sat down. He had on tan cowboy boots and a tan Stetson. I picked up a cloth that had previously been used for black boots; as I was swaying to and fro with the cloth, Jenny looked down and said, 'Marilyn, oh no, look at his boots!' They were not polished tan now but had great black marks all over them.

Luckily he didn't notice what I had done because he was simply mesmerised by Jenny's cleavage. I said to him, 'Sir, I'm sorry, but are these tan boots or black, which polish would you like me to use?' If looks could kill! 'Gee, girl, what have you done?' Jenny came to the rescue and gave him his money back, saying, 'Sir, please excuse my friend, she's just learning.' As he got up and left, Jenny said, 'Marilyn, you got the polish everywhere, even on his white socks.'

Eventually I told her the whole story about Kelly and asked if she could help me out. She told me she used to be a waitress in the Comedy Store downtown in Palm Springs Canyon. I went to apply for the job. Luckily, the head barman was a good friend of Danny Magano and so I got it. Just being a cockney girl serving drinks in an English pub is quite different from knowing a vast amount about cocktails. There weren't things like that in Islington as there are now. I didn't know that 'a slow screw up against a wall without a pillow' was a type of drink. And you have to use different glasses for short and long drinks.

On my second night working there, the place was full of people. My section looked as if they had just come out of *The Beverly Hillbillies* and the place was not air-conditioned. Well, there was a great big fat man, his fat wife and two fat kids. My job was to keep saying to the customers, 'Do you care for a cocktail, sir?' This fat guy said, 'Yeah, sure honey, I'll have two Rob Roys and two Shirley Temples.' By the time I had got to the bar I was sweaty, hot and tired. I said to Randy the bartender, 'I'll have two Roy Rogers, one Shirley Temple and a Clark Gable.' He burst out laughing and said, 'Marilyn, you're a hoot, but I don't think you will make a waitress.' Poor guy. He tried to be patient with me, but I just wasn't good at cocktail waitressing.

Also, I have to say I didn't like working nights, so I asked if I could work in the daytime with Lou and his wife who were managing the restaurant. They were great, real down-to-earth people from New York, and they treated me like one of the family. II a.m.–I p.m. was early bird special time with a set lunch at a knockdown price, so the place would be filled with wealthy, older people, mostly Jewish. 'Kikes' was the slang word for them if they had come from New York, which many had to get away from in the winter, because of the cold.

Well, every day I used to serve this little old Jewish man. I knew exactly what he wanted: a salt beef sandwich, no butter, tiny piece of mustard, half a slice of a gherkin, pickled cucumber on rye bread and a Martini straight up with an onion. This particular day I was really rushed off my feet and when I gave him his order he screamed, 'Miss, Miss!' Louis said to me, 'Go to table three and see what he wants.' 'Yes, sir, what's the problem?' 'You, where's my onion?' He was really shouting, 'Where's my onion?' 'One moment, sir, I'm sorry but I've forgotten, wait there.' Off I go to get this little 80-year-old, spoilt man from New York his onion, and by now everyone was calling out for me, 'Miss, you forgot my ketchup'; 'Miss, where's my food?'

This little man with his check polyester jacket and Crimplene trousers had started everybody off on me. But I finally got my own back on him when I leaned down and slipped twenty small cocktail onions into his Martini and whispered, 'Here's your fucking onions, you spoilt little bastard.' I just took my apron off, handed my till roll in and said, 'Lou, I can't work here serving those old snowbirds from wherever. They're the rudest, most ignorant people I have ever met. I've met better people in the pie and mash shop in my old neighbourhood; what is their problem? They are millionaires and they're eating "cheap early bird specials" and fighting in the queue over who's going to sit where. I'm sorry, I love you and your wife but I can't work in this place.'

So now I was out of work again. Jonathan – who had come

over and was living with me – was now aged eight and was going to school. Off he would go to meet the yellow school buses and I would make him his packed lunch. He would come home and say that the Americans were taking the mickey out of his accent. I felt so sorry for my son, as he was loved so much by my Mum and Dad; spoilt rotten like all grandchildren are, but I thought this would be a better life for us both away from the criminal fraternity of London.

My savings were dwindling away fast and I tried singing at different places in Palm Springs, but no one would give me a regular job. You'd get tips, that was all. A dollar here, five or a ten sometimes for a request. I'd have to split it with whoever was accompanying me. They knew I was an illegal alien and I couldn't squeal for a regular wage. One particular place was called Melvyn's at the Ingleside Inn, a very exclusive hotel where Errol Flynn, Howard Hughes, Shelley Winters, Clark Gable, Joan Crawford and many more great film stars used to stay. It was built on the side of a hill in a canyon with a very well designed interior and lovely gardens. Joe, the Jewish piano player, used to let me sing all the old ballads in Happy Hour and we would share the tips. But it really wasn't good enough to survive on, so I knew I had to find regular work.

Danny Magano had become a great friend and he and I took Jonathan to Disneyland, Magic Mountain and all the usual places in California. Danny would take us in a black Cadillac that he said had belonged to Al Capone, and I used to say to Jonathan, 'We're going in a Batmobile!' Weekends were great, the neighbours used to have a barbecue to which we'd be invited. The kids had their own communal swimming pool, so you see it was certainly a different kind of lifestyle.

As I got home at 10.30 p.m. one evening I found that Danny Magano had dropped a note through my door. Would I like to go to Vegas for the night? Would I? Twelve of us were going and I got my glad rags on, ready to leave at 11.30 p.m. My good friendly neighbour looked after Jonathan and off we all went with the Gaggi brothers from Buffalo. We were to have a five-course meal with Dionne Warwick and her new man who had been in *The Godfather* movie. I couldn't believe it. We arrived at about 4 a.m. and all went to the back of a restaurant and a beautiful dining room with the finest cutlery and cut glass. Dionne was a fabulous hostess and the Crystal champagne flowed continuously. There were no drugs, but by now I was falling asleep. The drive had been well worth it to see one of my favourite singers, not at the Albert Hall, but to actually meet her in private. She loved my cockney accent and Danny made me sing to her, 'You're Nobody Until Somebody Loves You' in B-flat.

Jenny would occasionally come and tell me about the boyfriends she had met, until one day she came to tell me something rather different; she'd had a visit from immigration. 'Oh no,' I said, 'I've just got my life sorted out.' My visa was nearing the end and I managed to have it extended for a further six months, but I would clearly have to do something serious if I wanted to stay. When Jenny went back home to see her parents, I reminded her to bring me some teabags.

It was after she had gone that I went to have a smear test. I always had one regularly every year from the time when I had Jonathan. In the States you don't have the NHS like you do over here; well, they do, but only if you are a true American citizen, so I had to pay for it. Off I went to the doctor to have it and then I forgot all about it because it had always been negative before. Then one morning I got a letter to say my test was positive and would I go and make an appointment. I thought, 'Oh my God, I have cancer and I'm only 28 years of age.'

The consultant said it was what he called stage three, in other words in the very early stages. I was under a very good hospital, the Loma Linda Riverside County Hospital; it was a veterans' hospital, so at least I knew I would have decent doctors there. I said to the consultant, 'Does that mean I have to pack my bags and go back to old rainy London and die?' He started laughing and said, 'No, nothing like it. Have you got Blue Cross?' I said, 'No, but my poodle used to belong to Blue Cross in London. No, sorry, I'm joking. What is it?' 'It's a good hospital insurance company for low-paid workers.' Anyway he was very helpful, gave me the details and then I started to subscribe.

My operation was due in three weeks' time, and as luck would have it Mum and my friend Maureen were coming over the following week. Jonathan was pleased to see his Nan and we did the usual things again – Disneyland and so on. Of course, I took Maureen to a few nightspots.

One night I had a date with a Puerto Rican guy who said he was in the recording industry. He and a friend made up a four with Maureen to a famous place where a group of male strippers performed like the Chippendales. This was just about the start of the male strippers. Then they asked us to go along to a party. On the way there we stopped off at one of their friends' houses and they left Maureen and me in the back of the car. All of a sudden we heard gunshots and there was my date running towards our car. He grabbed open the driver's door, but instead of getting in like we expected he lifted up the seat and there staring at us was a gun. I tried to take it from him, saying, 'You can't use that.' But he just snatched it away, then he jumped in, started the engine and began firing out of the window while he was driving away.

I wet myself with fright while my poor friend Maureen

ducked down yelling, 'Get me out of here!' Apparently they must have been coke dealers from Puerto Rico, all I kept hearing was '*Coca, coca*'. I must have been *loco, loco* to have got swept in. When it was all over and they dropped us back home, there I was saying to my friend Maureen, 'For God's sake, don't tell Mum about this. She'll have a canary fit.'

That was about at the end of the holiday, and Jonathan was asking whether he could go back to England with his Nan. He wasn't happy with staying on and going to school in Palm Springs, so we decided he had better go back to dear old London town rather than continue to be unhappy. The farewell at the airport was very upsetting for me, as all goodbyes are. We kissed and hugged and my final words to Maureen were, 'Try and come back for another exciting holiday.' I had to laugh at her; the reply was, 'You can't buy bullet-proof vests in Harrods, Marilyn!'

So there I was left by myself and facing the prospect of going to have my operation, very similar to a D. and C. They told me to arrange for somebody to collect me after the operation as it was to be an in-and-out job (just like Custer's words before the massacre). I had asked a Filipino friend of mine, Bobbi Brake, a real estate agent, but he was too busy and said his sister Mi-Mi would most probably do it. She was not over-keen until I offered her $50. She was the worst person possible to have been recommended. Off we drove to the hospital which was just over an hour's drive away and I reminded her, 'Mi-Mi, don't forget to pick me up at 4 o'clock this afternoon, please.' 'Don't worry, Malyne,' she said in her Filipino accent, 'I look up my old ex-soldier, Ricky, he live here, he take me for lunch and plenty of nookie. Be back in plenty time.' She rubbed her two fingers together, up and down, and I thought to myself, 'Lucky bitch.' Mi-Mi took the car keys from me and kissed me, and I said, 'Thank you' and gave her the $50. Mistake.

I was still groggy and tired when the nurse woke me gently to see the consultant. He said the operation had been a success and I could go home, but I nodded back into sleep until some hours later the nurse shook me and said, 'I'm sorry, honey, but we need your bed.' I said, 'Nurse, I still feel groggy from the operation.' With that another nurse handed me a gigantic sanitary towel which would have fitted a Sumo wrestler, then lifted me out of bed and sat me in the corridor. Well, I could not believe it. I was trying to keep awake as I knew in an hour's time Mi-Mi would be collecting me. I kept drifting in and out of sleep, plus I was feeling cold from losing blood and from sitting in the main corridor with mostly the poor working people, consisting of Hispanics and suchlike. I was glad I had brought my cashmere coat with me and had the brains to put it on when I drifted out of my sleep, as it kept me warm from the November desert chill. Finally when I could talk and think, I looked at my watch and saw it was 6.30. No sign of Mi-Mi with my car. I was calling her friend's house, but there was no reply. By this time I was doing my nut with temper.

Where the hell was she? Hours went by. 9 o'clock went into 10 o'clock. I was cold, bleeding and still feeling groggy. I kept going to the entrance of the hospital, calling her friends, going back to the entrance. The consultant came out and said, 'You're not still here' in disbelief. I explained what had happened, but he could not help. I would not have minded but I had hardly eaten before the operation and now I was starving. I did not have much money, only $20 to get the car filled with gas. By this time it was 11.30 p.m. I fell asleep again – this time for maybe ten minutes, when all of a sudden Mi-Mi appears with her ex-Marine boyfriend, giggling. 'Hi, Marilyn, I'm here.'

I said, 'Where the fuck have you been, you skinny little prat?'

'Hey, hey,' the man said. I told him, 'Soldier, mind your own business. Madam Butterfly here was supposed to collect me at 4 o'fucking clock.' I snatched the car keys and jumped in my car and drove back to Palm Springs just under 50 miles away, feeling a total wreck, with tears falling down my cheeks. The next day I rang Bobbi and told him that his sister was nuts. After that I stayed in bed and all I wanted was my family around me.

When I finally was up and moving I met an American guy called Ian Evans from Toledo, Ohio, who turned out to be a complete waste of space. Danny introduced us. Ian and I liked a drink together, and he made me laugh. He told me he was going to inherit loads of money from this Mildred, an elderly woman friend of his from Toledo, and I fell for it hook, line and sinker. I believed him totally, although in all honesty I have to say I did meet the elderly woman. At least she existed. I don't know that she was going to leave him that money though. She probably outlived him.

What I certainly didn't know was that he was a silent alcoholic – which means they hide the evidence. I think the only time he had his eyes open was when he was unscrewing a Jack Daniel's bottle. One day when I was cleaning and moving the three-piece suite in his flat, underneath I found loads of empty quarter-bottles of vodka and whisky. I thought, 'Now, I know we had a drinks party the other night, but it wasn't that full of drink.' Then it dawned on me that they were Ian's. It wasn't good.

Then within days Ian began asking me to marry him. As far as I was concerned the hook, line and sinker had been pulled up or out, whichever it is, and I said right out, 'You know it's only for convenience, for my citizenship?' I thought that at least I would have proper papers and be able to get a decent job, but it wasn't to be as easy as that.

The wedding chapel was arranged, but even then Jenny thought I was mad. She asked me if I loved him and I said, 'Yes, madly.' Of course I didn't, but I showed her the photograph of the big house with a swimming pool and a granny annexe which he was promising me. 'Oh yes,' I said, with a slight sound of stuck-upness in my voice, 'I won't have to worry about work no more.' 'Really, well done,' she said. 'Don't you worry, Jen, you'll be able to stay with us, I'll just say you are my housekeeper. I've only got to put up with him for a couple of years.' But in reality the burden of his drinking made my nerves bad.

At least the marriage to Ian at the wedding chapel was hilarious. Jenny was there with about six other people including Danny. We met at a Country and Western bar off Palm Canyon near the chapel. Ian had had a few drinks by the time he arrived and when we got to the chapel the fat woman reverend who conducted our wedding got the hump because I was giggling as we walked down the aisle. I was holding Ian up. I knew he'd been drinking, but I hadn't realised he had a full bottle of Black Label Johnny Walker in his right pocket weighing him down on one side. I had a problem because he was well gone and bending over to the right. I was pulling him upright and the flowers in my hair, which was red at the time, were falling all over the place. When the reverend was rabbiting on about taking this woman for a lawful wedded wife, Ian got slurry and was just saying, 'I love you, yes I do, yes I take this fucking English broad to be my nice tea cup.' He got so bad the reverend said, 'Shut up, or I will not conduct this wedding, period!'

Now I looked round at the congregation, but we were down

to three as the other half had left in fits of laughter. I left Ian being held up by the reverend and asked one of them to have a word with him. Up walked Leon, this Red Indian guy who was married to Melody, another girlfriend of mine, and half carried Ian out, put his head in a sink full of water and then rushed back to give the reverend $50 to continue. Jenny took the bottle of whisky and the service was rushed through. I thought, please stand up straight for 10 minutes. I said, 'I do', he said, 'I do' and with that we were man and wife. After the service when we all went to an English bar down in Palm Canyon I asked my friends why they were laughing, and they said Ian had farted really loudly as I was trying to straighten him up.

But, of course, it wasn't really funny. The weeks went by and I tried to get Ian put in an alcoholics' clinic. With a bit of luck and persuasion I did manage it – you have to be weaned off slowly . He lied and told them he only drank half a bottle a day, and doing cold turkey was such a shock to his system that the poor sod nearly died. I got a call from the clinic and they said, 'He's had a seizure, he looks like he's not going to pull through. Are you his next of kin?' I was very indignant at this stage. I didn't know what that meant, and I said, 'No, I'm not, I'm his wife.' He pulled through, but it was a lost cause.

My Mum and Dad and Jonathan decided to come over for a holiday and it was great to see them. The funny thing about it was the last letter I had sent them was full of Ian, and about how we were going to get married and I would have a house with a pool and I would not want for a thing. But through all the excitement, or maybe deliberately, because I didn't want to worry them, I had forgotten to tell them he had a drink problem.

By the time they came over, I was married to a complete

drunk. One day my Mum, Dad, Ian and I had a gorgeous lunch and plenty of wine, so Mum and Dad said that they were not sunbathing but going to take a nap instead. Ian was already slouched on the settee asleep, so I thought I would have a siesta too. All of a sudden, there was a noise like thunder and then a loud shaking sound; everything was rattling, things were falling off the window sills, pictures fell off the wall. I went to get my Mum and Dad and rushed out to Jonathan, who was happily playing in the pool. As I pulled him out I said, 'Jonathan, quick, darling, it's an earthquake.'

It measured 5.6 on the Richter scale and my Mum was screaming. Everyone was agitated and crying and we really did not know what to do. Mum, Dad, Jonathan and I just waited outside the house with Ian still asleep inside. Then I said to Mum, 'This isn't right, aren't we supposed to be standing inside of the door?' She replied, 'Ain't you supposed to be looking to see if your husband's all right?' I said, 'Oh hell, I forgot about him.' When I went in, there was poor Ian fast asleep with a bottle still in his hand.

Finally, after three months I called his woman friend in Toledo and said, 'You will have to come and get him, he's driving me mad.' But no one came to my rescue; I was stuck with a pest. Eventually I slung him out with his suitcases, but he kept coming round and waking up the neighbours, empty bottles all around the apartment block. By this time I had met up with a girlfriend and we were out having some lunch when I bumped into Danny Magano and Joey Gaggi. Danny said, 'Hey, Marilyn, what's up, you look whacked. I heard you sang on Keely's bill in Vegas. How come, a little cockney girl from London like you?' I said, 'Dan, it's not what you know, it's who you know, darling; I didn't want to, honest.' I thought he would be cross about my getting in on his friend's act, but he wasn't.

III

I stood up and pulled him outside the restaurant and said quietly, 'I'm having some problems.' He asked, 'What like?' I said, 'With that guy I married, remember, for convenience, for my papers?' He said, 'If I had known, I would have married you.' 'No, seriously, he really thinks he's married to me and refuses to leave, he's an alcoholic and it's stressing me out.' When I had told him everything, he said, 'Don't worry, Joey and I will take care of it.'

With that I thanked Dan and kissed him. Looking back I shouldn't have just done that; I should have gone to bed with him and held on to him while I could. Within a few days Ian was round at my apartment trying again to get me to go back to him. This time he wasn't falling about; he was standing and for once he was coherent. In fact he was more normal than I'd ever seen him since the wedding. It seemed to be a perfect time for me to call Danny. While I kept Ian talking Danny arrived with Joe and said, 'I'm sorry, Ian, but we want to have a word with you, outside.' They picked his aircraft travel bag up and as I looked out of the window I watched him being driven off in the car. Danny later said that they had put him on a flight to Detroit, and that was the last time I ever saw or heard of Mr Ian Evans, my first husband.

That, of course, didn't solve the work and money problem. For a time I worked in Churchill's fish-and-chip shop which was run by a Liverpudlian called Woody on Palm Desert Highway, and then I got what seemed like a better job at a beautiful hotel near the Gene Autry hotel at the bottom end of North Palm Canyon. I was a poolside waitress in shorts serving all these Jewish snowbirds who were giving me 25c tips and all these Cubans who were giving me $5, so you can tell which I preferred. By the end of one afternoon I was really hot and tired, and as I served a Cuban group one of the men said would I like to come out for a drink when I finished my shift. I said, 'I've got a better idea. I don't like this job. Give me five minutes and we'll meet then.' So I walked in and quit on the spot.

That was the first night I ever had what was then the 'new' drug, cocaine. Roberto and I sat at the breakfast bar of the apartment he'd rented until 4 in the morning. He had a razor-blade and he was just shaving slices from this block which was the size of a brick. 'This is straight from the horse's mouth,' he said. It was shimmering.

I stayed with him until his holidays finished and, although he left me with a couple of thousand dollars, now I had no job and the money went soon enough.

One afternoon I was looking through the *Desert Sun* and came across an advertisement for a receptionist required for a health club at a concession at a hotel in Palm Springs. 'No experience necessary' was just what I wanted to read, so I called and made an appointment for an interview. I got the job and started that day. The pay was a basic three dollars an hour. In fact it was a massage parlour under another name. The girls, two of them, were very attractive and wore white dental nurse-type dresses. So with my singing at Melvyn's and working from eleven in the morning until eight at night in the parlour, I was just making ends meet.

I must have been naïve. There were the girls counting their money to put up their noses, and I was counting the coins to pay the rent. For a time I didn't realise how they got it and they started laughing at me. When they eventually told me I thought, 'I'll have a bit of that for myself.' I wonder if that's why they call it Palm Springs.

So I began to work for Karen's escort agency. At the start I must have been the worst hooker ever, but at least I was a happy one when the punters paid.

Working for Karen was how I met Rina. She worked for her as well, and one time there was a call for two girls and Rina and me were paired up. She was about ten years older than me; very good-looking, very sophisticated. She told me what there was to know about the game; things like how to fake French when the punters want to see two girls getting it off together. After that we used to graft together. The majority of her friends were *maître d's*, and she passed on the customers she had spare.

It was fun but I met some weird punters; they come in all shapes and sizes. Rina and me had to do a regular double for one young man, about twenty-six he was, almost film-star good looks. You'd think he could have pulled any girl he wanted, but there again they probably wouldn't have stuck their hands up his arse. The first time I was horrified, but Rina knew what she was doing and she always carried these medical gloves with her. If it wasn't a fist, then it was a vibrator he wanted up his bum or clippers on his nipples. The first time he asked for that Rina said, 'They're in my bag', and I rummaged around and got out the toe-clippers. 'No, Marilyn,' she said. 'You'll cut him to pieces with those.' But knowing him, he might quite have liked it.

Another punter who comes to mind used to come to the desert to play golf at the weekend. His wife and kids had a room adjoining his, and he would want me to leave dead on five minutes before they would be walking along the corridor. At that moment he would ejaculate over a pair of his wife's beautiful expensive red lacy knickers, and I would have to run into his adjoining room, wait until they were in their room, close the door quietly and leave. This would happen once a month as regular as clockwork, but it was $400 for a half-hour's work. Not really work. He could have done it by himself really.

It wasn't hard work at all, two or possibly three tricks a night, and if they wanted full sex it was $1,000. But Karen was off her head with cocaine half the time, so one day Rina and me were talking and we agreed we should be working on our own. That's how I became the half-share owner of 'Pillow Talk – established since 1969' (we lied); 'Escorts for all occasions' said our card. So I was now a madam, the owner of an escort agency. The Americans just loved my English cockney accent, so often I would earn money for nothing. A lot of men just like to sit and talk, so quite often they would pay me to sit and have a few lines of cocaine and listen to my accent.

We operated out of the flat Rina and me were now sharing, and we split everything down the middle so to speak. It was simply a question of putting an advertisement in the local paper. Not advertising for girls but just the usual guff: 'New hot but discreet girls in town. Ring . . .' That sort of thing. As a rule we had six of them working for us. The girls who were arriving in town would read the ad and give us a call. You need to have a turnover of girls. They're better workers over there than they are here. Overall it's a better standard. They would usually show you a card with their last medical visit marked on it and, if they didn't, Rina knew a doctor she'd make them go and see before we took them on. We weren't worried if they tried a bit of blackmail on the punters, but usually the ones who did that were heavy on crack and had a black pimp. That's what we were worried about and the first thing I'd say is I hope you haven't got a black pimp. It sounds racist nowadays, but I was just wanting to avoid trouble.

As far as Rina and me were concerned, we worked only

hotels and apartments and condos that had security on the gate or the door. That way we had some safety. The rest we turned over to the girls. Once we knew what hotel they were staying in or the apartment, we'd suss out the quality of the punter and Rina and me would have the first pick. The better the hotel, the more we charged. We'd leave the cheaper punters to the others.

The punters would ring up and I'd tell them what the fee for a massage was. There was no question of mentioning a price for sex over the phone in case it was the Vice Squad. After that it depended on what the punter wanted, with straight sex going for $250 upwards. As I said, some of them were really weird. A lot of them liked having it when the girl was on. Then some of the girls would put up a bit of natural sponge to hide the fact. I did it once, but I lost the sponge and had to go to hospital to get a nurse to fish it out. I never did it again. I was really too heavy. My periods would last two weeks, which cut the earnings; I used to suffer terribly.

Then they'd like cocaine put on a dildo and shoved up their backside. Or they'd like to have cocaine on their dicks and have you blow them off or have it up your arse, which I did not do. If they wanted something like that, it was an extra $200.

Over there prostitution really comes under entertainment. It's a proper job. I never had anyone lean on me for my share. We charged the girls $50–100 for each referral, and what they charged depended on what services the punters wanted; that was up to them. When I was running the agency I never saw the punters except for my own. I'd be on the phone until 2 in the morning. It's funny how many of our clients who were big, important businessmen wanted things stuck up their backsides. I thought it was meant to be English public schoolboys who liked that. On the other hand the Americans didn't like watersports as much as the English. In those days you could really charge. Today it is not all it's cracked up to be, because of the very young girls who give it away free.

Rina and I had signed up with a gym so I was looking in tip-top condition. I would go three times a week and I hardly smoked. Palm Springs was an island in the desert surrounded by snow-capped mountains. I looked a picture of health, the pure air of the desert was marvellous, the streets were clean. OK, there was still your oddball at the local bar getting drunk, but you can't have everything.

Once we had a call from a group of guys down from Chicago; ten of them and they wanted as many girls as possible, so eight of us went including myself and Rina – who was a class act to follow when it came to her sexual appetite. The dinner was great and the wine was Italian – Barolo. One by one the girls would slip off to the bedrooms.

I was feeling great with $20,000 in my bag and loads of white powder up my nose, until one of the guys called Rudi turned round and said to me, 'Marilyn, gal, you have a lovely fanny.' I jokingly smacked his face and said, 'Do you mind, sir?' in a posh English accent. 'You have not seen it yet!' Rina, who was on top of another guy, straddled around him as if she was at a rodeo show, started laughing and said, 'Marilyn, he means your arse.' Everybody joined in the laughter and off we went skinny-dipping. Later in the evening it turned out that these ten guys I thought were businessmen were in fact FBI agents down from a convention in Los Angeles.

Being slightly deaf through too much nose powder, I said to Rudi, 'Oh, they have MFI over in London, where's your show-room based?' He said, 'What agency is that?' I said, 'It's a kitchen manufacturer.' He laughed and said, 'No, we are from the Federal Bureau of Investigation.'

Then Rina introduced me to a really lovely old man named Eric, who was another snowbird. He was in his sixties; he was lonely and sometimes he'd see me, sometimes Rina and sometimes both of us. He took me to Hawaii, put a deposit on a BMW car for me and paid a few months' instalments as well, but then with the better weather coming up there he went back to Canada.

As the summer and the hot weather came along the trade dried up. Rina wanted to have a bit of a holiday and she kept telling me about how great work was in Redondo Beach, so with what money I had left from Ian I decided to move to the coast and managed to get a job singing in a restaurant. The atmosphere was great. Rina kept in touch and came to visit. She now had a rich boyfriend there, so we used to meet and go for dinners or lunches.

One evening after she went back I was singing and a guy, Tony Wade, who used to tip very well, told me he admired my voice and asked would I like to join him for some late dinner after I had finished. He was very clean-looking, blond hair, wore a nice shirt and cotton trousers and drove a Corvette, so I said, 'Yes.' We had dinner, and he asked would I like to go to his apartment for a coffee. I said, 'Well, I can't make it too late but where do you live?' 'San Bernadino Valley.' 'Well, how far is that?' He said, 'It's only twenty minutes' drive, you follow me.' He wrote down the address in case I got lost, but anyway I followed him along the freeway playing my new Lionel Richie tape and The Gap band, singing away.

The journey was much longer than I imagined, more like an hour, before he pulled up and parked. The entrance to his house was on a slope, so you had to climb down the stairs to his door. I thought no more about it until I realised I had arranged to call in on Rina. So I said to Tony, 'May I use your

Me aged 2 months

Centre: *Miss Lovely Legs competition at Butlin's. I'm number 4 – and I won!*

Bottom left: *Me and my sister when I sang at Eddie and Charlie Richardson's party*

Bottom right: *This is me aged 10*

Top left: *Nanny Jane, Grandad, Uncle Lights and Aunt Jane*

Top right: *Dad and Billy Hart in Cornwall*

Centre: *Mum, Auntie Nellie, Jane (Light's wife) and Aunt Gladys in the 1980s (all my Mum's sisters)*

Right: *I was the star of* Young Love

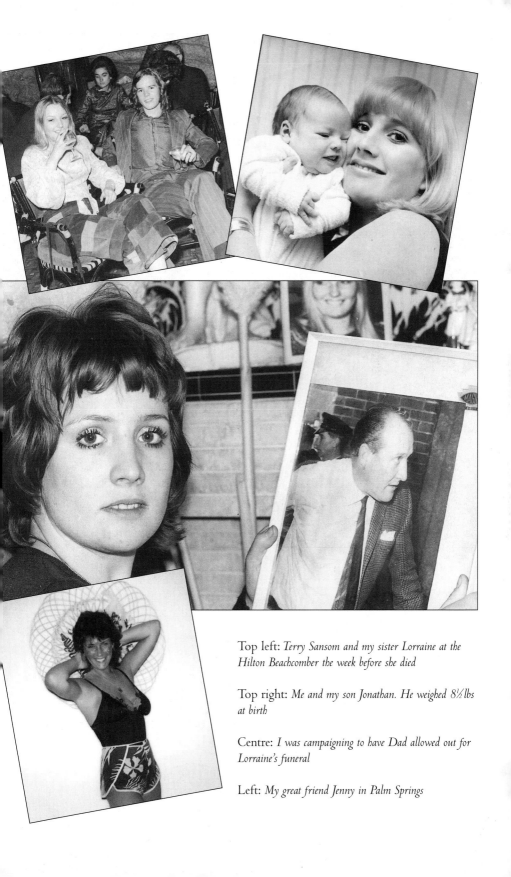

Top left: *Terry Sansom and my sister Lorraine at the Hilton Beachcomber the week before she died*

Top right: *Me and my son Jonathan. He weighed 8½ lbs at birth*

Centre: *I was campaigning to have Dad allowed out for Lorraine's funeral*

Left: *My great friend Jenny in Palm Springs*

Top left: *Danny Magano, who helped me so much, is surrounded by Jenny, me and another girl*

Top right: *This is me waitressing on my mum and Maureen — she's the one who was shot at with me*

Centre left: *Ian Evans, my first husband. He just about managed to stand up at our wedding — the bulge in his pocket is a bottle!*

Centre right: *This was the day of the earthquake, but it didn't shake Ia*

Left: *Me and Rina in Palm Spring*

Top left: *Me and mum at the races in Barbados. Richard Hannon, the Queen's horse trainer, is in the background*

Top right: *Jonathan and the Arsenal captain Tony Adams*

Centre: *Eric Hall, Terry Venables and me at Scribes in Kensington (copyright © Scott Mitchell)*

Bottom: *Let the train take the strain. Ronnie Biggs bought me this crystal train when I was in Rio*

Me, Frank and the former world boxing champion John H. Stracey

I've given Frank a hard time but here he's standing up to me

Charlie Kray, Frank and me

Frank and me lead a Gangland tour outside Turnmills, where Frank was shot

Top left: *Me, Arturo, Sinatra's valet, Rina, Dad and David in Palm Springs*

Top right: *This is me after Wade had beaten me up*

Centre: *Frank Sinatra signed this picture for me when we met in 1986*

Left: *Me and the medal Arturo Durazo gave me. I wish it had been solid gold so I could have pawned it!*

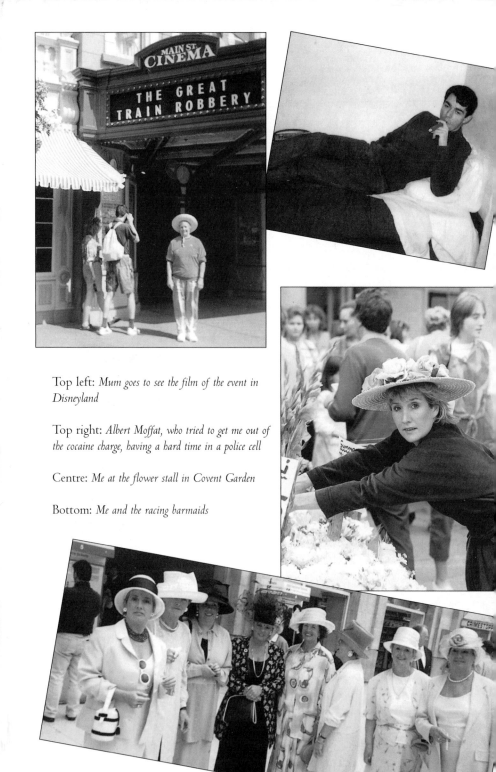

Top left: *Mum goes to see the film of the event in Disneyland*

Top right: *Albert Moffat, who tried to get me out of the cocaine charge, having a hard time in a police cell*

Centre: *Me at the flower stall in Covent Garden*

Bottom: *Me and the racing barmaids*

phone, I need to call my friend to tell her I won't be seeing her tonight?' He said, 'Through that door.' As I opened the bedroom door I felt a burning feeling; it was a crack on the back of my head.

I fell on the bed and nearly passed out, but I held on even though I felt a warm sensation around my head and his hands around my neck. I was gasping for breath, but I clawed at his throat and face. Now my head was dangling with the rest of my body. I had wet myself with fear. I could see a vision of me lying dead on a Los Angeles mortuary slab. I thought of my sister, then my Mum and most of all, my little boy. I thought, oh no, first my sister dead and now me. For some reason I did not scream, I couldn't, but with some almighty strength I managed to get his long slim white hands away from my neck. The sweat from his face was like he had been in a steam room. By now the blood was trickling down both sides of my temple and my face felt like a punchbag.

I managed to talk to this beast and said I would do anything he required. He seemed to relax a bit and asked me if he could stick his cock up my arse. I don't know why but I said no, very firmly. He didn't seem to mind the rejection and with that I just squeezed his erect penis and started to suck him. I knew if this blowjob never satisfied him I was truly, truly a dead piece of meat. I know it sounds far-fetched, but this was a fight for my life. Once he ejaculated he calmed down totally, and it was almost as if it had never happened. I started to get him to talk and I asked him if he had a mother or a sister and whether he had ever been in prison? He'd had a family, but he'd been in the Marines. Slowly, slowly, I thought. 'Let's have a drink and we can talk about things some more?' But when he looked at me, I thought, oh no, is he going to finish me off?

I slowly edged about two feet away from him and said, 'I

won't go to the police, Tony, please let's tidy up and go for some fresh air.' Can you imagine, this nut started to touch my face and said to me, 'Oh look, you have a swollen face, did you fall over?' I said, 'Yes, I need to use the bathroom.' He then resumed wiping away the blood. I thought, please God, let me see my son have children, let me get out of here. I knew I just had to get away from him.

I did manage to persuade him to agree to go outside. As I walked up his stairs to my car, my eyes were like slits, but I made out to him that I was OK and fine and acted like nothing had happened. 'We'll take your car and you drive,' he said.

As I drove down the Canyon the valley was lit up, but to me it had a steam effect. How I drove, to this day I do not know. As we drove along the freeway, many times I thought of pulling over to try and contact the highway police, but he had a knife at the side of me and just said, 'Keep driving!' It seemed like we were driving for hours, but finally we saw a sign to Long Beach and he said to turn left at this next exit. I did as I was told and there was a gas station. He told me to pull over and jumped out. Quickly I closed his door and locked it and just cried and cried and really thanked God that I was alive.

Although I don't go to church I felt as if my sister, Michael and Terry were looking down at me and helping me. It was a feeling that night that I will never ever forget. I finally got out to call Rina, who said, 'Give me the address on the phone box, the police will arrive soon, get back in your car and keep the door locked.' Within ten minutes a patrol car had arrived and I was soon taken to LAPD and seen by the paramedics. I must say that in 1982 the American police did handle me with great understanding and sympathy; they even thanked me for coming forward and reporting this guy.

I gave them his address, which was luckily in the car on the floor by the passenger seat, so that saved a lot of time, and within an hour I'd given a full statement and helped with an artist's impression. Tony Wade was his name and he was a Vietnam veteran, a woman-hater, and his room-mate said he was homosexual as well. I said he was just an animal who needed to be put away for ever, and the key thrown away. I had eight stitches in the back of my head, four stitches to my lip, three natural nails had just been torn off my nail-bed together with my acrylic nails – believe it or not, that was almost the most painful thing. I had a multitude of lacerations all over my head and six striped marks around my neck. All I can say is that I was a lucky girl that night, *very* lucky. My bruises and wounds soon healed up, but I used to cry and kick myself and blame my stupidity in going back to his place – especially after the precautions Rina and I used to take for ourselves in Palm Springs.

When I was growing up I used to watch the old-time classic movies with Doris Day and Rock Hudson. I would think that when I got a bit older my life would be like Doris Day's and I would marry somebody just like Rock Hudson. Darryl F. Zanuck films were very popular at the time when I was recovering and I met his great-grandson named Dominic. He had a beautiful home in Palm Springs, with dozens of dogs jumping around. The first time I went to see him I skidded on loads of dog shit and I thought to myself, I know it's lucky but this I can't believe – a well-to-do movie star's great-grandson, and the place is just littered with dog mess. When I got to know him a bit better I said to Dominic, 'Look at the state of this place. How can you let it look like this?' But all he said was that I shouldn't worry and that the housekeeper would fix it all up.

Gordon Liddy was a real gentleman that I had met in Palm Springs; not in the working-girl sense, but he was a quiet, reserved man. I never realised who he was at the time and Rina said he was a burglar. I thought, oh really, another American similar to George Chatham who was known as 'Taters' and who burgled those white Georgian houses in Belgravia. But no, this little man with a moustache had burgled the big White House in Washington in the scandal which was known as Watergate.

Well, after I met him the first time I was told about this and later I said to Rina, 'I've come over to the USA to get away from the criminal fraternity in England and I just seem to be a magnet for all these types. Do I have "gangster's moll" tattooed on my forehead?' Many of you readers must wonder why didn't I settle down with a normal hard-working builder, electrician or rich solicitor. While I was meeting these types, once they knew whose daughter I was, they somehow could not handle it. For some reason they seemed to associate the Great Train Robbers with thugs and gangsters, but to me my Dad and the others were not thugs, just men who went for it – who only wanted money.

A friend called Francis, the son of an Italian chef in Redondo, looked after me. He was great and really did his best until I told him I was moving back to Palm Springs. He said that I should go back to England. I said I wanted to find a rich, understanding, fun-loving American husband who would love me for myself and look after me properly. I'd completely forgotten I was still married to Mr Evans – if he was alive, that is.

I added, 'He doesn't have to be tall, dark, young and handsome, although that would be a bonus.' Francis laughed. He helped me put all the furniture in the U-Haul van I'd hired. I kissed him and thanked him; to this day I've never heard from him, but I would love to.

I went back to stay with Rina and I did a bit of work with

her spares. Then I rented a small studio myself. Arturo, Sinatra's valet, used to send Rina and me a lot of work. He'd give one of us a call and send a few guys our way. He was a good man, and he'd never take money from us for doing it. We stopped seeing each other when he had to go on tour with Sinatra. He adored him; he'd never stop saying what a good boss he had.

One day when I was feeling better and was over at her flat Rina took a call. 'Come on,' she said to me when she put the phone down. 'We've been invited out to brunch, 12 o'clock.' 'What, Crystal champagne and a smoked salmon bagel?' I asked. Rina said, 'Something like that, just be ready, bring your bikini and towel as well.' She collected me and we went over to a great big house in Rancho Mirage where she introduced me to this guy, Randy. Not my type at all, I thought. He seemed the usual rich American, with a check shirt and a beard. He told us to go out to the pool where a beautiful table was set for about 20 people; a few people were already there, talking and keeping to themselves. Then more guests started to arrive. Apparently they were all arriving from LA, quite stunning younger ladies and hunks. Finally, we all sat down to the so-called brunch, Eggs Benedict and plenty of champagne.

Everybody was creaming up to this guy Randy and I thought to myself that he must be loaded with either dough or plenty of cocaine or have a big dick, or all three, but it certainly was not the last one. As the champagne flowed, servants took away the plates and I said to Randy, 'I'm sure glad you have not asked me to help out with these dishes.' Everyone laughed at me, thinking who is this girl. I asked Randy if I could put some music on and he pointed to the sound system. I played my old favourites at that time, Lionel Richie and George Benson. I noticed some Sinatras, but thought better not as there were some really young people, and that I would save him for later. When I went back outside no one was there because they were in this gigantic Jacuzzi, all stark bollock naked. Rina had her legs around some guy's neck in the pool. I thought, oh no, but my 'No' soon turned to 'Yes' when I saw a whole saucer full of sparkling Peruvian flake and a great big mirror stretching from London to Glasgow.

Randy came up behind me and said, 'Sweetie, have some dessert.' I said, 'No, thank you, I don't like ice-cream', and he laughed, pointing to the lines, and said, 'Seeing that you're from England, you can use my platinum straw.' I took one big greedy line up my right nostril, then my left nostril, and then sat down. It just blew me away. I had never tried such 'coke' before; it relaxed me totally. Randy sat next to me and started to tease at my bathing-suit straps – I was not a bikini person. I said, 'Why don't you have some more of that ice-cream?' But Randy just kept on lifting back my shoulder straps and I was edging away with my chair.

He turned out to be a CIA agent. He desperately wanted to show me his gun which was in a suitcase, and when he did it soon brought me out of my Peruvian high. It did not impress me. I nearly fainted with shock and said such a silly thing: 'I wonder, Randy, if they will bring out a sequel called *Naked Gun 2.*' He laughed and put his suitcase away.

By this time I was seated at the top of the table like Al Pacino in *Scarface*, looking at the X-rated carrying-on with all these naked people. Randy said, 'Marilyn, why don't you go skinny dipping?' Stoned as I was I gave him a dumb answer, thinking what the hell is he talking about. I replied, 'I'm not skinny, I'm volumptious.' 'No, no,' he smiled, and said, 'No, take your bathing suit off so you can have some fun.' 'I said, 'I'm having fun just sitting here watching and listening to some of you lot talk a load of bollocks. 'Bollocks,' he asked, 'what's that?' I said, 'Balls, Randy.' There's a big cultural difference.

The hours were passing and they were all drifting in and out of the bedrooms. It was now 11 p.m.; little me was still helping myself to the nearly empty saucer-load of coke. Randy kept coming up to me, kissing me and trying desperately to get me to join him naked in the pool. He asked, 'Don't you like men?' I said, 'No, not on Saturday nights.' 'Do you like women?' he asked. I replied, 'Only on Sunday mornings.' He said, 'Well, it's Sunday night.' I said, 'Yes, Randy, another line.' It was then that Rina came to my rescue and took him away.

While I was the hostess with the mostest, by now people were wrecked and all deciding to go back to LA and party there. I was left trying to be straight, but after all that coke you finally end up talking a load of bollocks too. Rina came out and told me she was going but that I should stay; she said that I would be all right and that Randy would look after me. I then finally got to play my Sinatra songs and my swimsuit soon came off as Sinatra was singing 'I Get a Kick out of You'. So Randy and I danced under the stars naked and then he handed me a thick envelope. That was maybe the best part of the whole day.

10

Arturo Durazo

The weeks were rolling by and I became very homesick – also I was beginning to get itchy feet. I was even fed up with the sun and I was missing my little boy and parents very much, my English tea, the English sense of humour and, believe it or not, of all things, the rain.

I was still working, but really only with the trade Rina could not handle herself. One day she and I had to meet some high rollers from Las Vegas. The appointment was for 7 p.m. at the smart Ingleside Inn. I was feeling down and so Rina said, 'Let's get there early for happy hour, Marilyn. Joe's playing tonight; come on, you can sing with him.' When we arrived Bryan, the *maître d'*, gave us a good table. Then Joe, the Jewish piano player, introduced me and I sang 'As Time Goes By' and Errol Garner's 'Misty'. By the time I sat down it was 7.45 p.m. and our guys never turned up. I said to Rina, 'Perhaps they heard my singing and decided to leave.' She laughed and said, 'You know what these businessmen are like. They've probably lost all their money playing craps.'

Suddenly a waitress came up to us and said there were two gentlemen over there who would like to buy us girls a drink. 'Why, certainly,' said Rina. 'I'll have a martini straight up. What are you going to have, Marilyn?' I said, 'I'll have a bottle of Crystal champagne.' She told me not to be cheeky, but I was right out of sorts and I just said to the waitress, 'Vintage, please.' Rina said, 'My God,' but I said, 'Well, they did ask us,' and if it's being cheeky I'll say make it non-vintage. Anyway, Rina, I've had enough of this town. I'm flying back to England.'

With that the waitress brought a beautiful ice bucket with a bottle of champagne, nuts and canapés on a tray and said, 'The two gentlemen said would you like to join them.' I replied, 'No, tell the two gentlemen thank you for the drinks but we don't join tables.' She passed the message on, then Rina and I looked over to acknowledge their nice offer of drinks. One of the guys was very dishy, tall, dark and handsome and in his thirties; the other was like a Fifties film star, very distinguished, a bit like Anthony Quinn.

I said to Rina jokingly, 'I bet I end up with the old grey-haired guy.' She laughed, as she was ten years older than me even though it didn't show. The guys came over, asked if they could sit down and the older guy pulled his chair close to mine. I thought, here we go. Two more champagne glasses were put on the table and we got chatting. They said they had been to France and were both from Mexico but living in Los Angeles.

The older man of the two was Arturo Durazo Moreno who wanted to know if I was from Australia. I said no and that I was from London. I had a hard time as his English was not fluent, so every time we spoke it was through his friend Sanchez; although I could say a few things in Spanish I was not exactly fluent. That's why it's very important to learn a language when you're young. It's important for schools to teach our children a language – if only I had stayed at school! By this time we were having quite a fun night and when I got Arturo up dancing, he said to me, 'You can eat something?' So all four of us then had our dinner in the restaurant part with cognac and coffee to finish. They were actually staying at Ingleside. Every private suite had its own splash pool which I was amazed at. After dinner Rina was parting with Sanchez. I could not for the life of me get the courage to agree a price for my company, and even if I could have done I wasn't sure he'd have understood since he could hardly speak any English. So when Sanchez said, 'Arturo wants you to join him for some more cognac and coffee on the verandah,' it was a question of putting things off for a bit and I said, 'Fine.'

As we were sitting outside in his private garden, it was so romantic. Then I thought to myself – if I have any more drink I'm going to be sick. While we were trying to have a conversation his telephone rang, he went inside and I was left to gaze up at the stars. I could hear him gabbling in Spanish and I thought, I hope he remembers I'm outside here. I did not like to go inside to see what was happening, so I just made myself comfortable on a lovely padded sun-lounger and with that I'm fast asleep. I awoke when I felt a warm kiss and a warm hand on my arm. 'Ugh,' I said, 'go away, I want to sleep', and I rolled over. Then there was another warm kiss. I didn't respond, but I felt someone stroking my cheek. Then I felt a nudge and another rather sharper one. There, standing over me, were Rina, Sanchez and Arturo all looking at me. I had been asleep for almost an hour.

My dress had wrinkled up around my backside and back, showing my arse because I wasn't wearing panties, and I felt so embarrassed. Arturo was laughing and Sanchez said, 'Don't worry, your snoring was not that loud. He apologises for being on the telephone for so long and would you like to stay with him?' Of course I said, 'Yes.' I had a shower and lay on the bed with a beautiful soft bathrobe on. There was a knock on the door. Arturo was in the bathroom and I presumed he wanted me to open it, so I got up and answered the door. In came a beautiful bouquet of flowers, more champagne and sandwiches.

I thought, this beats going back to England. I'm beginning to like this. Arturo came out of the bathroom, signed the receipt and gave the waiter a $50 tip. I thought again, this man I like, as I don't care for greedy people, especially millionaires or multi-millionaires when they are really caked up with dough. Over the time, what I liked about Arturo was that he always really looked after the workers and did so from his heart. But that night I was full of being spoilt rotten. He gave me the flowers, then asked me if I would like a massage. I said, 'Oh, thank you,' thinking that's nice of him, he's going to give me one himself. With that he calls Sanchez, then there's another knock at the door and this time the housekeeper comes in with more towels and she goes to the bathroom to fill the large Jacuzzi. I thought, why could it not be my luck that it was somebody who I really, really loved and found delightfully sexually attractive? But then I thought, 'Never mind, just go for it, girl. Close your eyes, think of Mickey Rourke or someone very sexy like him.'

Arturo spoke in Spanish to the housekeeper, but I think it was to remind her to get something. Off she went and the telephone rang again. I was given more champagne; he was gabble, gabble another ten minutes on the phone, then another knock at the door – the housekeeper with some candles on a beautiful gold candelabra. I thought to myself, 'If he doesn't hurry up we will be getting ready for breakfast.' He put the telephone down and poured himself some tequila with salt and lemon. It was the first time I had tried this particular tequila, and it had a worm at the bottom of the bottle.

As I downed just one more tequila and he took my bathrobe off I thought, please God, don't let me spew all over him. We kissed and cuddled until we were just warming up to a mad passionate state when the damned phone started to ring again. 'Oh no,' I exclaimed. '*Un momento*,' he said. As he put down the phone he kissed me again and there was another knock at the door. It was all action. In came a big macho guy with white slacks and white tee-shirt and muscles on muscles, and I was led into a separate room where there was a massage bed.

I lay down on my front, a towel was placed over my backside and this hunk started to work on me. Now looking back on it, he was probably gay because he was really strictly taking no notice of me whatsoever. No conversation, and he looked as miserable as sin. He was probably hoping he would have a rich young boy to touch, instead he had a cockney blonde with only a towel covering her naked body to massage. But I'll give him this, he was a good professional masseur; I was in heaven, I was so relaxed.

Arturo came in every so often to see how I was. I smiled and gave him a thumbs-up sign which he understood perfectly. I said, '*Muchas gracias*, Arturo.' The massage had finished and Arturo then led me to the bathroom, which was softly lit with the candles, which of course always add something to a room. We both sat in the Jacuzzi and played around, then he led me to his bedroom and dried himself and me and kept gazing into my eyes and saying in Spanish, '*Tus ochos son del color del mar.*'

'He laid me down on the bed and I gave him a massage too, but he knew I was feeling relaxed; he stroked me and caressed me, kissing me where I liked and delivering me to the perfect orgasm. My Mum used to tell that saying, 'The older the fiddle the better the tune.' By this time I was thinking maybe I did have the right man. Now I know what she meant. I slept like a baby that early morning until 6.30 a.m. when the telephone rang yet again. It was the same scenario with Arturo gabbling down the mouthpiece, so I took to the bathroom. There was a knock at the door and in came a waiter with a beautiful trolley-load of the finest fruit, bacon, eggs, omelette, bread, champagne, orange juice, everything you could wish for. I had the sense to omit the champagne and got stuck into my bacon and eggs with a vengeance. Everything.

Arturo kept looking at me until he said, '*Momento*' and went to his drawer, got out a small wallet and then handed me a badge. I noticed and recognised the word '*policia*'. I thought, I don't believe it; with that I put my two arms up in the air, as people do when they are arrested. He roared with laughter; he was trying to tell me something. I just kept nodding as if I knew what he was saying, hoping Rina would surface early.

Sanchez knocked at the door; they spoke to one another and then Sanchez asked me if I would like to join Arturo for lunch. I said, 'Yes, of course, what time?' 'I p.m.' he said. Sanchez wanted to arrange for the chauffeur to take me whenever I was ready, so I told him to arrange for 8.30 a.m. I thought, I p.m., my God; I should be just getting up at that time, but Arturo seemed such a kind and caring person, who could communicate with me with his eyes. I wasn't going to turn him down, and anyway I was still out of my money.

I arrived for lunch at I p.m. on the dot and we sat by the pool. He was very attentive and this time there were no interruptions from the telephone. Rina had arranged to meet up with us later and I managed to have a proper conversation with Sanchez. He told me that Arturo liked my company very much and that he would like me to stay with him for that weekend.

Rina arrived with her loud American twang accent, Arturo finally suggested going back to our suite, and then I said, 'Siesta.' The weather was really humid and hot, so a nap was fine. I would have a shower, so would he, and we would cuddle up and sleep which I really liked to do in the late afternoon ready for the evening. During the afternoon Arturo taught me how to play the Spanish version of dominoes; at first I was useless, but by the end of my time with him I was getting quite clever at it.

We'd all arranged to go to a Mexican restaurant that night. After breakfast on the Sunday, they were leaving to go back to Los Angeles, Bel Air. I wondered what was going to happen, but we exchanged telephone numbers as I was leaving to be driven home.

Arturo gave me a thick envelope and I thought to myself, please let it be some money. I was skint and my bills were mounting up. I thought $500 would help and I couldn't wait to get home and open the envelope. I didn't want to do it in front of the chauffeur. Inside was the $500 all in $100 bills with a letter to say, 'For my love. See you soon, Arturo x.'

I jumped up and down and said, 'Right on, and now I can get back to England soon.' I really thought that was the end of that, but during the course of the week Rina had been in the Ingleside Inn, and she had been approached by one of the staff who told her that Arturo was coming down at the weekend and had arranged flowers for me; she was not to tell me, as it was supposed to be a complete surprise until that Friday. It was then I had a telephone call from Arturo in Spanish, 'Si, Si, Arturo, tiempo I p.m. at Melvyn's OK.' After the next weekend this would happen regularly.

In the meantime my parents were coming over the following week. Rina used to say, 'Marilyn, you know he's someone really high up in the government,' to which I said, 'As long as he keeps giving me loads of dosh, who cares?' But I knew I would have to tell him who I was and about my Dad because my father and mother would be arriving soon. When it came to it, it didn't seem to make the slightest difference to him. My parents arrived, staying in a rented apartment. After they settled in, Arturo arranged for lunch for us all at Melvyn's as he wanted to meet them.

We were playing our usual game of dominoes at the poolside and as I looked round I saw my Mum and Dad and Jonathan walking up towards us. My lovely Mum, bless her, was carrying a green Marks & Spencer carrier-bag. That was what caught my eye. So I got the large menu and was waving and pointing at the bag, because this hotel was full of Gucci and Louis Vuitton bag fans. I was trying to say put that carrier-bag away, this place is so posh, Mum, but I couldn't bring myself to.

It was a similar scenario to *Keeping Up Appearances*, that programme with Patricia Routledge, but anyway it did not bother Arturo because he seemed overjoyed to meet my Mum and Dad. We sat and had lunch. 'Ooh,' Mum said, talking out of the corner of her mouth, 'you're nice and comfortable.' 'Yes, Mum, it beats having pie and mash in Westmoreland Road, doesn't it, dear?' We laughed and when my father went to pay the bill, Arturo got upset and insisted he do the honours.

We later arranged to meet for dinner; it was a beautiful night – eight bottles of Vintage Crystal 1972. I knew it was expensive because it went down very smooth, not too gassy. I prefer Crystal to Dom Perignon. That night Arturo handed me a beautiful gold 50-peso Mexican coin and chain, which as I've said in Frank's book[1] has got itself into the pawnshop and me out of trouble so often when I have fallen on hard times. Looking back, I think Arturo must have had a supply of them.

I would love to have been able to tell Arturo how much he had helped me with this lovely gift. I suppose this was really better than all the cash because I would have blown the lot. Arturo asked me (through Sanchez) if we would all like to spend some time at his beach house in Laguna Beach as it was his birthday on 18 October and he had to be in Bel Air for his birthday bash – which, so Sanchez said, heads of state were attending, as well as his ex-wife. I had already met his son, whose second car was a brand-new Ferrari.

The idea was that Arturo would go to the party and come and join us later. Meanwhile we were to have the run of the beach house. His driver was to pick us up and take us there and so I went over to Mum and Dad for him to collect us all at their apartment. There was the toilet overflowing making a terrible mess, and in the bedroom Mum was sitting on a suitcase trying to make it close. Dad wasn't there and I asked where he'd gone. 'To buy a belt to put round it,' she said. 'Very Laguna Beach,' I thought. Arturo could have bought her a whole set of suitcases.

I thought it would be a little beach place, but it was big, more like a palace, right smack on the beach. We were left by ourselves. My Mum, being Renée, went into the master bedroom to unpack. As she opened the wardrobe, she gasped at the amazing sight of hundreds of men's shoes all neatly arranged with shoe trees, many of them different-coloured buck suede shoes to match the hundreds of neatly piled silk shirts. There

---

[1] *Mad Frank and Friends*, Frankie Fraser with James Morton, (1998) London, Little, Brown.

must have been at least 170 suits, all with see-through shoulder covers on them, and hundreds of coloured silk shirts.

Renée called my Dad and me, saying, 'My God, it's like Harrods' men's department.' I was half surprised that she didn't help herself for old times' sake. I said, 'I'm glad I don't have to iron all these shirts on a Friday.' Sanchez called us on the phone to ask how things were and if we were settled in. Saturday night was Arturo's birthday party. Obviously we were not invited as his family and those very special people were going to be there, but it did not bother me because we had our own fun time together and Arturo had told me he would see us on Sunday.

But after we'd enjoyed the Saturday evening out in a local restaurant, we came back home around 10.30 p.m. and unexpectedly there was Arturo's car. I said to Mum, Dad and Jonathan, 'Perhaps the driver came back for all those clothes or something.' But it was Arturo himself along with Sanchez. 'What are you doing back here so early? Have you left a pair of shoes that you wanted to wear?' Sanchez explained to Arturo, who smiled and said to Sanchez that he was bored with the party. He had met his family and now he wanted to be with us. So we finished up all of us drinking and celebrating with tequila, cognac and singing.

That's how I learnt that song 'Besame, Besame Mucho'. Arturo used to sing it to me. Now everywhere in the world whenever they play that tune I always think of him. We had a great time down at the beach for a couple of days before it was back to Palm Springs and then home for my parents. For a time I was in limbo as to whether I wanted to leave for England as well, to just leave everything behind and go back with them, but it did not take me much limboing to decide to stay. I kept thinking that while I was ahead I might as well enjoy it.

What I've learnt about this commodity called money is that it really is for spending and enjoying and sharing. The number of so-called English millionaires that I have met in my life are the meanest phoney types. They may have a million pounds' worth of assets, but have everything on the books and you really can tell the 'real' moneyed people from the plastic ones — you can meet those and they would not dream of buying you a drink, even the ones who are worth five million upwards.

My parents flew back to England again without me. I was sad, and I thought that it was really unfair that my life has always been full of 'goodbyes' and that I would have loved to settle down and have my family around me. Never mind, everybody in life has a cross to bear; no one goes through a perfect life, although at times there are more people than others who have far too much of a burden, which is so unfair. The most evil, jealous and meanest people seem to have all the luck in life; the people who deserve it don't get any.

But I soon enjoyed the weeks travelling around America with Arturo. He was the one who cured me of my cocaine habit. Before I met him I was stuffing $1,000 a week up my nose, but he didn't approve at all and so if I wanted a snort I had to go and have a line secretly in the bathroom. Then when we began to travel I simply gave it up. As I've said before, it's just a question of will-power. Then one day I had a telephone call from Sanchez to pack a light case and bring my passport; he would pick me up on my own. I said to Rina, 'Here's my car keys. If you like you can use it, I'll see you next week.' She asked where I was going, but Sanchez had said not to tell her anything and anyway he hadn't told me. That was the last time I ever saw her until the day of Ronnie Kray's funeral in 1995.

I knew we were going to Beverly Hills, but we were obviously going on somewhere after that. The journey there and not knowing where I was going afterwards, was so exciting. Looking back, I'm sure Rina must have thought 'crazy woman', but instinct had told me not to ask. Finally we got to Beverly Hills and drove down into an underground car park where Arturo was waiting for me. We both spoke in Spanish because by now I was getting quite good at it if he spoke slowly enough. '*Hola!*' He held my case. That's one thing I particularly notice about men with certain class, they hold your luggage for you. Frank always does it and so did Arturo.

He clasped my hand and led me to a beautiful if slightly dusty, red old-type Bentley and opened the boot. I looked in, thinking I hope he won't put me in there, why me? No, seriously! He then showed me a small compartment inside the boot covered with the best quality carpet. It was a safe. I thought to myself, so that is where he keeps his money. What a funny place to have a safe. With that he took out a small leather pouch which he handed to me. Sanchez said, 'It's for you to take upstairs, but now he wants to show you his car.' I said, 'Oh, it's very English', and Sanchez repeated what I said to Arturo. 'Yes, I know, I bought it from your Queen.' 'Which Queen, the one my Dad robbed?' The car was the one she'd been in at the Mexico Olympics or on a state visit or something. The adventures of my time with Arturo will always be with me. Certain people you meet through life may come and go, certainly in my case they did come and go. And the going next day was to Europe. In the meantime I'd had a look in the pouch when I'd taken it upstairs. It contained a number of fine diamonds and other jewels, and I lifted two of the diamonds. There must have been about fifty of them in all, but I didn't think he was going to be counting. If he did, then I'd have to start thinking of an explanation pretty quick.

While in Europe we stayed in the beautiful Four Seasons Hotel in Hamburg but, to be honest, it was then that I started to get bored with all the silver-set trolley, room service crap. We did all the tourist things, but I began to feel like I was a prisoner. So after a few days I said to Arturo, 'Shall we go out tonight? I've never seen a live sex show before.' Well, if I had seen one in Soho it was a tame one at that. Anyway, I got my own way as usual. Sanchez and Arturo were laughing because just when the lights were dimmed, a man with a black collar and chains brought on this Alsatian dog.

I quietly said, 'I thought this was going to be a live sex show.' '*Momento.*' And with that two blondes come out. Well, I'll leave you to imagine the rest. I'm sure they gave Rin-Tin-Tin plenty of Bob Martins that night.

When we got outside I told them this and the two of them laughed. Then a couple of days later we went up to Denmark and Sweden, and after that our next port of call was Amsterdam. It was always Arturo's decision. I just waited for Sanchez to say, 'Get packed, we're moving on.' Usually I didn't even ask where we were going. I just packed. But one day I said to Arturo, 'Let's go somewhere warm for a change, why not Spain? Perhaps we can visit my godfather Fred.' And so we booked in at the Marbella Beach Club Hotel.

The hotel paid us a lot of attention. Arturo knew they had a Mexican chef and he asked him to prepare a special Mexican feast. While eating our dinner three bastard cockney cab-drivers all wearing similar V-neck diamond-pattern jumpers, all the same pattern, everything brand new, were sitting eaves-dropping on our conversation and taking the piss out of our Spanish accents. All of a sudden Sanchez turned round, then Arturo got his fork and stabbed it into the tablecloth just by one of the guy's hands, muttered something and stared at them.

I've never seen three men get up and leave so quickly. I had to laugh because they picked on the wrong ones to take the mickey out of.

I couldn't find my godfather Fred at all, but our weekend in the Marbella Beach Club Hotel was very relaxing. I decided to tell Arturo that I wanted to go to London, seeing that we were so close, to stay for Christmas and have my birthday party there. He was quite happy and said he would be over to celebrate my birthday on 3 January. He waved me goodbye at Malaga airport and when I entered the lounge, who was sitting there but the three cockney taxi drivers? I stared them out until they turned their heads.

I've never seen Arturo again.

The Brinks-Mat robbery had just taken place in the November of that year and it played an important part in the way the chapter in my life with Arturo finished. He certainly thought my father had been involved, and he did not want any heat around him. He knew London, and probably England, would be alive with every undercover cop imaginable. So, no thanks, *señores*.

I really, truly believed he would be flying over for my birthday. Six weeks had gone by, and you might wonder why did I not have his phone number? To be honest, I really forgot to ask him. Arturo would always contact me, but looking back on it – when you see a telephone in a James Bond type of suitcase – I just thought, well, he would give me his contact number if he really wanted to. And I was not exactly head over heels in love with him. He was more than a punter, but I knew it was never going to last. I just liked the ride and the new experience. You have to bear in mind that I never knew the full extent of this guy. I just thought he was some high-up government figure from Mexico with plenty of pesos, and I eventually concluded that maybe he went back with his wife. The richer the man is the more girls he has in every port, and I didn't mind being one of the girls.

Even though the cold weather was biting, I decided that I would not go back to the USA. I rang Rina to tell her to keep the furniture and car, and that she could do what she wanted with the rest of my stuff except for sending over some personal things.

One cold Sunday morning I got my usual Sunday papers – another thing I did miss terribly when in America. After reading the *News of the World*'s juicy bits, I glanced at the *Mail on Sunday* and – lo and behold – there were pictures of Arturo in saluting position in his policeman's uniform and badges, and a story of how he was worth $380 million.

He'd been the Chief of Police in Mexico City for about six years from 1976 and he'd organised the security for the Olympic Games. On the face of it he was earning $200 a month, but he owned a string of racehorses and at his villa he had a greyhound track. He'd also paid nearly $8 million into bank accounts in Canada and San Diego, which is why he could splash out. He was suspected of running a drugs ring, but I don't think they ever proved it. He even used to charge the local council in Mexico City for use of the police cars. When I met him he was on the run, but he'd never seemed to hide. Perhaps that's why he wouldn't come to Britain. I thought to myself, all those millions, the greedy bastard; he never gave me any. I read later that he got captured in Puerto Rico in 1984 and he was sent back to Mexico where he got 25 years. I wrote to him in prison, but he never replied. I don't even know if he got the letter. Apparently his cell was just about as well furnished as his villa, so I suppose there was no problem about his getting the letter.

He came out in 1992 and, so the papers said, he went back to live with his wife in Los Angeles. But I'm glad I did get to meet him, even if only to see for a few months how the really wealthy people live.

As for the diamonds, he never discovered about them and I sold them for just under ten grand. It was as well that I took them; the mean sod only gave me $10,000 to come home with.

I was sorry to read in the papers that Arturo died in August last year[2]. He was 80 and the last few years of his life had been spent helping reform alcoholics in Acapulco. Well, he won't need the diamonds now.

2 Arturo 'El Negro' Durazo Moreno died on 5 August 2000. At his memorial service the former disgraced president Lopez Portillo described him as 'a magnificent policeman by vocation and devotion'. Durazo, who came to prominence after he foiled a pro-Castro plot in Mexico in the 1950s, was also highly thought of by the Soviet Union. For further details of his career see Alan Riding, *Distant Neighbours.*

II

Marriage

I got married in 1987 and it was a great mistake. To be truthful now I'm not sure it wasn't bigamous, because I sort of put Ian Evans out of mind. This time, in fact, the unlucky man was Olive Cornell's former husband, Alan Tear. Although his brother Bobby was in the Bank of America job with Frank's son Frank Junior, Alan was totally straight, a jeweller from South London; very straight and very boring. He looked like a fat version of Jack Nicholson and he'd been married to Olive Cornell after George got shot. Later Olive went out with Frank's friend Jimmy Robson.

I'd met Alan in the Tin Pan where I seem to have met most of my men. His stag night and my hen night was the night of the hurricane, 16 October 1987. The marriage didn't last much longer than the storm itself. I just felt I wanted to get married because I was being left on the shelf, plus the fact that I was pregnant again. I thought, I can't have another baby and not be married. I'd been going out with him for eighteen months when, out of the blue, he proposed.

After the usual headaches you have with organising such a big event and being six weeks pregnant, the wedding on 17 October (the day after the storm) turned out a right humping, bumping and jumping wedding! Four hundred guests, two disc jockeys and a five-piece band. My new husband had remarked to me that he didn't want me to sing on stage, but after a few guests sang my father and I got up and we did a duet, 'I Can't Give You Anything but Love'. The guests clapped and cheered; there was continuous champagne, smoked salmon, fresh lobster, eels, puff and cocaine. It was a great wedding.

A few weeks went by after the wedding and then I had a very bad bout of flu and was feeling under the weather. Alan said he had to go abroad for a jewellery exhibition in Amsterdam for the weekend, and I said that I'd have a few of the girls in to show them the wedding video that I'd helped to produce. 'Don't be going out' were his last words. That was his trouble, he wanted to be in control the whole time. I said, 'No, darling, of course not.' My friends came round and the wine went down a treat. It's fun watching yourself and taking the mickey out of yourself, especially as I asked the video company to interview the guests outside the church before the service and then again when they'd had a few drinks five hours later. We never stopped laughing. So when my friend Jackie, whose daughter Frenchie was one of the bridesmaids, said, 'Shall we go over the road for a couple?' I didn't need any arm-pulling to make me. It was now 10 p.m. – off the six of us went.

I'd told Jonathan, who was playing on his computer, not to be up too late. 'Just ten minutes,' he said. 'I'm finishing this game, Mum.' We left him and all trotted out, tiddly-pissed and playful and giggling. Two hours later, when my girlfriends dropped me home in a mini-cab, I noticed a fire alight in one of the great dustbins. I've never run so quickly to telephone the fire brigade, with the bin being so close to the flat.

As I went to put the key in my door it was ajar. I thought, 'Strange'. I was sure I'd closed it, and I couldn't believe Jonathan had gone out. Then when I opened my living-room door, standing there was a guy about 5'6" tall wearing an overcoat and holding a briefcase. My first reaction was for my son. 'Jonathan, Jonathan! Jonathan!' I shouted. He was half asleep and I screamed out to this intruder, 'Who the fuck are you?' I don't know how I managed to get to the kitchen, but I picked up a knife and I got hold of his collar. I called out to Jonathan to phone the police, then I heard him shouting to my neighbour. In all the nervous shouting, I was trying to push the man into my neighbour's flat across the little landing. I told her I had found him in my flat. He was sweating and I was digging this bread knife into his fat neck, shouting at him, 'Who sent you here, you bastard? You know who I am?' He cried out, 'Please, please don't hurt me. It was a mistake, wrong door!' 'Don't give me that, I'm a police officer,' I said. 'You're under arrest!'

With that the real police came and when they questioned me they asked if he had attacked me sexually and was there anything missing. I said 'No' to the first and 'Give me time, I'll look' to the second. Then I could see the man had left all these drawings – some of them were sketches of nudes – in the living-room. The police did a check on me at the Criminal Records office although I thought I was the victim. After that the woman police officer said, 'Are you sure he's not an ex-boyfriend?' I replied, 'Are you joking, have you seen the state of him? Do you mind, I've just got married.' I was so shaken, my darling son was white and shaken, and the WPC just said,

'We will be in touch.' When I shut the door, I was totally disgusted at their attitude and was bewildered because I didn't know why the man was in the flat. What was he up to?

I put Jonathan to bed and kissed his forehead, saying I was sorry that this had happened to him when I'd been out. He said, 'Don't worry, Mum, you're just like a lioness protecting her cubs!' With all the trauma that we had just been through, these words from a teenager cheered me up no end.

Later in the week when my husband came back I told him what had happened and he was none too happy, The policewoman had said that they couldn't charge the man, because there was no forced entry as I had left the door open. I then said some money was missing, to try and get some action. Weeks later I had to make a statement, but by then I declined.

In the end it turned out that the guy had got drunk with a gay neighbour, had a quarrel and left. He went back, but became disorientated and this time went into the wrong entrance of the block. When he'd rung the buzzer, my neighbour thought it was her son drunk, and she'd released the security door. The gay drunk then wandered upstairs and with my door being ajar he strolled in. I must have walked in a few minutes after him.

The gay neighbour himself was a bit of an oddball. His dog was even the same, because he and our Danny always used to growl at one another even before this incident. It's quite amazing when animals and children have this sixth sense towards us.

A week later I was rushed to hospital and I suffered a miscarriage. Christmas that year, I had to entertain friends while feeling absolutely dreadful with another bout of the flu, and with no help except from my husband's business pal, Nugget McGee, who carried in the turkey. One Christmas of many that I didn't enjoy, although everyone else seemed to have enjoyed their dinner. Little did they know that I had accidentally dropped the twelve-pounder on the kitchen floor and cooked it with the giblets inside. I certainly wasn't going to tell them.

In January, Alan and me spent a week down in Bournemouth in a chalet we'd bought by the beach. But that didn't go any better. My new husband had appendicitis in the early hours of the morning; we didn't have a phone in the chalet and there were no such things as mobiles, so I walked two miles along the beach to call an ambulance and he was rushed to Christchurch Hospital. The doctor said that if I hadn't got to a phone box in time he would have died. A few days later the consultant said, 'Mr Tear, we have never seen such a big appendix. In fact we are going to keep it and put it in our medical college to show our new students.' He was really amazed at the size of it. Alan made a speedy recovery – quite unlike our marriage.

Later that month he came home one afternoon to tell me he had met a younger woman who worked in a dry-cleaner's, and that he wanted a divorce as soon as possible. I knew we weren't really getting along, but I couldn't believe it when he just dropped it on me. We'd been living at my place but he'd always kept his own flat and he just left. Then after a couple of weeks Alan came over again and this time said he wanted to come back. I said I couldn't see it after what he'd said and done. How could it ever be the same? I told him just to have the divorce papers sent round.

So he settled with the dry cleaner's young woman. I'd like to say I took him to the cleaners, but it was the other way around. About three days later he came round again, with a van, and said he was taking the three-piece suite along with my mink and he wanted the diamond engagement ring given back as well. It was a good one because, being in the business, he knew what he was doing when he bought it. I really lost my rag at this and I got a pair of pliers and pulled the stone out. Alan burst out laughing and said, 'Well, now you might as well keep it.'

After he'd gone Jonathan said, 'Mum, we're sitting on the floor. What are we going to do?' I told him not to worry; there was a sofa bed we'd intended to put in the chalet and we'd use that.

Then in June that year, when my mother and I had the cocaine rap charge, Alan sent me divorce papers stating that he was entitled to the custody of Jonathan, that he owned my flower stall which I had got before I even met him, and he also named a flat in Eltham that I owned which he said was his. It was meant to be a secret. I thought, 'Give me a chance, I've just got out on bail.'

Things couldn't have got any worse for us at that time. I contacted a local solicitor and he sorted things out. Alan dropped the claim for custody of Jonathan and I kept my flower stall but after Tommy got convicted for the cocaine the flat in Eltham went as one of his assets. In the end I was so pleased just to sign those divorce papers and let Alan get on with his life. At least he managed to have a baby boy. It must have been those giblets that Christmas put some stuffing in him. The last time I saw him was a couple of years ago at Lottie Sansom's funeral (Terry Sansom Junior's grandmother).

If my family are disappointed in me, they don't say much. They let me get on with things. Sometimes I think I'm a black sheep and not a goat at all.

Things did pick up for a bit after I'd split with Alan. Three of us girls from South London opened a spiel in Parkfield Street just off the Angel: Jenny Bond, Kenny Sansom's cousin, and Vicky Richardson – no relation to Charlie and Eddie –

and me. It came through Dad and Harry Hicks. The fellow who let us have it had a snooker hall with a great big bar area he wasn't using. Actually, I would say I was one of the first to open at 2.30 in the morning. We had no licence, of course. I called it 'Pal Joey's'. If I had called it 'Pal Tommy's' I might have been able to stay open longer.

It was round the corner from that club Ra-Ra's where poor Tony Adams, the Arsenal footballer, accidentally fell down some stairs. But us girls, all ex-shoplifters, ran the place; no doormen then. We didn't need them, bearing in mind that in 1989 the rave thing had only just started. If a guy was drunk and being a nuisance we would just politely say, 'Pal, your cab's here, darling', and off they would go. Today you have either these steroid plastic gangsters on the door or what I call squeaky middle-class prats with their guest clipboards. You can see that their buzz for the night is ticking off names and acting like little Hitlers.

This idea with having all these doormen is another form of making money for the police. They say it's to stop the drugs and fights, but I think it creates more drugs and fights. I liked the clubs in the old days where the bouncers used to be mingling inside quietly dressed like customers, so all the heavy players would know who's who anyway. Frank and his friends used to look after places in this way. The more people you have running clubs, pubs and wine bars, the more risk you take with corruption. But the three of us running Pal Joey's soon got closed down, not by the police nor the local neighbours but someone from a North London family who said it was a new neighbourhood watering hole, and thought it was competition.

They were jealous.

Then that year I started going with Albert Moffat, from

Glasgow. He was a shoplifter really. His proper claim to fame was that he was the first man to cut Dennis Nilsen – he did it in the Scrubs. Nilsen was the one who chopped up young boys in Muswell Hill, not the Black Panther; I think you spell him differently. Albert was prosecuted for the attack, but the jury slung it out. He said he'd been repelling Nilsen's homosexual advances, and when he did so Nilsen took a piece of metal to him. Albert had gone and called him a big poof as well. Albert was only 21 when that happened.[1]

I'd met Albert at Pal Joey's and we'd gone on holiday to Spain and then to Switzerland, touring Geneva and Zürich doing a bit of kiting. While I was out there I rang up one of the girls to see how things were and she told me the whole place was boarded up and they couldn't get in. Poor Vicky come out of it worst. No dough, and so she bought and sold a bit of puff to make ends meet. She ended up getting nicked later on for drugs. Someone grassed her up and she got a five.

When we lost the club I said to my Mum, 'The difference is people. Remember the Head brothers. They brought custom to us when they could have said we were in opposition to them in the pub.' I didn't tell her I'd been having it off with the

---

[1] From 1979 until his arrest on 8 February 1983, Dennis Nilsen lured a series of young men to his flat in Muswell Hill, a north London suburb, and killed them, cooking parts of their bodies and disposing of the remainder in the drains. He was arrested in 1983 after neighbours complained of the smell. Found guilty on a 10–2 majority after the defence argued that he was incapable of forming the intent to murder, he was sentenced to life imprisonment with a recommendation that he serve not less than 25 years. He should not be confused with Donald Neilson, the so-called Black Panther, who on 14 January 1975 kidnapped and later killed 17-year-old Lesley Whittle. He also killed three others in a series of robberies.

fatter one of the brothers and that may have been why he was looking out for us. I could understand the local clubs getting the hump if we were open at the same time as them, but we opened after they had closed and we weren't no challenge. Three women getting a couple of grand each wasn't going to break their bank accounts.

It didn't work out with me and Albert. He was a good-looking man but he had terrible teeth. I said if he had them fixed he'd look like a film star. In fact, while he was on remand for the cocaine troubles he had them done.

But by this time Albert had already left me, so I was back in London pregnant again. And that was when I went to the abortion clinic and the police come round. As I've said, he really did try and do the decent thing by me in trying to take the rap for the cocaine.

Jonathan had started to work on the stall. He wanted to be a builder, but the training schemes were hard to get into as there weren't enough of them at that time in Conservative Islington. So I got him working as I didn't want him laying about and ending up getting in trouble. Looking back over my life, I messed up in business. I let my heart rule my brain.

12

Cocaine

That June in 1988, Mum and I eventually arrived at HMP Holloway after being remanded in custody on the cocaine charge. The screws, they unload your possessions and then tell you what you can have. I told the officer I had some make-up and she said, 'Yes, you can have some lipstick.' She opened an Elizabeth Arden blusher with a mirror that I had just bought while we were shopping in Harrods the previous week and snapped it in my face. 'Oh no,' I said, 'why have you done that?' 'You're not allowed to have mirrors in case you hurt yourself!' I kissed my teeth and shook my head. They gave you two pairs of cotton pants, and a brown paper bag with blue powder in it. I looked inside and said, 'What's this for? To clean out the toilets with?', thinking it was Ajax. The screw laughed but not very nicely and said, 'No, it's tooth powder.' Then we were taken to another part where we had to have a shower and then a physical, and I saw a few girl shoplifters I knew in the reception. My Mum and I were sent down to the mothers-and-babies unit and my Mum was given her own cell.

I was to have to share a dorm with three other girls. All you had was a bed and cupboard; really it was a bit similar to a hospital, but with prison of course your door is locked. Next day we were woken very early at 7 a.m. to get ready for breakfast; then it was back to your cell and be locked up until lunchtime – except for one hour's exercise, that is.

Our first full day in Holloway, I can remember my mother handing out her cigarettes. The girls were all round her like pigeons at Trafalgar Square. I said to Mum, 'What are you doing?' 'Oh,' she said, 'I'll get some later.' I said, 'Apparently we have to wait to place orders for what we need at the canteen. We won't get nothing till the end of the week!' 'Oh,' she said. 'No one told me.' She soon learned though.

We were then required, or at least I was, to see the prison doctor. I told him I was eleven weeks gone and that I wanted a termination. He asked me the usual questions, name, date of birth, but he didn't seem to be interested about my condition, so I said, 'When will we be leaving for hospital for my operation?' All he said was, 'Don't worry', and that was it. Next thing I was back to my dormitory with three African ladies who'd been accused of bringing in weed. All had been used by men in Africa and all had done it expecting to make a bit of money to feed their children and to have a decent roof over their heads. Little did these women know that at the end of the day, say two out of four would be tipped off to the Customs, while the others would get through. I tried to explain this to them, but they didn't understand. It still goes on today, from cannabis to cocaine, heroin and 'E's. The runners will tip off Customs about a couple of mules. They build the lost drugs into the price and they don't care what happens to the women.

My sleep would be broken up at 4 a.m. with one woman

praying, and then she would get a bowl of water and stand in it to wash herself down. My mother and I would meet up on exercise; the cons in the mothers-and-babies unit used to let us wheel their babies around, but it did nothing to make me think I was going to keep Albert's baby. In the canteen before I was separated from Mum we were queuing up for lunch when I heard her say to the woman who was serving, 'I don't want any onions, thank you.' The reply was, 'Onions? They're not onions, this is cabbage.' It was not cabbage but transparent gunge. I do hope the food regime has changed now.

As we were walking around, Mum looked over to another wing of the prison and said, 'Oh look, I didn't know men were on remand here as well.' I looked and there were three or four butch-looking girls with donkey jackets on. I started laughing and said, 'Mum, they're dykes.' 'Oh,' she said. 'Lesbians.'

After I got back to my dorm I was ordered to leave and move to another wing, so I never saw my mother on exercise again. This time the three girls I was with were in for petty thieving. The girl in the bed facing me had apparently thrown a brick through a shop window and got six months. I asked her why she'd done it and she said, 'All I wanted was to get a roof over my head.' Many of these women didn't have a place to sleep, and without one they weren't able to get a job and vice versa; so you see where all this unnecessary taxpayers' money is wasted. To keep a prisoner on remand costs more than £500 per week, and they are there for maybe three months. It doesn't make sense at all. After a few days in Holloway I would be awake and hear a van pull up outside in the yard and I would think, 'Oh, perhaps my Dad has sent someone to rescue me,' but it would be an ambulance to take a girl to hospital to have her baby.

The food in Holloway was vile. You ate from blue plastic

plates and drank from blue plastic mugs. What amazes me —
and don't forget with remand prisoners by rights with our so-
called law, they're innocent until proved guilty — is how
everything against them is totally biased. Heaven knows what it
is like when you are a convicted prisoner.

One particular day, after I was moved to 'D' wing, I was
walking along the corridor with no slippers when I heard, 'Put
your slippers on!' I just carried on walking. I never knew the
screw was talking to me, I was miles away. I waited by my
dorm, but no screw came to unlock the door. As I was trying
to find one there were two big fat butch screws with a girl in a
white gown in between them, and as they were approaching me
I smiled at the prisoner. That did me no good. She made a
jump towards me and shouted, 'Ugh! Who are you fucking
looking at?' I thought, keep quiet, Marilyn, but I put my slippers on.

The following afternoon a screw said, 'Who would like to
join the art class?' I put my hand up as if I was at school and
said, 'Yes please, Miss.' I thought anything to get out of this
dormitory. In fact I did love art at school and while in my last
year I think, primary or secondary school, I was awarded a
commendation for a painting that I had done, of all things of
a signal train worker sitting in his signal box. He was at his
table with his pot of tea and had the signal in the background.
I was so proud of this award.

The screw said I could, but my enthusiasm to join the art
class lasted until all the prisoners had been seated and there
were only two seats left. As I got into the room you would have
thought I had committed a murder. Not one person said hello
or smiled. Kiss my arse, I thought. I was looking to see where
I could get my paper and paintbrushes until heads looked up at
me. No one never said a word to help me. So I opened my

mouth and said, 'Can one of you please tell me where I can get a fucking paintbrush and something to paint with?' With that a girl said, 'In that box under that table.'

I sat down at a table by myself until Hannibal Lecter's sister walked in with her white gown on. I thought, 'Oh no', so I put my head down, the screw got her a paintbrush and some paper and said, 'I will be back in a minute.' Who does she sit facing? Yes, me! I couldn't keep up the pretence any longer. I felt her eyes staring at me and I slowly brought my head up, smiled again and said, 'Hello, you know I wasn't staring at you yesterday.' Before I could finish she said, like a really slow 33rpm old-style record, 'They won't let me send any flowers.' I said, 'Ah, won't they? Look, give me the address and I will get someone to send them as I have a flower stall. What's the person's name and address?' She just looked right through me, very vacant, and never spoke to me again.

The art class was soon over and we went back to our dorms until our teatime break when one girl came over and said to me, 'You know that girl who was sitting opposite you?' I said I didn't. 'Well, don't you know what she's in for?' 'No!' She said, 'Apparently she stabbed her boyfriend thirty times and killed him!'

The following day when a screw came and said, 'Who would like to join the gym?' I said, 'Yes, I would. Where is it?' We were led through different wings, about three of us until we approached 'E' wing where about ten more girls joined up with us. We were asked if we wanted roller skates. Well, I thought, this I haven't done for a while, it will be a laugh. I was buzzing around and it brought back memories of when my sister and I, Rachel Rumble and Carol Cooper used to get about eight of us together all holding hands and skate fast. The last one would be pulled and then we would move up to a fast skate and really get wickedly fast; nine times out of ten you would all let go and fall over.

So because I felt like being a child again I got some of the girls to all hold hands and do the same in the gym. I explained to them what you had to do, but this particular bunch (unbeknown to me) were not like the girls in the other wings, so as we all skated very fast the end girl didn't know what had hit her – she was going so fast she could not stop herself and ended up falling on top of the coconut mats. One of them said, as we were all in fits of laughter, 'You'd better get away from that one.' The girl who fell over got up and she was squinting her eyes looking right across at me. Soon it was a case of her chasing me around the gym. Luckily I really had lots of stamina and strong legs. I must have skated around that gym fifty times, and knew that if I had to fight I would. The whistle had blown, gym was over but no way was my back going to be in front of her. I quickly got my skates off and she started putting her fists up to me. I shouted, 'Come on then now, me and you. Don't keep shouting about what you are going to do to me!' As I stood there another screw came in to take 'E' wing girls back, but she was still screaming and shouting. I remained standing there until a few more screws came in and said, 'Right, you lot, upstairs!' With that 'E' wing girls were led upstairs. Until us three girls who were in 'D' wing were talking in a break, I didn't know that 'E' wing was the nut-nut wing. No wonder that as I was skating and saying to them, 'Come on, girls, faster!' they were in another vacant world and wouldn't answer me. I was lucky I really didn't get done.

Over the days I kept asking to see the doctor. Just to be given a date to go to hospital would have helped my anxiety, but I was kept in limbo and getting very worried, until finally one day I was told that I would not be allowed anything to eat or drink after dinner time, which in prison was 5 p.m. My operation was for the following day, but they never told me where, what time or anything. I then was woken at 4 a.m. to be told to get my overnight stuff, wash and wait. Once I had my shower and got ready, a screw proceeded to take me inside another part of the prison and waited again, then I was led into reception where two screws handcuffed me and put me into a mini-cab and I was taken to UCH twenty minutes away.

I was taken into a ward still handcuffed, and by this time the women patients who were in for gynaecological problems were all seated having their breakfast. I walked between the two screws and was led through the ward to a private room where I was told to get undressed and put on a hospital gown. Then I got into the bed with the two screws either side of me with the door shut, and one arm was handcuffed to the bed. The doctor came in and asked me the usual things: name, address, next of kin (which was my mother), next of kin's address. I said, 'Holloway.' 'No,' he said, 'full address.' I said, 'HMP Holloway, Parkhurst Road, N7.' He coughed and said, 'I'm sorry.' 'It's OK.' He asked how was I feeling and I said, 'Fine, what time is my operation?' He looked at the screws and said, 'Sometime this afternoon.' Off he went and my blood pressure was taken by a nurse. Then I was asked to give a urine specimen. The screws had taken the cuffs off and when they went to put them back on, the nurse said, 'I don't think it's necessary, do you? The bathroom is just over there.' With that they held my arms and led me to the bathroom where I pissed into a plastic container while they watched. I handed the sample to the screws and was allowed back into my private room. God knows what the other patients thought.

I had the usual plastic band around my wrist and was hand-cuffed to the bed again. I managed to fall asleep, but this time I was woken up by the smell of food. The screws had got their sandwiches out, although they did politely ask me if I minded. I said, 'No, go ahead, I shall be eating at least some decent food after my op.' 'Oh,' the screw said, 'there's no way I can eat right after an operation.' She was just trying to be friendly. 'Can't you?' I said. 'Well, perhaps your guts are not as strong as mine.'

The orderly came in to give me a 'pre-med'. I'm glad UCH sent in a good-looking one as it brightened that day up, instead of just having the two ugly butch-looking screws in my room all day. Forty-five minutes later, I was wheeled through to have the termination. As I was being given the main anaesthetic I could hear, 'Sorry, but you'll have to wait outside.' I drifted off . . . and was now back in my private room, where I woke from my operation to dinner being served. Finally I was allowed to have some food, but almost before I'd finished the consultant came and told me it was all right for me to leave whenever I felt OK to do so and the mini-cab came to take me back to Holloway prison.

I had one visit from Jackie Saintey – who at the time was the girlfriend of Tommy Falco's son, Tony – and also from Maureen who was with me in America that time. They came to see me in the first week of my stay in Holloway. I asked them if they had brought any cigarettes, so I could have a smoke, but they said they didn't think I was allowed to. I bit their heads off. I said, 'If you don't know you should ring up the nick and ask. If you don't ask you don't get! They can either say yes or no!' I was gasping for a cigarette until a screw supervising the visit kindly could see, and offered me one. Whoever you are, thank you. But I did think the world of Jackie and Maureen coming up to see me. Some people who I thought would have come up never did. When it came to it, many of my so-called friends weren't there.

Finally our bail arrangements were made. My Uncle Len and Aunt Gladys Hancock (Mum's sister) stood bail for me, and my Uncle George and Aunt Dot stood bail for my Mum. To this day I will never be able to thank them enough – them being hard-working people and helping us, considering being on a drugs charge back then still had a big stigma to it. It's not like today when everybody in all walks of society is taking either coke, E's or cannabis.

The date was set for the bail application to a judge in chambers. My mother's was granted and she was allowed to come up to my wing to say goodbye. I looked through the latch at her with tears in my eyes and said, 'See you later' and she said, 'Good luck darling.' Really, once Mum had bail it was only a matter of time before I was allowed out, and a few days later my application was granted.

I was quite upset and angry that of all the people my parents and I knew not one person had been there at the gates for Mum to pick her up. We were finally reunited with our Jonathan minus my Dad, who was on his toes and nowhere to be seen or heard of. It's true what you read in articles – that when you've had a trauma of some kind, be it rape, a bad attack, or have been in a police cell or prison, the first thing you want is a lovely bath, and that's what I had.

Jonathan had been looked after by Kathy Dudley, the daughter of Reggie Dudley who was done for the so-called Epping Torso murder of Billy Moseley and Mickey Cornwall in the mid-1970s. Along with his mate, Bobby Maynard, he did about 25 years just because he wouldn't admit his guilt and so become eligible for parole. Kathy was really good. She'd been done herself over the murders, but rightly she got a not guilty. In turn Dad had kept an eye out for her while Reggie was away.

All we knew of Dad was from a certain face in North

London — who has never been in prison, but in my opinion seemed to know everybody else's business — that he might be in a police cell. At that time, because of overcrowding people were being kept in police cells up and down the country and not in prison. It could take some time to find out where a relation was actually being held, and by then he could just as likely have been moved. In fact the man wasn't correct and he got a message to Dad to say I would take the blame for the drugs. Dad got a message back saying thanks but not to be ridiculous. In fact it was not until the next spring that he got picked up. Meanwhile Mum and me were like lepers. People who should have known better just wouldn't come near us, but we kept our spirits up and managed to carry on at the stall.

My mother had already suffered enough. What a strong lady she had been over the years, but after Dad was arrested over the American Express travellers' cheques business with Billy Gentry she had a small stroke which took it out of her.

One of the bail terms was that we both had to sign on twice a week between certain times, I can't remember the actual ones, at our local nick which was then in Upper Street, Islington. One particular night we had had a good drink in Covent Garden with a lovely old lady who was a character from Neal Street, along with her two sons Harry and George Goody, in Jimmy Ryan's White Horse. We said our goodbyes, went home and got into bed. It was now 12.30 a.m. and I nudged my Mum and said, 'You know what? What day it is?' 'Tuesday.' I said, 'Yeah, Tuesday, and we've forgotten to sign on last night.' We both jumped out of bed and I called up Upper Street police station and explained what had happened, saying, 'Can we sign on this evening?' The desk sergeant said, 'No, you'll have to come now!' So with that we put our coats on over our nightdresses and walked the half mile or so from our flat along Upper Street at 1 a.m.

Cocaine

After you've been signing on for a bit some officers will just
let you wave from the door, but not this one. In fact it's more
of an inconvenience for them than anything else. I gave the
desk sergeant my number and apologised for being late, but he
said, 'What are you charged with?' I said, 'I don't have to tell
you that, I've just given you my number.' He said, 'You will tell
me, otherwise you will be back in Holloway.' My Mum nudged
me, so I kissed my teeth and said, 'Conspiracy with intent to
supply a class A drug'; then he looked at my Mum and said,
'You can go now.' Mum said, 'Wait a minute, do you want my
number?' 'Oh,' he said, 'another Wisbey, Mrs?' He still insisted
she must say what she was charged with. As we were leaving and
going home I said, 'What a perv, that's his kick. I should have
sung that song, "I Get a Kick out of You".'

That was the only day we ever missed signing on, something
that was to last a year, until my father was captured in
Wilmslow, Cheshire, and charged with the same offence along
with Jimmy Hussey, me and my Mum and Albert Moffat, my
ex-boyfriend who was done for trying to pervert the course of
justice by saying the cocaine was his.

Albert had heard I was in trouble and he did a really decent
thing. He came forward to say the drugs were his, and he swore
out an affidavit about it. It took a man to do that. They weren't
his of course, and his story was full of holes. The police never
believed him for a minute, so they charged him with perjury. I
was really pissed off with both Dad and Jimmy Hussey. I was
just upset to think the pair of them had been through it all and
had gone and done it again. It wasn't even as though Dad
hadn't had a bit of a lesson with the Billy Gentry case. Mum
had told him even after the Train that if he got into any more
trouble that was the end of the marriage, but she still stayed
with him.

Of course, it didn't stop us going to see Dad while he was on remand. After all there was three of us – Dad, me and Albert – all willing to say the stuff was theirs. In fact it was quite simple because Dad was quite firm that he was going to take the blame.

I had changed my solicitors to James Saunders in Harrow Road and Albert had that Scottish QC Sir Nicholas Fairbairn come down to defend him. I had met Nicholas Fairbairn, he was a good man. You could see as soon as he walked in there was an aura about him and that in the justice department he was a strong lawyer who wouldn't take any shit from anyone.

The day of our trial at Snaresbrook, my Mum's defence lawyer had his wig and gown on and he was calling her as we waited for our case. 'Mrs Wisbey, Mrs Wisbey.' I said, 'Mum, that man's calling you.' He lifted up his wig and said, 'Mrs Wisbey, it's me, Mr——' I forget his name. 'Hello, I didn't recognize you with that curly wig on.' My lawyer briefed me and in we went with all five of us now in the dock. I stood there. I have been in some situations in my life, but this one was second to losing my sister and boyfriend Michael; I had tears in my eyes not knowing what the judge was going to do. I was also feeling very bad for my father, Mum, Jimmy and Albert. Our defence counsels asked if my Mum and me would step down. I was oblivious to what was being said, but what had happened was that in return for the others pleading guilty Mum and me were to be acquitted without any evidence being given. Then the prosecution read out Albert's convictions and he got 18 months for perjury. He was given his sentence and went down, then we sat through to listen to the prosecution talking about my father, Thomas William Wisbey, who had been caught living with another woman up in Wilmslow.

I was shocked and my mother was worse. We didn't know that he was living with somebody else. Tommy was sentenced to 10 years and Jimmy Hussey got 7. Also they confiscated everything of Dad's that they could find. As I said before, my flat in Eltham which I'd bought with my American money but was in Dad's name – that went, and so did about fifteen grand which had been in a drawer by the bed. I'd said all along that about £3,000 was mine which I was using to stock the flower shop, but it didn't do us any good.

Before he went down I waved to my father who looked at me as we came out of the court. I kept silent with tears running down my face, and my Mum who was also in tears was saying, 'Who the hell was this bird?' The prosecution could at least have kept that from us. I then said to her, 'Oh, don't worry, you did have your affairs when he was doing that bird for the Train Robbery, Mum. Call it quits, eh?' She looked at me and said, 'I didn't think he liked women all that much, and I didn't think he had it in him.' I put my arms around her and said, 'Well, at least you won't have to worry about cooking his dinner by six o'clock.'

Afterwards Roy James, who'd been on the Train with Dad and Jimmy Hussey, said it was all wrong and the pros was just trying to wind us up. He'd not just been staying with a woman; he'd been with her and her husband.

13

The House of Fraser

The last two years previous to meeting Frank I'd felt very lonely. I was missing my father, not having him around in the background. Having to see him once more in Her Majesty's Prison really upset me, although I must say he got on with his bird all right and never moaned. Then there was the case over my divorce, especially when I was out on bail and had enough on my plate without my ex-husband hitting me with the papers. But I continued to carry on with my life. My friend Jenny from Kent used to visit me and we would go out to have the odd dinner or lunch. I continued to work on the market stall, which I didn't like. I much preferred having that spell at Pal Joey's club underneath the snooker hall until we got turfed out.

In fact things hadn't been going well for me for those couple of years, mainly because it was after the case at Snaresbrook that I'd run into Giacomo Pavanelli – who I called James, since that was his name in English. Well, actually Albert Moffat introduced us. James was in Pentonville when I was visiting

Albert who was doing his 18 months over trying to protect me with the cocaine. We'd finished our relationship mainly because Albert, lovely as he was about trying to help me out, was such a dreamer and a fantasist. He was forever going to rob the bank at Monte Carlo when in reality he was a petty shoplifter. He was the sort of man who couldn't go out for a walk without having to rescue someone in a fire. I met him again not long ago, and he was still rabbiting on, but I'll never forget how he tried to get me out of trouble at his own cost.

James was doing four years for fraud – he'd been involved with some promissory notes and securities and a South American bank – and, being Italian, he didn't have any visitors. Albert asked me if I would visit him and, of course, I said I would. Anyway things went on from there. I kept ringing his sister in Turin for him, and when he was in an open prison near Newmarket he was given home leave and all his stuff including his passport. It was almost as if they didn't expect him to come back. And he didn't. He stayed with me in the Islington flat and as the time came for him to go back to High Point he said he wanted to go to Italy and would I come with him, where we could go into business together. So we flew to Rome and then drove to Turin to see his sister and on to Genoa.

James had this thing about museums and art galleries. He said he had to show me Lucca, and we went there with his nephew and his girlfriend. It was baking hot and you had to park outside the old walls of the city and walk. We arrived just about 3 o'clock and all I wanted to do was go and have lunch and a cold bottle of wine. There was an old man sitting by the museum gates and he was just about to shut up for the afternoon. I was standing behind James with my hands closed in prayer that he wouldn't let us in and for once they were answered.

James's idea was that he'd buy some special Italian wine from a vineyard crop and sell it in England, but of course after his trial he didn't have any capital. It sounded like a good business and I had £25,000 left from what I'd brought back from America. Fool that I was, I agreed to put it in the business; I came back home and sent it to his sister.

I didn't hear from him so I just went over again on spec. James was away but his sister put me up. Then when he came back he sort of manufactured a row. I said send the money back, and I came back to England. Sometimes I think I keep my brains between my legs.

The clever thing was having me send the money to his sister in the first place. I never thought he'd have me over, and I certainly didn't think his sister would help him. Probably he never told her what he was going to do.

Then he wrote to Daddy saying he was sorry about everything, that the chemistry between him and me wasn't right but the money was safe. Of course it wasn't. After I met Frank I asked him if he knew anyone in Italy and he spoke to Battles Rossi who'd been done with him when Frank slashed Jack Spot. Battles made a phone call and someone went round to James's house in Turin, but all that was sent to me was £1,000 and he's still floating around the world somewhere on my money. There's no point in trying to sue him, but I do think our representatives in Italy could have leaned on him a bit harder.

I got made bankrupt about then. £19,000 was all it was – all gone on Pavanelli and the money seized over the cocaine case. Fortunately they couldn't take my flat in Duncan Street. I'd bought it when the council offered it, and as I couldn't sell it for five years the trustee in bankruptcy couldn't get it from me. It's worked out that the original £19,000 doubled, and the costs and everything came to £40,000, so eventually I was forced to sell the flat. There was no way Frank and I could get a mortgage. It seems amazing that you go bust for something and with lawyer's fees and so on it ends up costing you twice as much. I think the bankruptcy laws should be changed. Lawyers and accountants are the ones who make money out of small people.

There were some good bits. I was the only girl in a group from Henry Brown's pub to go to the Hearns–Hagler fight in Las Vegas. There was a good bunch of Chaps including Jimmy Saunders who was done over the Ilford bank robbery, and who got out when Bertie Smalls the grass told the police that Jimmy hadn't been on it. Poor Jimmy, he got a fifteen a few years back for trying to do a snatch in Baker Street. Mickey Green, who was grassed up by Smalls over the Wembley bank, came along with us too. A bit ago Mickey was meant to be the most wanted man in Britain. I still knew a couple of people in Vegas and they warned me there was a team in town likely to try and roll the punters, so I passed the information on and told the boys to be careful. I knew what I was talking about because I'd done a spot of rolling in Vegas myself.

It was after Pillow Talk closed and I went to Redondo that a couple of friends of mine, Shelley and Brian, were a bit skint. She suggested we go to Vegas to roll a punter and so off we went in Brian's Mercedes. We hadn't $200 between us, and we had $25 less when we got pulled for speeding near Barstow.

Then when we got to Vegas it was dead quiet. You could have rolled a bowling ball through Caesar's Palace and not hit anyone. Brian went off, leaving me and Shelley, and we started showing out to a couple of men and they were doing the same to us. Then they came over and asked if we wanted to play craps. I was very nervous because since I'd worked in a casino

I knew about the holes in the ceiling through which the games were watched and videoed. 'Don't worry,' said Shelley. 'Just do what I do.'

We went to the tables and she leaned over when the punter was playing and nicked a few chips, masking herself from the camera. It isn't a thing you can do too often. After playing a bit, one of the guys asked if we wanted to have some fun and we all went off to his hotel room. One of them was really drunk by this time and he soon went off to his own room, but we had the other send for canapés and smoked salmon and champagne. That's when he wanted us both to stay the night. We put him in a deep sunken bath and played around with him and by then it was 2 in the morning. He said he was a bit sleepy and I went and lay down on the bed with him, and within a matter of a minute he was out like a light with his arm over me. Shelley went through his pockets and got his wad out. I was whispering to her not to take it all, just say $500. It's easier that way if the punter starts to complain. If there's nothing there, then it's more difficult to explain; it looks obvious.

Then she just left me to stay the night. Next morning he wanted to know where she was, and I said he'd been asleep so long she had to go and I would have to leave soon as well. He wanted me to meet for lunch downstairs and I agreed. Then I legged it back to our hotel and we were out of town in five minutes. It turned out Shelley had nicked a grand, which wasn't bad for a night's work. That and the champagne and smoked salmon.

Anyway, as I say, this knowledge should have come in handy for the party but Jimmy and Mickey can't have listened. Jimmy had taken his son to Vegas as a 21st present, and I was waiting with him at Caesar's Palace where the fights were. For once it was pissing down. Finally Jimmy turned up. I've never seen anyone look much more bedraggled, and it all came out. They'd met a couple of hookers who'd slipped them Mickey Finns and taken Mickey's top-of-the-range Rolex and their dough. Poor Jimmy said he felt too ill to watch the boxing and he just went back to his hotel.

Now and again I would venture into the Tin Pan club – it's now a wine bar – in Denmark Street just off the Charing Cross Road. In the old days it was an old-fashioned after-hours drinker, but then when people no longer wanted their feet to be stuck to the carpet it went up-market and became a smart wine bar. In fact I'd met my husband Alan Tear in there. It was run by Frank's nephew Jimmy Fraser and Frank Junior. In fact Jimmy's still got it. They knew who I was, of course. I'd known them since I was 18 when they used to come and drink in the Alliance during that short time when my Mum and me had it. In fact I knew Frank's other sons, David and Patrick, much better. David is so handsome. He and the other Fraser boys all took after their Dad. They are real gentlemen – and so has Frank been. He's never laid so much as a finger on me, not even when I've steamed into him something rotten.

Jimmy and Frank Junior used to take care of me when I went to the Tin Pan. If I was drinking too much, and sometimes I was, they would make sure I was put in a taxi to get home.

Then in April 1991 my life turned around. Apart from meeting one of the best singers in the entertainment business of the twentieth century, Francis Albert Sinatra, later in that same month I met, for the second time, one of the most feared post-war gangsters, Francis Davidson Fraser. It took a bit of time, but I changed him into an ex-gangster – but for those people who have met him they have said to me, 'He is a gentle-man.' It's nearly ten years I have been with him, and it has been one roller-coaster ride to say the least, but what has amazed me is that for such a small man he has so much strength, both physically and mentally. I always say to Frank about being a soldier, 'You would have been a great leader for our country.' As a woman, and having met a whole range of different types of men in my life, in true honesty I wish I could wave a magic wand and turn the clock back to see this little man with so much strength become another great politician like Winston Churchill. At least he's truthful and answers a question to the point.

This one particular night I went to the Tin Pan to see my friend June McCarthy, who was Jimmy Fraser's long-standing girlfriend of twenty years, to see if she could get me a job. As I was singing on a bar stool that song 'Crazy' by Patsy Cline, Frank Senior came over to me. He was with Val, a girlfriend of his that used to work in the Log Cabin for Tommy McCarthy in the days way back before he had met Francis junior's mum, Doreen. He said, 'I hope you're not referring to me! You know I have been certified insane three times!' 'No, I hope you know whose daughter I am?' Laughing, he said, 'No, whose?' 'Tommy Wisbey's.' 'Ah, how is he?' 'He's in the nick right now.' Frank said, 'Give my regards to him – and by the way you have a gorgeous voice. You should be singing in a club.' I said, 'They don't have clubs like years ago, do they, Frank?' and I added, 'Would you like to come and visit my Dad with me one day?'

Of all prisons, Dad was back in Parkhurst working off the time for his cocaine sentence, and Parkhurst was where Frank had all that trouble when he led the so-called riot back in 1969 when after it was over the prisoners got beaten black and blue. We exchanged phone numbers and made plans and arranged to meet at, of all places, Waterloo Station where the train used to leave for Dartmoor prison. Frank said that's how he'd know where to go. But he was only joking. He has a great way of making me and others laugh.

Frank was dead on time. I've found out over the years that he's never late. He's always there ten minutes before time, and if you're more than half a minute late he'll be looking at his watch and making a joke when you come up. Something like, 'I thought maybe it was tomorrow.' This time I was dead on time, which must have made a good impression on him as well.

I took with me a sort of picnic – more champagne than smoked salmon sandwiches – for the journey. It was always sad seeing Dad in prison again, but I was determined to make the best of things and I knew he'd be pleased to see Frank.

The day was good from start to finish, as it turned out to be a very amusing and interesting journey to be listening to an intelligent older man. It made a nice change from some of the arseholes I had met in the past. I got to know more about my Dad as a thief and person than from anyone I had ever spoken to. Particularly about how loyal Frank said my father was, which was something I loved to hear.

The train journey soon came to an end and the ferry across seemed much quicker than it had been all those years ago when I was a child. I could remember way back in the 1970s when Lenny the taxi driver was waiting for us at Ryde Pier. Lenny was a terrific Isle of Wight person, who used to really help everyone. He was always on time to pick up all the waiting prisoners' wives and girlfriends at the Pier. With Dad there time and again, Lenny became a good friend of ours. Poor Lenny was hated by a lot of prison officers because he would say what lovely people we all were. Apparently, over the years he came up against a lot of problems from the other local taxi drivers and off-duty prison officers. What a pathetic society of people who were narrow-minded, just because he showed kindness to all of the visitors no matter who they were or what their loved ones had done.

There he still was and Lenny was pleased to meet Frank, as of course he knew of the famous riot, and he asked about all the old faces and how Eva (Frank's sister) was. He wanted to know how Ronnie, Reggie and Charlie Kray were, and all about Dolly Roberts, Harry's mother.

When we got near the gates there's a little road which leads up to them rather like there is in most prisons, and I thought it looked much newer to me – and about time too. I hadn't been there for something like twenty years, and of course I wasn't out of my teens when I last went. When I look back at how the prisoners and the screws have to stay in these old Victorian buildings, and still do, it's a wonder that the Prison Officers' Association has never made more of a complaint about the conditions. Someone might listen to them; they'd never listen to the cons. It really has amazed me that only now in the twenty-first century, the Home Office has started to wake up and smell the coffee! But from what I read of the reports of the Prison Ombudsman I'm not so sure they have. He's forever condemning prisons and the way prisoners are being held. At least when Frank and Dad were in during the sixties they weren't three in a cell made for one. No wonder there's no reform and people commit crimes again the moment they're let out.

We waved goodbye to Len and asked him to pick us up at 4 p.m. and then our troubles started. As we went in a young prison officer naturally asked me for the VO (Visiting Order) which I gave to him and then for some ID. I gave him mine but, silly me, I'd forgotten to tell Frank to bring his ID and he hadn't thought of it. 'I'm sorry,' the handsome young rookie said, 'but I'm afraid you can't come in without any ID.' 'Oh, no,'

I thought, and looked across at Frank in case he was going to explode. Then all of a sudden an older prison officer asked what the problem was. When the rookie said, 'This visitor has no ID, sir,' the older officer looked at Frank and said, 'Well, hello there, Mr Fraser.' Then he said to the younger man, 'I know who he is, all right. Let him in.' But turning to Frank and me, he said that next time we should remember to bring some ID. Luckily this man was the senior officer in charge of security. It was good of him in fact, as we had come a long way. Given the riot he could easily have cut up rough and, despite the journey we'd made, not let Frank in. Funnily enough at the time I never knew about Frank being the man accused of the Parkhurst Riot in the seventies. After all I was only going on 12 when it happened and it didn't make the papers that much. Dad had been in Parkhurst along with Gordon Goody at the time, but the Train Robbers were kept in a special security wing and took no part. I don't think they even knew the demonstration against conditions which led to the riot was going off.

We then went through the same system as everybody else; the usual metal detector, in one electronic gate then another one, waited, got told to leave everything in a locker, and then told to wait in a separate visiting room until visiting time. All the visitors for the A4 Category prisoners had an even more strict procedure as well. To me, you could not get any prison today more secure.

When we were finally in the pre-visitors' room I made Frank laugh by saying, 'Thank Christ they let you in, otherwise they would have had another riot on their hands over a poxy ID.' My Dad was very pleased to see Frank. Over the years things have got so much easier. No question of glass between prisoner and visitor, with a screw at your side. Now you can talk to other prisoners who are in the room, and we chatted with Cyril Birkett who had been doing time inside with my Dad during the Train; he was a character too. There was also a Yugoslavian guy who was painting a mural for the visitors' room. He came over to shake our hands, Frank's and mine. What a nice person. I have to say this, when you have decent surroundings in a prison it does help.

As I say Cyril Birkett had been in Leicester with Dad when he was protesting about conditions and was up on the roof. The Governor asked Cyril if he would go up a ladder and try to persuade Dad to come down. Cyril went up the ladder and then when he got to the top he joined Dad and sent the ladder crashing back into the yard.

Frank knew him quite well after he came out and before he was nicked again. Apparently Cyril liked having guns about him and one day he gave Frank a lift. Half-way he told him he'd got five in the car. Frank nearly had a fit. No one would have believed he knew nothing if they'd had a pull. I asked Frank if he made Cyril stop so's he could get out, but he said they'd carried on so he can't have had that much of a fit.

The Yugoslav guy stayed on the island after his release and he was killed in a car accident there a few years later. The mural was of a man, woman and a child standing on a quayside. Dad always used to say it represented the three of us, but I suppose just about every prisoner with a daughter said the same. That's what made it such a clever painting.

You have to remember that travelling miles away with children is no joy for anyone. Years ago when I was a young girl, you never saw an area for small kids to play in so that they would not disturb everybody else's visit.

When the visit was over, Len was waiting for us and dropped us back in time for the ferry. We chatted non-stop on the way home and when we were pulling into Waterloo Frank asked me if I would like to go out for dinner. I said, 'Well, actually, I've got plans,' so he said maybe another evening and we made plans for two evenings ahead, which was Friday. With the champagne and smoked salmon I'd spoiled him rotten on the way down to Parkhurst, and that night it was his turn to look after me.

Being like any other woman I do like to be made a fuss of and Frank certainly made a fuss of me. That night he was contemplating going home to Val when he suddenly said, 'Fuck it, I'll stay with you.' It was then that he told me about a book he was writing and which he had nearly finished which I thought was a great idea. He asked me if I would like to meet his co-writer and of course I said I would. Judging by some of the stories Dad had told me, I said to Frank that I thought he ought to get a literary lawyer to give him some advice.

He didn't have a lawyer so I arranged for one to meet Frank and his writer, but the wanker sent his friend to discuss everything and the writer himself never turned up. This wasn't encouraging, and Frank's lawyer asked us what publisher the writer had. Frank said he didn't have anyone at the moment, and the lawyer asked where the co-author was. Frank lost confidence and decided not to go ahead as it just seemed a waste of time. I kept saying to him, 'But you have a lot to tell; don't throw it all away, Frank. The media have been mentioning your name since the year dot.' Well, in fact since he was 16, and he goes back in amongst the criminal fraternity in every decade from the thirties to the nineties. 'No,' he said. 'My time has been wasted.' 'Yes,' I agreed, and I was getting a bit angry. 'Not only inside but outside as well!' He laughed, so now he was no longer giving up but he was without a writer. I said, 'Don't worry; I think I might be able to help you as I know Gollancz publishers.'

Our flower stall in Covent Garden was only a few yards from their offices and one of their staff bought from us. What had happened was that one rainy night as I was closing up a man came and asked if he could buy some roses. I unlocked and he bought an enormous bunch of the roses we had. We got chatting and he told me that he was at Gollancz and gave me his card. He knew about Dad, and I said that I might have a very interesting book for him. At the time I was thinking of my father's book to be written. I kept the card years before I met Frank, so a day later I said to Frank, 'I managed to find his card and I've made an appointment for you.' The man remembered me; his wife Liz had seen us in Henrietta Street. They were very much interested, but all the writers they suggested were busy doing other projects and months went by without Gollancz being able to find us a suitable writer.

They tried their hardest to find Frank a writer, but they never managed to come up with one. What was so sad, Liz (we heard later) died of cancer. Frank and I were so upset because she and her husband were such a lovely couple and had so much faith in Frank's book.

In 1991 Frank and I had been invited to a birthday party at a restaurant; afterwards we continued on with our friends, going from one wine-bar to another until I said, 'Let's go up to Ra-Ra's, seeing as it is on our way home.' It's good fun there because they have karaoke, and when we got into the pub there were people Frank hadn't seen for years who started buying us drinks. No one would let us spend any money, which was handy, but also it was nice to get respect. There were people from both East and South London coming up to him; it was a terrific atmosphere. I got up to sing on the karaoke, and I never got off.

Finally Lisa, a girl I had known for years, said, 'Mal, are you going to Turnmills?' 'Where's that?' She said, 'It's a new rave place in Farringdon.' I was always on the lookout for business arrangements. I thought perhaps I could open a club. Maybe that was one of the worst decisions of my life.

Turnmills is just about a hundred yards from Farringdon tube station and as we got inside the dark smoky atmosphere, you couldn't talk to one another because of this 'Boom! Boom!' sound. Once again Frank had young guys coming up and shaking his hand. It's a wonder they recognised him in the dark and smoke. I had to laugh when Frank asked for two vodka and tonics and the gay barman said, 'Oh, I'm sorry, but we don't serve alcohol.' Frank said, 'Why, are you closed then?' The barman laughed and said, 'No, it's only non-alcoholic drinks.' So we just made do with our company, although there was a man to buy us drinks. Eugene Carter from South London was in there; his Uncle John had a long-running feud with Frank and the rest of his family. In fact Frank told me he did him badly while in prison with Frank. Jimboy, a funny character who used to be a friend of Lorraine, Michael, Terry Sansom and I way back, was there and he also offered to get us a drink. Frank was amazed at all the people there. It was packed and the music was really thumping. Frank disappeared and for a time I was left talking. When he came back he whispered in my ear, 'Someone in the toilet gave me a tablet.' I asked, 'What sort of tablet?' 'It's an A.' I laughed and said, 'You mean an E.' I went to the toilet and looked at it, it was a 'Dove'. The last time that I had had one of those was in a studio place off Wandsworth Road. I said to Frank, 'Do you want half with me?' But he replied, 'You know I've never puffed [meaning cannabis]. And the coke I've tried don't go up my knife and shooter. What will happen?' I told him it would make him feel both relaxed and horny. I broke the tablet into two and we had half each. When a minute later I looked down at Frank's feet, he had started to tap, and I was also feeling switched on to the music and got up to dance to 'I Wanna give you Devotion' and 'Where the Love Lies' by Alison Limerick.

By now it was about 4 a.m. By this time Turnmills was heaving, and I felt as if I was floating. On the other hand, Frank by now was OK but obviously he'd had enough, and he suggested we went home. We said our goodbyes and started to creep out, but as we were leaving, people who recognised Frank said, 'Come back in and have a drink.' Although he said we wouldn't, Frank was as polite as always, saying we'd been out all night as it was. Personally, I could have carried on and wanted to stay because that 'E' had really kicked in.

We wanted to get a mini-cab and there was a firm outside the club which called itself the African Car Firm. A man there pointed with a clipboard to a car across the road for us to take. Looking back, that road looked miles wide and the kerb seemed a foot high. I held Frank's arm and we walked over to the car, when all of a sudden a guy appeared from nowhere. He was well over six foot tall with a baseball cap on and was holding a white cloth over his mouth and a gun in the other hand, although at that instant I never noticed the gun. Frank later told me he'd already thought, 'This guy is going to shoot someone.' As he stood by Frank, he tilted his gun into Frank's face and fired. There was a loud crack and a flash. I'd never been that near a gunshot before. Even when I was in Palm Springs that time it had seemed well away. It was clear that Frank had been hit and I grabbed him and held his face down. I turned around and yelled, 'You bastard!' With that the gunman stood about 8–10 feet away and fired a second time. Now the bullet ricocheted off a car and then the gunman ran off to a van where there was a fair-haired, smaller guy standing. They jumped in and sped off. Frank was back on his feet, but he was bleeding badly and I held him back to stop him trying to run after them.

I remember calling out for the ambulance, but no one seemed to be able to help until Jimboy got us into his car. Frank was still standing up, which was something I couldn't believe. He kept saying, 'Fuck the hospital, take me somewhere out of here,' but I demanded that Jimboy take him to the hospital. What Frank wanted was some doctor who could treat gunshot wounds and not report them, but I didn't know of any and I wasn't sure he did. Anyway Bart's Hospital was pretty near.

Of course, Frank was covered in blood; all over his face and suit and shirt, but I had only a small amount on me from holding him. The bullet had gone in one side of his cheek and came round to the other side. Once we were at the hospital the police never once asked to take a statement from Frank. They tried with me, but not too hard, though perhaps that was because all I kept saying was that I wanted a tablet for my headache. I suspect they'd looked up my record and seen I'd been fined at Highbury Coroner's Court for wasting police time years and years ago. All that had happened was that I'd taken Dad's car out and a boy had driven off in it. Rather than tell Dad, I'd reported it stolen.

When finally I was allowed to see Frank at Bart's Hospital the police were surrounding him. He had two officers wearing bulletproof vests in his room. Frank was sitting up in bed in a side room and I turned round to him and said, 'Fucking hell, Frank, that was a powerful shot of vodka we had last night, what proof was it?' He looked up and started coughing. 'Don't make me laugh,' he said.

I'll always remember the detective who tried to interview

Frank. He was a tall man with a gut, and pockmarks on his face, and he tried to ask Frank questions but he got absolutely nowhere. By now Frank was convinced it was the police themselves who had tried to have him killed. 'Just fuck off! You've already tried to kill me. What, are you gonna try again? Just get them lot outside and out of here.' And when it came to it that's about what they did.

They kept a presence for a bit though and they even had the audacity to search my bag when my Mum and I went up to see Frank. Of course, the newspapers had a field day and said Frank had given his name as Tutankhamen. My friend, June McCarthy, took me to stay with her while Frank had the operation, because I wanted to avoid the press. I really needed to go home to get Frank's bits and pieces from the flat, but I was frightened of who might be waiting there. June offered to come with me and I thought the world of her for that. As we got to the door of the flat in Duncan Street Mike Sullivan, who is a top crime reporter from the *Sun* newspaper, was there. It gave me such a fright and it really threw me because I thought he was an undercover cop out to kill me. But once he politely said who he was, June told him that I was too distressed to talk and he was very good. He didn't press things like so many would have done.

We then went upstairs to collect Frank's toilet bag and slippers and so on. By now other people from the press had turned up and were ringing the entry-phone bell. I was trying to remember the list of things that Frank had asked me to bring to the hospital while June was tarting herself up asking where my make-up bag was. I said, 'Why do you want make-up, June?' and she replied, 'Just in case we get our photographs taken.' It really made me laugh at such a traumatic time.

The newspapers made it out to be a gangland war, which

they always do, and it's a good excuse for a few columns. They said he'd been shot over a drug deal with a top North London firm, which was absolute rubbish. I don't suppose the police complained either. Frank has always said to the TV and media that, far-fetched as it might seem, it was an undercover cop. It was common knowledge that Frank was writing a book, and maybe they thought that it would disclose a lot of his past about bent coppers who were high up the ladder. When it came to it, Frank didn't write much about the police at all. People have often asked me what it was like that night and I say to them, 'I'm glad I was as high as a kite.'

There's a funny story about when Frank lay in hospital and had the bullet taken out by one of the top doctors at Barts. The consultant said to Frank, 'Well, Mr Fraser, I'm pleased to tell you that you are a very lucky man.' Frank asked him why and the consultant said, 'That bullet was an eighth of a centimetre away from your left temple.' Then Frank said, 'Doc, do you mind if I keep the bullet?' 'My God, whatever for?' Frank replied, 'I have a pal in the scrap-metal business and he collects them and puts them on the scales.' The consultant gave a big smile.

Frank came out two days later. It shows how fit and tough he was that he could have a bullet in his face and be up walking within such a short time. I went to collect him and as we walked out together there on the hospital board were the names of all the different wards. One was called Francis Fraser Ward, Floor 3. We looked at one another and, like that Victor Meldrew in *One Foot in the Grave*, said, 'I don't believe it!'

We stayed away from my flat. I knew I had to stick by Frank, but I was also thinking of my son's safety – and a bit of my own, I've got to admit. If there's a shooting in the Underworld and it's botched up, then as a general rule someone goes to see both the victim and those who've done the shooting to see if something can be worked out. So there isn't usually a second attempt. But in this case Frank could hardly go to the police. Eva, Frank's sister, told us we could stay with her, but I said no as she had already been through enough. When it came to it a friend's son gave us a place to stay at over in South London, but even there my nerves were shattered. Every time I heard a car backfire my heart went in my mouth.

Then Alan and Mona Stanton from West London offered us their villa in Gozo for Frank and me to have a little holiday. Frank had known Alan through being in the nick with him. Alan and John Bindon had a wine-bar together in Fulham and Mona, who is Swedish, is a drop-dead-gorgeous ex-page 3 girl. We drove over there and parked the car with them. I don't know what we were doing because we left a gun in one of the side pockets with a couple of dusters over it. Fortunately it was there when we got back. Mona never knew anything about it.

Malta was lovely and relaxing. There's a story amongst the faces that I was Dom Mintoff's (the premier's) mistress, but it's not true, I'm sorry to say. The only time I was near him was when I was in the sea throwing a ball about and it hit his shoulder. I've never seen bodyguards move more quickly, but they soon realised it was nothing.

While at the airport I'd bought a book to read. Of all the books I had chosen it was the hardback version of *Gangland* written by James Morton. There's nothing nicer than to read a compelling book while under the shade on a sunbed. Whilst topping up my coffee at the airport Frank said to me, 'I thought you might have bought a Jackie Collins book to read.' I said, 'Before I met you, I liked Sidney Sheldon and Jeffrey Archer. Now I'll see what things are really like.'

Even though I'd been around the scene all my life this was

such a good book. It gave me an insight into different sides of a life through which it seemed I had just been tiptoeing around. After all, Chaps don't make women their confidantes if they've any sense. The fewer people who know what you're up to the better. If you want an example, look at poor Billy Gentry and my Dad and that grass Tina Meer. My father Tommy was mentioned in the book and Frank was mentioned many times. During the holiday I had the opportunity to ask Frank some informal, silly questions such as, 'Did you really kill Dickie Hart?' I'd met Dickie's wife many times years ago when I was with Mickey Morris. By then she was married to Stan Naylor, who got convicted along with the Tibbs over their quarrel with the Nichols family.

Frank had told me that it was Dickie's wife who'd told the police that when Dickie was in Mr Smith's on the night the fight took place he (Dickie) had gone home to get armed. Dickie shot Frank and nearly smashed his thigh-bone; in fact he was lucky he didn't lose his leg. While we were sitting on the terrace of the villa one evening I said to Frank, 'Looking back, it seems like it was like a Wild West saloon fight at the OK Corral,' and he replied, 'Yes, John Wayne would have been proud of us.'

Not long after we got back we were in Mona's restaurant-wine-bar over in Wandsworth, where Mona's cooking was the attraction and Phil the Bomb used to come over. Phil should really have been called the Pied Piper because of all the different kids that he had fathered. He thought the world of Frank and offered to give any help we might need. But things had quietened down and we moved back to Duncan Street soon afterwards.

Alan introduced us to some guy who later on became a grass. This guy, Steve Mahood, apparently said he had shot a

Catholic policeman over in Northern Ireland and had been in prison there. Unbeknown to Frank and myself, he was working with Alan and together with Blue, their gofer, a guy from Fulham, they were importing coke. The Customs caught Mahood with it and he turned Queen's Evidence and helped them get evidence on Alan. Poor Alan was charged with importing and supplying. The grass was then sent to a remand prison over in Dover, to spy and inform on any remand prisoner so he could get his sentence cut in half.

Mona called to see if we could get Alan a good brief and we asked around and were recommended to an Egyptian, Moby Shah. Moby would have gone on to become a very good barrister as he had plenty of balls and intelligence; he was a good friend of Rudy Nurayan, the well-known radical lawyer. While Alan was on remand in Canterbury, we would visit him and we did what we could to support Mona as a friend. As I know only too well, once your old man is nicked the false friends and ponces stay away. Mona coped pretty well seeing that she was from Sweden and really didn't know what was going on. Meanwhile poor John Bindon's health was deteriorating slowly.

We kept in touch with Moby Shah and would often have a drink with him. He was at the place that night when the father of Ronnie O'Sullivan, the famous snooker player, got done for murder. Ronnie's dad was provoked because of being the father of Ronnie, and a fight broke out and the other punter got killed. Moby decided to go ahead and be a witness for the defence. Unfortunately the week after Moby vomited and choked, and he was found dead in his sleep. He did like his champagne and he dabbled with cocaine on the side. Whether that night he overdone it remains a mystery, because his girlfriend said they were just drinking loads of champagne. It was a tragedy, as he could have really helped as a witness for Ronnie O'Sullivan's dad.

Alan's trial was a really hard one, with Alan making speeches from the dock. In the end, on 15 December 1992 Alan got 14 years and Blue was found not guilty. I suppose to this day Steve Mahood is still at large working for this new system of a Drug Enforcement Agency in this country. Poor Moby didn't live to set out the grounds of appeal.[1]

It got even worse for Mona because Alan didn't last a year into his sentence. In fact he died before his appeal could be heard. It was while he was in Maidstone that he was taken ill with pneumonia. I think it was an infection from the pigeon shit on the roof as he was on the top floor of the wing. Later he was put in an intensive care unit at Maidstone Hospital, and the prison apparently had him handcuffed to the bed with a couple of screws in the room so that this dying man couldn't escape. I don't know how they thought he was going to manage it. Mona complained; even the hospital complained, but it didn't do no good. Poor Alan died on 26 July 1993.

John Bindon gave the address at Alan's funeral. 'If Alan had not introduced me to the Peruvian Marching Powder, I would have made it as a good actor.' We all cracked up laughing and even the young vicar had a smile on his face. Many ex-girlfriends of Alan's were there and so were a lot of faces, as well as Vinnie Stapleton and umpteen actors and actresses. John didn't last long after that. He was dead within two months and he had a great send-off. People said it was AIDS.

---

[1] Saiyad Mubarak Shah was called to the Bar in November 1983 and two years later was suspended from practice for 30 months. At the time of his death in December 1992 he was practising from the chambers of C. Patel at 76b Chancery Lane.

I don't know if they were right, but he'd had a pretty rackety sex life. It was also said that he could hang half-pint glasses on his dick. I never went out with him, but one of my girlfriends did and she said it was true. After John died she went and had an AIDS test herself and I'm glad to say it was negative.

It was after we got back from having that relaxing holiday – there were no sounds of any back-firing cars in Gozo – I said to Frank that he should try to get James Morton to do his book for him. I said to Frank, 'It's worth a shot at, I'm sure.' 'If it's the same one, I know him,' said Frank. 'He defended me over Parkhurst and he defended Eva as well.' I rang up the publishers Little, Brown, and they gave me Mr Morton's office telephone number. Anyway Frank called James Morton up, and they arranged an appointment. Poor Mr Morton must have thought that he was going to have his back molars pulled out over an article he had written. But yes, it was the James Morton who had defended Frank in the Parkhurst Riot. We laugh about it, because Parkhurst prison keeps coming up over and over again in our lives. Frank once said to me after Barbara Windsor's 60th birthday party at the Holland Park Restaurant, 'Let's get married, and have the reception here.' I said in jest, 'Nah, we can't go against the grain; we gotta have it in our old meeting place, Her Majesty's.' 'Her Majesty's?' 'Yes, Parkhurst.'

Frank thought he had a publisher lined up, but that was another deal which fell through and I am pleased to say the outline was accepted by Little, Brown. James used to come over to the flat in Islington and I'd leave them some sandwiches and go off to work down the road while they reminisced.

I still hadn't recovered my nerves from the shooting incident and so while Frank was writing his book with James, I went off with my Mum to a holiday in Turkey. The idea was to stay in a hotel for two weeks and go on one of those gulit boats for

the third. We made friends with one couple, a schoolteacher
and his wife, but there was another pair which we didn't get on
with at all. He was a broker from Lloyds or something like
that, and he behaved like a small child the whole time. He was
always demanding where the boat should go and when it
should stop so he could swim. From the first day, when we
came from lunch to where we'd left our towels while we'd been
suntanning we'd find they'd been moved. Then one day when I
was handing him the pepper, which was in an open cruet, it
blew over his face and I'm sure he thought I'd done it deliberately. In an evening, when we were playing Sinatra and jazz
tapes he'd want them turned off. He used to go to bed at 9
o'clock while we and the other couple stayed up. Then on the
fourth evening we were playing tapes after he'd gone to bed and
he started banging on the ceiling of his cabin saying we were to
be quiet. I was fed up with him and his manner by now and I'd
had a couple of rakis, so I went down and banged on his cabin
door and I told him I'd had his type in my massage parlour.
'You like domineering,' I told him. His wife called out, 'Do you
mind?' and by now I was in a real temper. I said, 'Yes, he's a
regular at the massage parlour.' Mum was tugging me saying
we were going to get slung off the boat if I didn't stop, and
eventually I went back up on deck with her.

In the late afternoon of the next day when we were sitting
on the deck, with Mum with her rollers in, the holiday rep.
came and asked us to leave. I said there was no reason why we
should, but they were already moving our stuff. I told them I'd
pack myself but Mum wasn't for leaving. I said I couldn't bear
another three days and the rep. said we'd be better off on
another boat or in a hotel. We were put in this small boat. It
was getting late and the sea was up. Mum still had her rollers
in and she was convinced we were going to die. I'd ask the

boatman how long we were going to be and he'd say 20 minutes and I'd tell her ten. It was then she started on me, saying I had to go and see a psychiatrist. In the middle of the ocean! When we got back to England she kept on and on at me and just to please her I went to see my GP and he referred me to one. I think I only saw him three times before he said there was nothing wrong with me.

When the book came out there hadn't been too many gangsters' memoirs at the time, and it caused quite a stir with reviews in the *Sunday Times* as well as the tabloids. By this time, Frank was appearing on radio shows and became his own unique identity. He's got a good line of repartee and he goes down well with listeners. I believe this was the making of 'Mad' Frank into 'Sane' Frank. I think he'd have been a success at anything he tried and if things had been different for him when he was growing up would have made a good leader in Government, a good television presenter or an actor. But at least he has made something of himself and I feel that the fact he has kept out of prison the last ten years speaks well for him – and for me. It's the longest time he's ever been out since he was a teenager.

One day we got a telephone call from James Whale's researcher, as Frank and I had been on one of his previous late-night shows 'Whale-On'. The researcher said the programme, which was going to be at a Birmingham studio with an audience, was about lifers and women who visit murderers in the nick. Mike Mansfield was the producer. Gary Jacobs, a good lawyer, was also on the programme, and so was Tony Lambrianou from the Kray days.

To be honest I really didn't want to go, as I still felt very nervous talking on television. I can remember being on the BBC early-morning programme one day with Anne Diamond and Nick Ross. I was so excited by my first TV appearance. I had seen this new baby blonde highlight, and knew I had to have that hair colour so I had gone to Nicky Clarke's hair salon to have it done. Well, when I looked in the mirror the expanse of this canary-yellow hair left me devastated – and a big burn mark in my purse! I just died. I should have known not to try a new hairstyle, especially with just a day to go.

Frank and I had got made up by the make-up artists and after the previous hair-do this time I just left it to the experts. I came out of make-up at the same time as Frank and we almost passed one another in the corridor. We didn't recognise one another. He looked like Groucho Marx with bushy eyebrows and I looked like Lucille Ball with this bright canary-coloured hair and shocking-pink lipstick. We screamed out with laughter. He had loads of powder on too. It was so strange seeing this tough ex-gangster with all this greasepaint and powder made up like a poof. I was crying with laughter which was starting to affect the powder on my face and I said, 'I can't go on looking like this,' but of course I did. Anne Diamond was not interviewing – I think she was on holiday – but Nick Ross gave us a very good interview. He asked me a question, but I was just so shaking with nerves I completely lost what the question was and I just could not open my lips. I could have died. But now I'm all right since I've done shows like *Gangsters' Molls* and been on with Johnny Vaughan and Lowrie Turner.

Never again, I had said to Frank. Not after that episode. But Frank didn't want to go up to Birmingham on his own and he begged me, saying this time I should have a couple of drinks beforehand. I said, 'No, they'll have that cheap wine.' 'Take some Smirnoff in with you.' But instead of Smirnoff I took a flask of Jack Daniel's.

We were special guests in the audience, plus there was three women who visit murderers. One girl was Sandra Lester whose story was that she had become one of Peter Sutcliffe's groupies. You get this certain kind of woman who gets her kicks off writing to famous criminals. There was another girl whose boyfriend had killed her granny with an axe. The actual topic was 'Why women fall in love with murderers'. Sandra's reply to James Whale's question, as to why she had fallen in love with Sutcliffe was that he had been trying to reform, that he had given her money to have a breast enlargement and that she was writing a book about him. Then James Whale turned to me. 'Marilyn, you are married to the most dangerous man in Britain who murdered someone in a fracas many years ago at that famous fight at Mr Smith's club, "Mad" Frankie Fraser. What do you think?' I said, 'First of all, James, Frank and I are not married. Secondly he was accused of the murder of Dickie Hart, they all said he had done it but he was found not guilty. Thirdly, what do I think of Sandra Lester? I think Peter Sutcliffe, Ian Brady, Dennis Nilsen and Myra Hindley should be twenty feet under the ground, and as for you' – pointing at Sandra Lester – 'you should be with them for visiting Peter Sutcliffe. How dare you sit on that podium and visit a man that has murdered thirteen women? You're a disgrace to all us women; you are nothing but a pervert.' The Jack Daniel's had worked a treat.

Poor James was trying to calm me down and then he got this prison psychiatrist who was sitting in front of Frank and me to voice his opinion. He gave the usual crap. What amazes me with these so-called professional people is that they never seem to support ordinary decent criminals. They always seem to think all criminals are the same, but then they favour people like Sutcliffe and Hindley.

Some time later I wrote to Wensley Clarkson of the *Evening*

Standard, after he had said what a very dangerous man Frank was. I said that I would feel a lot safer walking along a common on a dark November night with an armed robber, or a drug-dealer or a killer of police than with the likes of Sutcliffe. Although my letter was never published I did get a nice reply back from Max Hastings, the editor.

In our audience along with her husband (unbeknown to us) was Olive Smelt, who was the only woman to survive an attack by Sutcliffe. In the Green Room she came over to me and thanked me for what I'd said. Olive showed us the inch-deep dent in her head, and told us how her marriage nearly collapsed through the police trying to accuse her husband of doing it; making it worse after the most gruelling attack on this poor woman. The fact that most of these women were prostitutes should make no difference. Everybody is a human being and if the police had really done their homework – instead of prob-ably just having the attitude, 'Oh well, they were only prostitutes, what do we care?' – they might have got him sooner. It's amazing the amount of time and money being spent on the killer of Jill Dando. If she were an ordinary person her file would be on the back of the desk by now. It must be dreadful for some mother whose young daughter has been killed to be told the case is more or less filed away, and yet there's hundreds of thousands of pounds spent on trying to find the killer of a celebrity.

We met up with the tall lanky psychiatrist in the Green Room as well. I had a copy of the new hardback version of *Mad Frank* in my hand and he said, 'Oh, what is that book about, may I ask?' 'About his life in prison and Broadmoor. He's also been certified three times.' 'Oh, really, what were you certified as?' he asked. Frank then looked up at this very tall man and replied, 'Being a psychiatrist.'

The amount of publicity good and bad made Frank an in-famous celebrity, much to the annoyance of clergymen and the like as well as a number of our so-called own people who were jealous of his celebrity status. One clergyman up in Liverpool who should have known better made a remark to the Liverpool *Echo* that Frank should not be making money out of his past in crime. What Frank was doing in Liverpool then was a show for a thalidomide charity with the comedian Gary Strike. The media wanted Frank's opinion on this clergyman's remark which was made public in the *Echo* and his reply was, 'As a clergyman one of his objectives is forgiveness and he was far short of practising what he preaches. Plus I've served my debt to society. I broke the rules but that was the road I went down. Surely people would rather see me playing a cameo role in a film and advising students in universities on criminology – or would society like to see me using my pliers again?' Well, to me there was no answer to that.

When I think of all the young offenders who really want to be straight and in their hearts want to break into music, acting or even football, but because of their criminal records are get-ting no help from the famous pop stars, actors, actresses and footballers, or the Government, I despair. There's no real train-ing in prison for those who want to make a go of things. People from all these sides of life want to think about the slogan 'Charity begins at home'. Famous people don't always realise that street kids on the block are quickly ignored and one of the only ways out is through the boxing clubs. But, they get hardly any lottery money and the young kids are boxing with torn gloves.

The Prince's Trust has been a great help, but once when I tried to apply when I had the flower stall and wanted some financing, I discovered you had to fill in questionnaire after questionnaire. That would be no good to half the talented kids on the street who can't even read or write but who have creative minds that need bringing out. The only people who could really help are their idols.

One day after the book came out Frank and I were passing Wesley's Chapel off Moorgate when we saw a poster advertising Derek Lewis as coming to speak, and afterwards we went and spoke to him and had a photograph taken with him. The rector, Paul Hume, heard we had been in and seeing that he had had the top man in charge of our prisoners speaking he thought he should hear from the other side. And, fair man that he is, he invited Frank to give a reading at this chapel where Lady Thatcher was married to her husband Denis and also had her children christened. There's been a lot of famous speakers, so you have here a good man of the church allowing a prisoner to voice his opinion. What a difference from the man in Liverpool! I wasn't too sure who John Wesley was and I asked Paul Hume what he was about. Paul told me, 'He used to look after prisoners, as part of his religious path in life', so we were in the right place.

Frank got a full congregation and was well mentioned in the *Guardian* newspaper. After his talk Paul Hume looked after us and invited us back into the rectory for sandwiches and coffee. He made me feel honoured because I asked for an ashtray and he quietly said, 'My dear Marilyn, we do not allow smoking, but my friend will get you an ashtray. In fact out of all the people who have been here, you and Denis Thatcher have been the only two allowed to smoke.' I beamed and said, 'Yes, but he likes Gordon's Gin and I like Smirnoff.' He just laughed.

Another time we were on the radio was with Terry Christian who used to do that very good programme on Channel 4, *The Word*. At the time he had a late-night show on Talk Radio. In fact he sent a car to pick us up from Arthur Sutty's place in Epsom. On the programme was this girl ex-cop from New York who became a topless model, and a bouncer whose name I can't remember, something like Thompson. After Miss American Big Tits left, Terry told the listeners that Frank would be answering questions and the phone line was jammed with different people calling from everywhere. I was sitting in the Green Room looking through the glass partition when the producer asked if I would like to sit in on the panel, and I was ushered in and put on the green mike. Terry was very good at putting me at my ease. He'd been a presenter in Manchester, and I have found that people from up North are more down to earth than Southerners and they have great personalities. No need for the Jack Daniel's.

The news was read and questions started again. The next caller was a lady from Lewisham. Terry said, 'Good evening Megan', and then there was a silence. We all looked at one another and then Terry said again, 'Hello, Megan, can you hear me?' All we heard was a woman crying and howling. Terry went very quiet. Frank looked down, the bouncer from the East End looked blank and I grabbed my microphone and said, 'Hello, Megan, can I help you, what's your problem?' She said, 'I . . . I . . . cannot sleep. My . . . my . . . boyfriend of twelve years never comes home at nights; never gives me any housekeeping money. I'm . . . I'm . . . I'm on Valium tablets for five years. I . . . I don't know what to do.' Poor Terry didn't have a chance as this poor lady from South London was in great despair and suicidal, so I just said, 'Well, if that was me, I would firstly change your doctor, get rid of your boyfriend and join a social club.' In my heart I really wanted to say, roll a big fat joint and get your hair done.

But this was when we were on something of a roll. If you've

been away for twenty years straight, you don't exactly have a lot of money. Frank didn't, and mine had gone as I've said, so before Frank's book came out our financial situation was minus zero. I admired the success of Jimmy Fraser's Tin Pan Alley and the way he had updated it. I wanted us to get going with a wine bar for when the book came out.

Instead I went into the sauna business.

14

Sauna Days

One day in Islington I took Danny – the beautiful black and white dog I'd had since he was a puppy – for a walk. I'd bought him in Harrods' pets department years earlier, so I suppose I was following my Mum's footsteps. He was a Lhasa Apso and Gina Lollobrigida had his litter-sister. That day it was pissing down with rain and I was looking at the empty shops to let. There was also one I had read of in the local paper that I wanted to see. It was in quite a good street and when I looked round the owner asked me what I wanted it for. The rent was low and I said maybe a wine-bar or perhaps a beauty parlour.

Out of the blue, as I was leaving I bumped into a girl who had been in Holloway prison with me when I was on remand for the cocaine. She told me that she was a masseuse and that it was good money. It's funny since I'd worked in a parlour in Palm Springs that I'd never thought of the idea. I half asked if she wanted to go into partnership, but she didn't have any money herself so all we did was exchange telephone numbers.

The idea of a wine bar would have cost me far too much, but on the other hand a parlour or sauna didn't require much overhead. A bit of decoration and hiring the girls plus a couple of ads was all it would need. It wasn't like buying stock and having it left on the shelf. The only thing was that I would have to change into an attractive blonde now and again. I walked back home soaked from the rain, told Frank of my plans, and off I went down to the pawnshop which, about that time, was my favourite shop apart from Harrods – and in went Arturo's gold peso.

The place was very discreet behind a ladies' dress shop, and with a basement and its own front door. In fact, it was an ideal place where men in suits could come. I never went to a solicitor; the agreement was just signed on a bit of paper. So then I had to get the place kitted out with the help of a good decorator. George and his crew from Folkestone did all the hard work for nearly nothing. Bennie Harris helped out with some furniture, Bob Boxes with televisions and Parker's security camera firm put in a lovely camera on loan. What terrific people; they all said they would wait till we got up and running and then I could pay them back, and I really thought the world of them for that. I didn't even have the money to put a telephone in. My new friend Jennifer (not the girl I knew in Palm Springs) sent me over a couple of girls. One of them even arrived before the ad was in. In fact by this time I was so skint, I had to use her mobile phone to give as the number to call. It was sad because eventually I had to get rid of her over the problems she was having with her black pimp boyfriend.

I called the massage parlour Canonbury's and it had the Arsenal cannon logo in the corner. It took off almost from the start. I was so busy that gradually I managed to pay everybody back. We kept Parker's security camera on loan as we did need it for any 'baby fathers' knocking on the door.[1]

If people asked, I would say we were in the ironing business. Frank would do the cleaning, and I would iron the girls' school uniforms and French maids' outfits. They loved working for us as we weren't greedy with them. The customers were happy and the girls would give a good service. I tried to keep a good cross-section of girls – a Thai, a tall Brazilian, a busty blonde, brunette, redhead and a more mature woman.

I used to take £5 a customer from the girls and a £20 shift fee. Everything else they kept for themselves. The shift was 11 in the morning until 9 at night, but of course when we weren't busy they'd go out for tea or coffee or to do their shopping. The ones from Manchester and Birmingham were the worst trouble; they would ring up and ask if there was a job going, but if they had a quiet day they wouldn't come in the next and they'd go somewhere else. Often they had black pimps and were unreliable. One girl got really badly beaten by her boyfriend and Frank had to go and have a word with him. He was really giving it large until Frank sorted him out, and after that he was all right. A lot of them were using drugs in a heavy way. Once I'd learned to suss out the accent I wouldn't take them on.

The place was spotlessly clean. Two cubicles and our VIP suite which had red carpet along with a mirror, couch, candles and low lighting. You would be surprised at the type of gentlemen we would get in – smart guys in suits, even the local council workers would come and the odd off-duty policeman, a couple of solicitors plus one or two raincoat pervs. There was also a judge and a film producer as well as a couple of journalists.

[1] Specifically black pimps.

Some evenings after work we would call in at one or two local restaurants and eat. One particular evening at work I was on reception and a man came in who I had recognised as being the owner of one of the places where we used to eat regularly. When he asked me how much a VIP service would cost him, I turned my face aside as I told him so that he wouldn't recognise me. I don't really know why I was doing it – after all, we were both in the same game. I introduced him to the six different girls and he picked one and spent the usual half an hour. Then the girl came out and said he wanted another half an hour. I thought, 'His wife's going to be mad; he'd better hurry up and come, otherwise the waiters will be waiting for their wages.' Then he wanted another half an hour; he must have been in that room two hours in all. Frank and I never went back to his place to eat again though.

One day we had a call from a very politely spoken man. Did we do bondage? I asked around but the girls said, 'No.' It's something of a speciality. You have to be careful in case the man gets really hurt. I then asked how much he was paying and he said £400, so I thought, 'Well, why not? I'll do it myself.' I asked him what he wanted specifically and he told me, and that he lived in Bishop's Stortford, so I arranged to go up the next day. I took a cab into Soho and bought the gear – chains, leather, a dog-collar and a rubber mask. It cost £150, so it was just as well he was genuine.

Next day he met me off the train from Liverpool Street and drove me out to his home. The moment I got through the front door I saw all these chains and collars hanging from the banister rail and I thought, 'Oh God, he wants to start here.' And then a big golden labrador came bounding out to greet us. Just as well he didn't want to join in or I'd have definitely been out of the place.

When we got upstairs it didn't go too well. He wanted me to really mark him with stilettos. Then when I put the mask on him I realised it didn't have any hole for the mouth and so he was spluttering 'I can't breathe' while I looked for some scissors to cut one. I notice he didn't ask me to take it off him though. I'd have done better if I'd taken up one of my mother's green balaclavas. Afterwards I was sick in the bathroom. 'Is this the first time?' he asked. I thought he might be so pissed off with me I'd have to make my own way back to the station and he'd stiff me for my fee. But no, he was a perfect gentleman. He didn't call again though. I'm not cut out to be a dominatrix, that's certain.

Frank and I worked in the sauna seven days a week and it was getting us a steady living. I suppose I was making a grand in a good week. The customers were happy and some repeaters would often bring a bottle of champagne or a box of chocolates.

Frank would do the cleaning early in the morning and leave just before the girls arrived. One particular morning, however, we were late getting the place cleaned and I was waiting for a new 20-year-old brunette to start. I had got a phone call from a regular guy who worked night shifts and must have felt 'fruity', so I sent him his favourite blonde, Shelly. While she was with him the doorbell rang and when I looked at the camera a tall man I'd never seen before was standing there. Before I let him in I shouted down the stairs to Frank, 'Frank, don't come up yet, we've got another customer.' He was from Ireland, and I asked him to sit down. Now it was 11.15 a.m. and I didn't want him to know there wasn't a girl available in case he pushed off somewhere else. I switched on the television so he could watch a soft porn film and gave him a copy of *Penthouse* to thumb through. I told him I had a young brunette new starting today and she wouldn't be long. The punters always like to pretend they're getting something new and untouched even though they know in their hearts they aren't. Then I asked him if he wanted a tea or coffee and he said in his strong Irish accent, 'Oh, tank yer, I'll have a tea.' So I stood on the top of the stairs and shouted down, 'Gladys, Gladys, one tea please, no sugar.'

I couldn't say 'Frank' because it's not nice for men to know that other men are on the premises. I don't understand why that is, but it's just so. Frank looked up from the basement and gave a grin. The Irishman asked, 'How long will the young lady be as I've got to take some bricks over to Kilburn.' 'Oh,' I said, 'not long, about five minutes.' I tried my hardest to keep him there and he looked at me as I met Frank part of the way down the stairs. Paddy sort of gave me that up-and-down look and then said, 'Look, I have to be at King's Cross, I only want a hand relief.' I said, 'Oh, I'm only the receptionist, sir.' 'You're pretty, I'll give you £40.' I said, half grinning because I knew Frank downstairs could hear, 'The girl won't be long.' With that he said, 'I can't hang on much longer, what about your friend downstairs, that Gladys?' I laughed and said, 'Oh, Gladys is 85 years of age. She's the tea lady.' With that he got up with a raving hard-on bulging through his trousers and said, 'For Christ's sake, I'll have to go.' When I had shut the door on him, Frank came running up the stairs with a pair of Marigolds. We really did laugh. I couldn't get my breath back and Frank said, 'Good job he didn't request an extraction from his back teeth.' But if Frank hadn't been there I'd have helped him out so to speak; from time to time I'd do relief work.

Business was always up and down. People seem to think that there is plenty of money to be made in a massage parlour. There is if you're taking the piss out of the girls – in other words taking most of the percentage, which most of the pimps do with their women. Our house was very good and once I'd got the Northerners sorted out most of the girls stayed with us. The only problem was that when some weeks or days were dead quiet, the girls who had black or Thai boyfriends wouldn't come back; they were just sent somewhere else. These girls were very foolish to allow themselves to be treated like that.

One girl in particular was very pretty. I found out later that she was the girlfriend of one of the guys who'd made a terrible vicious attack with a cheese cutter on an innocent office worker in Brixton. Another girl told me how her boyfriend tied her up one night and put a knife to her throat. I said, 'Tell him to piss off', but these girls are intimidated by their so-called boyfriends – scumbags is more like – who tune into the girls' weaknesses, and get them hooked on drugs to sell their bodies. Most of these girls are from up North from decent middle-class backgrounds or who have run away from home. Frank used to try to persuade them to break away, and to protect them, but eventually we gave up trying because they would soon go back for more abuse, mentally and physically.

It's a terrible shame. If we were to be practical and legalise brothels like in Germany, Holland and Nevada, the Government could have the extra tax and girls would be safer – regular, controlled check-ups, no sexually transmitted diseases, no HIV. I just can't understand why everybody has to be so narrow-minded and not make it legal. Isn't it much better to have certain brothels in certain areas in London without having all those cards in phone boxes?

Frank and I were getting worn down with the work and with these girls letting us down, so I was glad his book was soon to be published; he deserved it. I felt sorry for him because he didn't deserve to be put through all of this after everything he had been through in his life.

So then I thought I'd go legit and I took an aromatherapy massage course, but even that was a con. I paid £500 for it in Stoke Newington. Apparently the woman was an oddball, and she took all the students' money but it turned out it wasn't very good. I was asked by one of the girls who had investigated her if I wanted to take the couple to court, and I said, 'I can't do that.' I just wiped my mouth. I wanted to achieve my certificate and open up a proper salon and be licensed by the council, but it wasn't to be. Frank and I had even applied so that we could have a proper business.

It was while we had the sauna that we had a call from Roy James. He was one of my favourites from the Train. I liked them all, but him and Jimmy Hussey and Roger Cordery were my favourites – Jim because Gill was so good to me and my Mum, and Roger because he tried to help me get into show business. Roy didn't marry until after he came out and I remember taking his girls to a panto. Steven Berkoff had introduced me to the girl who was the star and I'd got in touch to ask her to come down to say hello to the children after the show. We waited and waited but she never came. Not like Barbara Windsor, who turned up at a benefit I was holding for June McCarthy who's got a rare blood disease. Not only did she turn up but she wouldn't take any money for her taxi. That's the difference between star quality and the others.

Anyway, Roy phoned me and Frank at the sauna in the seconds after he'd shot his father-in-law. He was so emotionally upset of course. He was separated from his wife; he gave her every penny he could for the children and he was having a hard time over visiting and things.

After he came out from the Train Roy was acquitted of a

VAT charge with Charlie Wilson. Roy had a nice little jewellery business and he married one of his assistants, a girl named Anthea whose father worked in a bank. We used to see him and have a drink with him here and there. Then he got separated or even divorced (I never knew which) from Anthea and he was in trouble over paying her £150,000 as a settlement. He thought her dad had been advising her against him, although as it turned out he hadn't, and one afternoon when they brought the kids back after a day's outing he went and shot her father and gave Anthea a beating with the pistol.

When Roy called, Frank shouted over my shoulder, 'Get out, get out now!' down the phone. If he wasn't there when the police came, then Frank thought it might still be possible to do something. Then when Roy told me he'd phoned the police we didn't know if it was safe to speak over his phone, so Frank rushed out for a phone box. When he come back he said that there'd been someone in the nearby boxes and when he'd finally found one a policewoman had answered and he'd just put the receiver down. We went to visit Roy quite a lot on remand. He got six years and we visited him during that time as well. Then when he came out he had a heart by-pass and suddenly he died of a heart attack. He'd had a by-pass earlier but it hadn't lasted.

Of course Dad and Mum went to the funeral and there was a really good turn-out of what's left of the Train Robbers. He was the fifth of them to go. Charlie Wilson's widow was there, so was Jimmy Hussey and Bruce Reynolds, of course, and Bobby Welch who was on sticks after the operations he had over his knees. Of the others, Billy Boal's dead and so is Buster Edwards.

We finally took a week off after over one year spent building up this business. I left one girl, Samantha, and a lovely pretty girl in charge. About 12 a.m. she called to tell me the security camera had broken, so I called up Parkers and the man said he would try to get down for 5 p.m. I said, 'OK then, but we really do need this on asap.' I said to Frank, 'The first week we have off, as soon as our backs are turned things go wrong.' It's always the way, as those of you in any business will understand, that as soon as your back's turned the takings start to drop. We went down to the place about 4 p.m. I had already told the girls not to open the door without looking through the spyhole, as they waited for the repair man Bryan to arrive. He called sooner than we had expected, I thought. Frank asked him to look at our video players down in the rooms, as they had decided to go wrong as well. Seeing that it was a very quiet day we managed to get all our odd jobs done in one.

Frank and Bryan were down in the rooms when the doorbell rang and Samantha called, 'Marilyn, there's three men outside.' I said, 'Don't open the door – quick, grab your coats.' I called out to Frank and said, 'Frank, get out quick!' The girls followed me downstairs, asking, 'Where can we go?' Bryan packed up his box of tools and the girls were running around like headless chickens saying, 'We want our purses, whips and uniforms.' Looking around, they were all flapping. The doorbell never stopped ringing and now the phones were going. 'Where to?' one girl asked and I told her, 'Up that ladder.'

Luckily we had a fire escape and all five of us managed to climb up the old rusty ladder onto the roof, where we looked over, hiding. I crept to the entrance and there were three guys who I thought were Vice Squad, but one had a camera so I knew it was the newspapers. We knew we had to get away from the premises. Next door was a shoe shop, where the girl was just packing up. And as we all looked down I called, 'Rose.' She wondered where the voice had come from. 'Rose, you daft prat, up here, it's me, Frank and Marilyn.' She looked up at us five – these two with their sexy black basques and stockings and with their raincoats over their shoulders, me, Frank and the electrician Bryan. 'Quick, get Tom's ladder.' Rose was giggling. 'It's in his workshop.' Before I could say 'Ronnie Biggs' Frank had jumped down this 15-foot wall. I couldn't believe it. My knight in shining armour, and he calls to Bryan, 'Throw down your case.' 'But Frank, my tools are in there.' 'Just drop it down slowly, then,' Frank said. So Bryan dropped his case, and then Frank grabbed the bottom of Bryan's legs as he was much taller and got him down first; then one by one us girls managed to get down for the 'Great Escape'. We all climbed over fences until we were at the back of a French restaurant. I noticed one of the waiters in the kitchen and I shouted, 'André, André!' He was looking around, the kitchen-door was open. 'Psst, over here, let us in!' He opened the gate and we were into a restaurant that we used regularly. I whispered, 'André, for fuck's sake! Get us out of here lively! Is the lady boss coming tonight?' He said 'Yes' and he told us to go out as if we had been to use the toilet, and off we all went in single file. The chefs made us laugh as we walked through the kitchen. One of them was cutting the onions, and as Samantha and Cindy walked in with their sexy underwear on, he said '*Oh là là*'. I had to laugh as I reminded the girls to put on their coats and do the buttons up.

Outside the restaurant we grabbed a black taxi and went back to our flat in Duncan Street. Someone had tipped the press and our home phone was ringing non-stop. We just left it to ring until the heat had died down. Frank insisted the girls stayed the night and by the next morning things had quietened down and then they went home. Back at the sauna Frank and I cleaned out the stuff, but that of course was that. Earlier I had had an anonymous phone call at the massage parlour to say

I was under observation, but when I told Frank this, he'd said, 'It's probably some jealous bastard that's having a joke.' Some joke! There was a bit in the *Sunday Mirror*: 'Train Robber's daughter' and so on. I think we were bubbled by one of the journalists who used it. We saw the man I thought had done it in the Groucho a bit later and he definitely looked shifty. But, of course, we had no proof.

Years later I did have another go at running a sauna, but this time it was more as a favour for a friend of Dad's than anything else. They used to say if you sat in Piccadilly Circus long enough you'd see the whole world pass by, and I think it's the same for Upper Street, Islington, because it wasn't long before I ran into Bobby Mackew. Bobby had been a great adventurer in his time. Back in the 1950s he was involved with 'Dandy Kim' Waterfield when they did the safe at the film producer Jack Warner's house in the South of France. Bobby had fled to Tangier and he was nicked and swagged over to the French Quarter so he could be extradited back to France. I know him and 'Dandy Kim' both got a good bit of bird over it.[2] Anyway, there he was and he said a friend of his who had a sauna in the

---

[2] In August 1953 the man-about-town 'Dandy Kim' Caborn-Waterfield and Robert Mackew were with Barbara Warner, the daughter of Jack Warner, the film magnate, at Warner's villa in the South of France. According to Barbara Warner, Caborn-Waterfield needed money to pay a hotel bill; she took him to her father's safe intending to give him the equivalent of £100. He saw there was a considerable amount of money and the prosecution's case was that while Mackew decoyed the girl with a 3 a.m. walk in the garden Caborn-Waterfield took £25,000 from the safe. Both were convicted by a French court in their absence. In 1959 Mackew was indeed captured in Tangier where Caborn-Waterfield was running a skiing school which was alleged to be a front for a cigarette-smuggling operation. Mackew served a sentence of three years. Caborn-Waterfield returned to

Holloway Road wanted someone responsible to look after it. The man who owned it was the nephew of Horace Cutler, the old man who'd been the chairman of the GLC. There was a bust of him in the living-room because it was more or less done from a private house; and that's why they called it Cutler's. It was all telephone work; no one called unexpectedly. I only ran it for about six months and then I handed it over to another girl. It's long since been shut.

Funnily enough, it was while I was running Cutler's that I heard again from Rina. She wanted to come over on a semi-working holiday and she arrived just the day of Ronnie Kray's funeral. Frank was invited to be a pallbearer, but I didn't want to go out of respect for Olive Cornell and so Rina was a god-send as an excuse. She stayed with us at the flat in Duncan Street for a time and then we found her a studio. She only intended to stay a month and she ended up staying six. She did a bit of work in Cutler's, playing the older woman which of course she was by then, but as elegant as ever and even more experienced, and she was a great success.

England with, it was said, the help of the Kray twins. In June 1960 he was extradited to serve a similar sentence. It was said that Caborn-Waterfield was the only man Diana Dors ever really loved, and he certainly remained a close friend to her death.

15

Work

I think Shirley Pitts was the best hoister of my time. She was a bit older than me, but I'd still think she was the best of my generation. Once she nicked a fifteen-grand fur-coat from a dummy in Harrods' window. She had the cheek to put her old Aquascutum mackintosh (which she'd nicked anyway) on the dummy in its place; that must have been one of the best things she ever managed. Shirley got me my dress for my twenty-first. My hair was red at the time and it was an oyster-pink ball-gown. She hoisted it for me and sold it ever so cheap; really it was a present. I think I only had to pay her the cab money. Of course she came to the party at the Leigham Court Hotel in Streatham owned by Charlie Taylor – who was a friend of Billy Hill and who died while on trial for fraud at the Bailey. It was a wonderful party until someone ruined it. Mum organised it as my present and there was a lovely cold running buffet with everything possible on it. About 1 o'clock the DJ said there was a bomb alert and we had to evacuate the hotel. There we were standing outside in the January cold without even coats round our shoulders. There was police and the fire brigade everywhere, and the hotel guests in their pyjamas and nightdresses. Then we were told it was a hoax and we could all go back in. But the evening was ruined and after a bit we sort of just drifted off home.

The best hoisters will shoplift to order. Of course, if you were ordering you'd have to leave a lot to them, but there's no problem because they know what us South London girls like.

In the old days they'd have a driver and go out of town, say to Stratford-on-Avon or up North. The best time was during the lunch hour when the store would be short-handed and probably there'd be a lot of punters. They'd load up the car, and then they'd come back on the train themselves so that if they got a pull at the station on their arrival they'd be clean. Quite often the police would be on the trains to try and catch them. The driver would just get a day's wage.

They'd have one main fence who would lay out the gear. Over the years I did a bit of fencing, but I didn't have much luck and sometimes I'd end up with the gear and not being able to sell it. The aim is to knock it out inside a week.

Say they had a parcel worth five grand, I'd pull up just under a third. So I'd give them one-and-a-half and I'd reckon to make just under a grand for myself. If it was just one dress or something, I'd as soon keep it for myself. But most of it's stopped now because of the security tags; you can still do it but it's got much, much more difficult.

Say I wanted a cashmere overcoat or a Chester Barrie suit, the hoisters would go for that. Even shirts could come to over a hundred. They'd put together a man's outfit worth say £800 and you'd pay them two-and-a-half to three.

I was quite a good shoplifter but I wasn't a pro. I'd take

clothes or sunglasses, but really when it come to it I didn't have the bottle. It takes a lot of guts to do it professionally.

The A. and R. Club – it stood for Artist and Repertory – was based in Charing Cross Road. When I knew it best Mickey Regan and Ronnie Knight, Barbara Windsor's ex, had the place. I would say it was the best afternoon drinker, especially on Mondays and Fridays. There was more piss-artists and reps (as in salesmen) in there than any other club I knew. Singers and musicians would be allowed to get up and sing or play. You would also have the hoisters selling their wares; one day in fact I bought a beautiful top-of-the-range set of Chef knives, it was only £80. Then there would be all different firms popping in and out, and also madams. There was one who used to have apartments all over London. 'Mary from the Dairy' she was known as.

Malcolm Allison owned the A. and R. before Knight and Regan, and the ex-football manager Jimmy Logie – who used to play football for Arsenal and Scotland before he fell on hard times and ended up as a newspaper salesman at Piccadilly Circus – helped him.

Mickey Regan's brother, Brian, used to be on the door to make sure everyone signed the members' book. There were never any fights in the place, although you could occasionally hear the thud of a body going down the stairs a bit sharpish. Any girls who drank there were always treated with respect. The old songs would be playing; the vodka or gin would be flowing, most of the Chaps – whether they worked in the street selling swag jewellery or were hoisters – would never let any girl or older woman buy them a drink.

Alice Gilder and her friend were a lot older than most of us but it made no difference. When it was Easter time it was nothing for them to walk in with their bonnets on. Maureen, her daughter, would get up and sing 'Hurt' with her fine heavy chains around her neck and gold rings on every finger. Today there is no way she could have had that amount of tom on her. She would end up hurt by these scumbag muggers trying to get it off her.

The other thing I would do was minding a bit of gear. When I had a flat in Langdon Court off the City Road I was looking after 40 kilos of puff. It was in blocks known as soaps. Puff can give off a real horrid smell and someone called the Gas Board and reported a leak. The man come in to check it out and he said, 'Funny smell, but it don't smell like gas.' I didn't know if he'd twigged so I had the man come and get the puff twice quick. I got a couple of grand for minding it.

What I did do back in the early Eighties was a couple of drug runs. I had the contacts here and over in Las Vegas and I brought out two lots of cocaine. I was the only person who knew when I was going or coming back or which airport I was using, because I didn't trust anyone not to make a telephone call tipping the Customs off against me.

The people in London loaned me the money to buy, but I didn't tell them where I was going to get the stuff and I knew it would be cheaper in the States. I strapped a kilo round my waist, went into the back of the aeroplane and slept all the way to London. No one looked twice at me. I paid $15,000 for it and by the time I ounced it out back here I'd cleared £60,000. I did a second run, but then my bottle went. I kept thinking of Jonathan with his mum doing a long term in the nick. By the time I arrived I was really sweating, but no one took any notice of me that time either. It sounds as if you make a great deal of money, and you do, but if you get 12 years then what are you making – £5,000 a year? And anyway, you don't get to keep anything. I went and spent all the money on my flat and that went in my bankruptcy. In those days I thought if you had money you had to spend it. That's why I'd like to see schools playing a major part in helping kids get an insight into what finance is all about, teach them how to pay a bill. I'd also like to see them shock the kids into staying on and getting a better education and not just simply dropping out.

Funnily enough, when I went out to Spain recently my passport was out of date by a couple of weeks but no one noticed.

When I was in Brazil visiting Ronnie Biggs there was a girl hanging about the reception area in the hotel and eventually we got talking. She told me she was from South London and she was stranded. She was meant to get down to São Paulo, pick up a consignment and come back to England with it, but her contact hadn't turned up. She'd been ringing England and getting no reply. I told her that she should just walk away from it. Then she said she had a ticket from São Paulo but not one from Rio down there, and I simply gave her the money for the flight. I never gave her my name but I did say she should never, ever do something silly like that again.

One evening at my flat, out of bravado and a couple of drinks, I was talking to a guy known as 'Cartwheel Charlie' because he would do handstands and cartwheels in shops and in the street. You'd be walking down Bond Street and all of a sudden he'd do a couple of flips. It didn't half distract the shop assistants. That night I said I would love to rob a bank – through the wall, not go in with guns, that is – and that I knew that the branch of Williams and Glyn's at the Angel, Islington, had a derelict building at the side of it. It's always good when that happens because it often means there's a way in. So 'Cartwheel' said, 'Um, that sounds interesting.' With his having done time for robbing security vans I knew he would be up for it. The next day him and his cousin Tim went up to the Angel to look at the derelict building for themselves.

Within a couple of days they had managed to open up the building and they came back and asked if I was still game. 'Of course,' I said, although I must say I was having a few qualms. The three of us were dressed all in black and we had high-powered torches. At about 12.30 p.m. we climbed down to the basement of this empty building. Well, to be accurate, they climbed down a 15-foot drop and I stood on top. My bottle had gone; I didn't think I'd ever make it back up. 'Cartwheel' and his cousin had a good look round but it was to come to nothing, as really first it would have needed money to invest to get the electricity put back on without no one knowing. Second, you would have had to have hydraulic machines – and I'm sure there was a third and fourth but, looking back, we lacked one thing and that was the money to set it all up. You can always put a job like that on offer and get a finder's fee if it comes off; just like in business, but we never bothered.

Years later when it had changed to the Bank of Scotland, I asked the manager for a loan. He refused me point blank on the grounds that I never had any equity. I felt like saying, 'No, if I had equity I'd have turned your bank over years ago.'

The other thing was that I used to lend my flat out. I suspected (but I never knew exactly who it was going to or why they wanted it) that it could be someone on the run from the nick or wanting to hide out after a job. I'd be asked where I wanted to go for a holiday and I'd be given a ticket and my exes and told to ring before I came back. Sometimes I'd be told a bit about things later. I know Johnny Hilton had the flat once. He was a man who never gave up; he had a few years over the killing of a dairyman in a robbery in the 1950s, and later he escaped from the nick after another robbery. Eventually he got captured trying to rob a jeweller's in Burlington Arcade off Piccadilly. The men in the shop just ran after him. The next thing was he put his hands up to the murder of another jeweller who got shot in a raid. Then he also put his hands up to killing his partner who he'd accidentally shot in the same raid. He was given life. He was in his sixties then and he'll be a very old man before they let him out – if they ever do. Another one the flat was lent to was Frannie Pope who got done recently with Charlie Tozer. He used to meet his wife there when he was on his toes some time back.

When I first met Frank and before his book come out, there was a couple of little tickles we did; just delivering things. Funnily, we got a pull both times. The first was after he was shot. We went and lived in Croydon for four months and we'd only just come back to Islington when Frank had a telephone call: would he deliver a gun to South London? I was driving and we took Danny the dog along with us. Danny was on Frank's lap and the gun was in a carrier-bag on the floor behind his legs. Down the Tower Bridge Road I went through a red light; I was looking out for a turning and I just went straight across. As soon as I had done it I knew there was a copper seen me and he flagged me down. Frank was getting nervous because if they'd found the gun he'd have been straight back in the nick on a conspiracy. They'd have said he was the armourer letting out guns for murders and robberies. 'Calm down,' I said. And I gritted my teeth and wound the window down. I'd intended getting out of the car, show them respect is always a good idea, but then I couldn't undo the seat-belt. The copper stuck his head through and said, 'You know you've jumped a red light.' 'Sorry,' I said. 'It's the first time I've ever done it.' They all say that, don't they? Frank had his head turned away so the copper won't recognise him.

'Is that a baby you've got there?' asked the copper. 'No,' I told him, 'it's my little dog.' Then he wants my licence and of course I haven't got that. He was very nice. 'Always carry it with you,' he says. And off he goes.

The next time we had to deliver some money – a couple of hundred grand – up North. Again the money was in another carrier-bag under the passenger seat. The car was an old banger and I was just carrying on in the middle lane doing about thirty when there's a flashing and I'm being signed to pull over. 'It's all right to do thirty,' says the copper, 'but not in the middle lane.'

That was the last time. I realised I wasn't cut out to be a wheel girl.

On the other hand I did do jury service once. It was at Middlesex Crown Court, something like October or November 1997. I was perfectly entitled to do it. I was waiting along with the others and, just before a big case involving about two tons of puff came on, my name was called by the usher. 'Are you Marilyn Wisbey?' And of course I said I was. I was told I couldn't sit on this particular case because she was Sammy Oesterman's sister-in-law. I'd never met her but that was that. I was off. So when it came to it I sat on two smaller cases. The first was a woman in her fifties who'd had ten grand from a friend of her boyfriend for some business venture, and she'd never repaid it. She bought and sold goods and she'd told this bloke he could double his money.

What I thought was unfair was that there wasn't a single person on the jury except me who'd had a business of their own, and I'd only had the flower stall. As far as I was concerned it was a deal which had backfired; he'd taken his chance to make a big profit and it had gone wrong. After we'd listened to the pros, the foreman said over the lunchtime that she was as guilty as hell. I said, 'You haven't heard her defence yet. Any business is a gamble. There's loads of people lose money when goods don't come through on time.' There were two others who went along with me at first, but the foreman was very strong and in the end it was just me. She got a bit of bird; she'd a few previous.

In the second case a foreign student was being accused of shoplifting. He walked out of John Lewis or somewhere like that without paying. No one asked how much money he had on him and I sent a message to the judge. It turned out he'd got over a hundred, so he could easily have paid. He got a not guilty. I think I did my duty.

16

Chaps

'Chap' is a term that perhaps some of you won't have heard of before. That's not surprising as it's part of the underworld language. You could put the Chaps into three categories. Top of the league would be security van robbers, train robbers, bank robbers, city financial scams and jewellery robbers. Second would be top-class shoplifters, hijackers and credit card frauds. Lastly you'd have fences, buyers of stolen goods, spivs and unlicensed street traders.

The Chaps, as they say, came from all different sides of London, but in my opinion the best ones came from South London. You only have to look at the long list of robberies that originated from there – the Train Robbery, Brinks-Mat, security van robberies – you name it. In the old days the Chaps would always look smart in well-dressed designer silk, Crombies, cashmere overcoats, crocodile shoes and Turnbull & Asser shirts. They would never dream of wearing an earring or loads of rings as knuckledusters; they usually wore smart watches and definitely were not like today's plastic gangsters who have tattoos and muscle that makes them look as if they have just come out of *Gladiators*. The Chaps would drive a proper saloon car and would never let a woman buy a drink; they felt very offended by the thought of it.

I've known them all and some of them have become my best friends. There were some great characters when I was growing up, not like today where selling drugs to young kids is the norm. Crime today has changed and the scumbags of crime are people like burglars, muggers, handbag thieves, and drunk drivers who go around killing people. I'm not trying to say that mine was a rose-tinted era, but it was different. And whatever people say about the East End, the best of the Chaps were from South London.

I've found that people who came from West London were very false. They were the so-called Chelsea and Fulham lot, but really they were brought up in Notting Hill and Kilburn, which were tough areas at the time. East End Chaps on the other hand were basically hangers on, usually market traders who tried to act like the real Chaps and be in their company. When it was their turn to buy a round of drinks they would always leave quietly. Some were taxi-drivers who used to drive the real Chaps around, and it made them think that they were part of the team. Some hopes. The North London Chaps tried to emulate the South London Chaps. They could only have a fight if they were in a group, but they were shit-scared when it came to a real man-to-man fight. I miss the old school of gentlemen Chaps back in the seventies, but it's all changed now.

East Street Market was the centre vein of South London for me. It was filled with top thieves and gangsters. I can always remember young Terry Sansom Junior telling me that an old-time thief in his seventies was walking along in Brixton when Fred, Terry's dad, had been eyeing up a Post Office that he and another fellow were going to do that afternoon, just before it closed. Fred had asked the old man how he was and he said, 'Terrible, Fred, I'm down on my luck. I've gambled everything down at the dogs last night at Catford, and it was money to get my old woman's tom out the pawn-shop.' Fred said, 'Never mind, Harry, jump in,' and he asked his partner in crime to take the car around the block and park it in a side street. The old boy was bewildered and kept saying, 'I've got to find £300 by tomorrow morning.' 'Never mind, Harry,' said Fred. 'Just sit there and listen to the racing at Haydock while Slim and I go and do some betting.' They locked him in, took some tools out of the boot and in 45 minutes they were back with four big money-bags. Off they drove and Freddie Sansom gave the old boy a grand. He said, 'You sure, Fred? You must have had a good tip, what was the horse's name?' Fred said, 'Father Christmas.'

Of course even the best of Chaps can sometimes lose their nerve. One friend of mine did a jewellery shop in a hotel when he and a mate caved the windows in, but then his bottle literally went and he shit himself. He had me take his trousers to the dry cleaner's, and the man behind the counter was sniffing and rubbing at the mess saying he thought it was mud. I was nearly pissing myself trying to stop laughing.

Sometimes I've thought this book should really be called 'Sleeping with the Underworld' because an awful lot of the Chaps have been my boyfriends. And many of them have been top-class villains.

But it's really the women who are the heroes in gangland. They are the ones who have to stay behind, and go out when they're taken out. 'Behind every successful gangster there is a strong woman,' as I said on a BBC documentary *Molls*. Frank's sister Eva Brindle was a tigress. For the love and support for her brother while he was inside and out, Eva fought like a tiger, and if you read *Mad Frank* and *Mad Frank and Friends* you'll know just how much she did for him. Eva was married to Jimmy Brindle, and gave up shoplifting when she got married. Poor Frank never forgave her for that, because until then he never had to buy a new shirt.

Maureen Walpole is a great woman who went through trials and tribulations with her husband Derek. She sold me her blue Mini once as it had the registration plate MW, the same initials as mine. Jeanie Savage was another great person who stood by two men in her life; one was Mickey Ishmail and the other Johnny Lloyd, both of whom did a lot of bird over the years. Poor Jeanie went down for receiving part of the Brinks-Mat money. Rosie Davis is another good East Ender in my books; in fact both Rosie and Jeanie used to come in the Traf all those years ago. Rosie Davis gave it her all for the 'George Davis is Innocent' campaign, along with many of George's family and friends. I know it was a great sadness for her when after all that hard work in getting him released he was nicked again doing the Bank of Cyprus in the Holloway Road. Another great lady was Flo Sutton, who sadly has died, but she was a great fence and a good friend to Nicky Carling and Albie Woods, who was the one who cleared the glasses off the bar in the Blind Beggar on the night George Cornell was shot so the police couldn't take them away for fingerprinting. Frank has always said what a good man he was; a good friend of Bobby Welch. He got two years with Eva when they did her for conspiracy for trying to get Bennie Coulson to tell the truth in Frank's 'Torture' trial. A couple of years ago Frank heard he'd got cancer and was in a hospice down in Sydenham, and we went down to see him. He'd lived with Flo Sutton for years, but they'd split up. Now they were in the same hospice; they died within a fortnight of each other.

A funny thing happened while we was with Albie. We were sitting joking, saying that if Flo could come up from her room we could have a wheelchair race with Frank pushing her and me pushing Albie, when in came a nurse and said she'd seen Frank before. He said there was no way it was possible, but she was sure; she said that he'd come to visit Gary Kray, Charlie's son, when he was dying in the very same bed a few months earlier. If only Frank had known he'd a double, think what alibis he could have put up!

Shirley Pitts was always well loved for her strength and being a go-getter. Another great shoplifter along with her was Colleen Warner; both have died of cancer too. Even if I didn't admire her for her choice of husbands – although I should have learned from her experience – Olive Cornell was ultra-special. She was another who had cancer, but I never once heard her moan and groan. I particularly admired her for her courage when she went round to the Krays' house and broke the windows after Georgie got shot. That took some real courage. Frank went to Ronnie's funeral, but as I say I wouldn't go out of respect for Olive.

Dolly Roberts, Harry's mother, is another I admire for her courage. Even when she was really ill she was campaigning for her son for a much lesser sentence. He'd got a recommendation of 30 minimum after those three coppers were shot in Shepherd's Bush. Of the other two guys sentenced, one died in prison and the other was released and was killed a few months ago down in Bristol. Poor Harry got most of the blame put on him, but hopefully he'll be released soon.

Pat Wilson, wife of Charlie who was on the Train with Dad, is another who stuck by her husband through all those years. In fact I can't think of a single Train wife who didn't – which must be some sort of a record. Charlie was a lovely, lovely man, one of my favourites. He was coldbloodedly shot down in front of Pat by two animal cowards in the Costa Del Sol and I wasn't at all sorry to see that one of them, Danny Roff, got his come-uppance in 1999. Someone took two attempts to do it, but it was well done at the end.

Diana Dors was another who campaigned over the Train sentences. As a thank-you, when Tom was in Parkhurst he made her a fort for her son out of matches. I was working at Royal Ascot and Mum asked me to deliver it. She lived at Orchard Manor near Sunningdale and I took it before I started work. I'd always thought of her as such a big star, but there she was with the washing machine going.

And the women sometimes come out of it more harshly than the men. Take my poor friend June McCarthy. For a long time she was the girlfriend of Frank's nephew, Jimmy, who had the Tin Pan. Then she became involved with Patsy Murray who'd absconded from home leave when he was doing 12 years for robbery. They both got done for drugs, but he got another 3 and she, who'd never done a day in prison, picked up 5 years. Even with the rest of the time he had to do over the 12 he was out before her.

In March 2000 Frank and I organised a benefit for June. She's got a very rare condition, Wegener's disease, and now she's got osteoporosis as well, and is having chemotherapy. We had the benefit down at the Thomas à Becket, and as I say Barbara Windsor came. She and I went to the Ladies' together and my heel broke as I came out. When I had it fixed, there she was chatting to the DJ Jimmy Miller and she saw he had her CD. I said I'd bought it and Jimmy played it.

I admire Charmaine Biggs for her love and support to

Ronnie while he was on the run; giving him up when it seemed the best thing for him. Last but certainly not least there's my mother Renée, who stood by my father when they both lost a child of 16 while he was serving the 30 years. She went on every visit except for two during the 12 years he served, and in those days she never knew what condition she'd find him in. He may not have suffered as badly as Frank did, but if you tried to escape or you assaulted a screw then you were bound to get your share of licks. She watched my Dad go on hunger strikes and she campaigned more than any other Train Robber's wife over that outrageous sentence of 30 years.

She still stood by him through two other jail sentences. The 15 months he served on remand may not have been too bad, but the other was for 10 years and she was put away at the beginning for that herself. She's suffered two strokes, witnessed burying my sister with no husband by her side, experienced the loss of not having a father at all as well as the loss of her mother aged 66 when she was only 32 years old.

I have to say that these women were genuine wives or girlfriends of the Chaps – not like some women who write to infamous criminals and child molesters hoping to gain recognition for being a jailbird groupie, to gain excitement with their titillating letters, and with luck to get their knickers wet, away from their humdrum boring lives in a quiet suburban town. I've seen and met enough of these so-called groupies to be able to tell the difference between the genuine do-gooders and these prats who will do anything to be either visitors or be seen out with an infamous criminal. These jailbird groupies are very similar to the groupies that pop stars and actors have to contend with. None of them think anything of breaking a marriage or relationship to get there.

What I can say about Barbara Windsor – who supported

Ronnie Knight in court when he was charged with Tony Zomparelli's murder – and Renée, Charmaine, Eva, Flo and the others is that they all deserve a medal.

17

Looking Back

The end of the sauna, Canonbury's, came as Frank and me was filming *The Underworld*, a series for the BBC. It had six episodes and Frank was in four of them. The last one was to open at Frank's birthday. Then the producer wanted me to sing and seeing that it was Frank's 70th we combined the two things together. Frank's birthday is 13 December – he was born on Friday the 13th, which is maybe why he's been a bit unlucky. Jack Trickett, the boxing manager, who owns the Acton Court Hotel in Stockport, allowed them to film us at the hotel. He always puts on a great show at Christmas time.

Frank had known Jack from the early 1990s when he'd been staying up in Manchester over some business, and again when he'd gone up there the night poor Jimmy Moody was shot. Anyway, Frank was able to help out some friends of Jack's in return. Jack told us about a guy called John Ruskin who his wife Avril had been going out with before he met her. I think she met this Ruskin while over in Marbella. John Ruskin was a square character; owned a villa, a yacht, Range Rover, dog

226

kennels – you name it, he owned it. So when you see these types of people hanging around the Puerto Banus with their Rolex watches it would make any woman think well, here's a successful man, and us women do tend slightly to be impressed by all that. Avril is a successful businesswoman in her own right and this Ruskin preyed on her success. He got her to loan him some money on some property with the intention of selling it and splitting the profit 60/40. Avril had some money she had inherited from an uncle and she had loaned him a considerable amount – we're not talking about £1,000, rather more than £30,000. What happened is similar to what happened to me with the Italian James Pavanelli. She was left waiting over a year with the usual problems, until Jack called Frank up and said, 'Please could you get hold of this John Ruskin and find out what's happening with the money.'

Frank made the phone call from our flat and we arranged to meet at the Hilton in Park Lane with Jack and Avril, Ruskin and a friend of his, Frank and myself. We sat upstairs and Ruskin looked quite together as if he was ready with all the answers; just the way a professional con artist does. Frank let him do all the talking. It was great because Ruskin said how he was waiting for this bank to release a sum of money and then how he had to re-mortgage some property. Frank was very clever and said, 'Do you have the time?' In a flash manner, Ruskin lifted his sleeve to show off his gold and diamond cufflinks and sitting on his wrist was a beautiful top-of-the-range gents' Rolex, so Frank said, 'Um, no money, John? Well then, first of all let us have your watch.' Ruskin took the watch off saying it was a snide, so Frank said, 'We'll soon find out,' looked at it and slung it right across the foyer, hitting a window display of diamond rings and necklaces. It smashed; lock, stock and two springs, and the bits went rolling across the marble floor. So maybe it was snide.

Well, Avril and Jack and I were purring. It was like a dog had licked this pussy's cream. With that and in a quiet, slow mode, John Ruskin and his friend got up and Ruskin said, 'Avril, you'll have your money as soon as the cheque is passed through and cleared.' Then he left. And a couple of weeks later he paid.

Then in 1999 Ruskin had managed to do the same thing again, this time to two lovely people called Ernie and Yvonne from Kent, who had skippered his yacht for years. They were in their late sixties and they'd let him have their life savings to invest. This time, he had changed his company name and gone into liquidation, but he was still owning and driving a top-of-the-market Range Rover and off to Australia for holidays. Jack Trickett asked Frank if he could do anything. Ruskin had got some kennels up in Suffolk somewhere.

I didn't go up with them, but Ruskin caused all sorts of aggravations. He went to the police saying that Frank had threatened to shoot him, and in the end poor Ernie got arrested and told he would be charged with demanding his own money with menaces. Fortunately Yvonne had gone with Frank and her husband, and Ruskin never mentioned her being in the car. So the police bailed him out, telling him to come back in three weeks' time. Ruskin got in touch with Frank and he got a solicitor who asked why they hadn't arrested Frank. Apparently the police said they couldn't find him, but they can't have been looking very hard because he was in the papers all the time. Fortunately the police dropped the charges, but poor Ernie hasn't got his money back.

When we went up to Jack Trickett's for Frank's birthday there was the two of us, my Mum and Dad, and my Uncle

George and my Aunt Dot came as well. We all got there on the Saturday and the do was on the Sunday evening.

Then on the Sunday morning came the shock. There on the sixth page of the *Mirror* was 'Train Robber's daughter sells sex!' It was all I needed. I had to be in my long evening gown ready to be filmed singing at 10.30 that morning and I said to Frank, 'For fuck's sake don't let my aunt and uncle see it.' Luckily my Uncle George only reads the *Sunday Times* and doesn't look at the tabloid newspapers.

That night Frank's birthday party was terrific; there were over three hundred there. People came from all over – Liverpool, Leeds, and London, the Manchester Mob, Vinnie and Louis Schaivo, Ray Ellis, Tony Ellis, 'The Golly' and Stan Freeman, David Gardener and 'Giro' and the footballer Lou Macari were all there. All through the evening people kept on coming up to Frank's table and bringing him bottles of vodka, champagne or claret, sitting down and having a drink and a few minutes' chat and then moving on. Poor old Stan Carnell, who once saw a flying saucer from his cell one night, was there as well. Frank had also seen it from his cell, but they didn't dare tell anyone in case they thought he was really mad. But later it was in the papers. It must have been some sort of comet. Stan brought over half a dozen bottles of champagne. I was sorry to hear he's just got 10 years in Scotland over some drugs. That night really was like the wedding scene in *The Godfather* – people rightly paying tribute to Frank and his status amongst them. I went on and sang before the real cabaret, who was that brilliant comedian Franklin James, and this is what opened the last programme of the *Underworld* series. I was so sorry to hear that Franklin died of cancer last year.

The programmes got a lot of stick, but many people did find the series a good documentary. No one had ever tried to do anything like that before. Lorraine Heggesey and Frank Symonds produced it and all those on the team were great people. When the BBC do a documentary, they do it well and fully research it. They must do because they are masters at the game, although television on all channels has come on as well.

The timing for the book and series couldn't have been better. Frank got asked to do radio interviews up and down the country. Alex Stein, the boxing promoter, got him up to a charity boxing do in Leeds, and at the book signings all over the country there were queues miles long.

It was then that I got taken ill and had to go to hospital for a hysterectomy. Reggie and Ronnie Kray sent their best wishes and Ronnie sent me a beautiful bouquet as well. It's funny how after all these years when Frank was meant to be their arch-enemy that they turned out such good friends. I was under a top gynaecologist, Mr Setchell. Apparently he was one of the Queen's consultants, so at least I was in good hands.

After Frank had been to see me, the girl Linda in the next bed to me said, 'I know that man who's been visiting you, that's Reggie Kray.' I said, 'Reg? No, it's Frankie Fraser, my partner.' 'Oh yeah, he's that mad one!' I said, 'Well, does he seem mad to you?' She replied, 'No, in fact he's a lovely gentleman. In fact my husband's in one of Her Majesty's prisons but he's nearly at the end of his sentence though.' 'Really, what prison? Latchmere House?' That's where people finishing their sentence often go on day release. She said, 'No, Maidstone.' Margaret, the woman across the ward, was grinning. She was rather well spoken and she said, 'I work for Her Majesty.' I said, 'Are you the governor at Holloway then?' She burst out laughing and said, 'Oh, my God, no! I work for one of the ladies-in-waiting.' I said to her, 'Oh, not one of the ladies of the night up in Soho?' She tut-tutted and said, 'No! At

Buckingham Palace.' At that Linda laughed and said, 'Marilyn, please don't make me laugh, I have still got my stitches in.'

When Frank visited again, all the patients in our ward and their friends were coming up in their nightdresses asking for his autograph. I wouldn't have minded, but Frank is not the greatest hospital visitor. He was 'in and out', but he did come up every day, bless him. I told him to stay and get on with promoting his book, but he said, 'No.'

I remember feeling very tearful after the hysterectomy thinking, I'm only 41; now all I'm going to be is a granny. But then I was watching Richard and Judy's *This Morning* show and they had on Lily Savage. I think it was the first time he had been on their show. I'd just finished crying and feeling blue when Lily came on. In fact, Richard and Judy were on top form that morning; they are such a funny pair. Lily, he just had me in stitches. It was one of the best shows I had ever seen on *This Morning*, and from that moment on I picked up. Thanks, Richard, Judy and Lily.

The consultant came round to tell me that everything was fine and I could go home. I thanked him for doing a good job and thanked him or whoever done the stitching. Frank thanked him too, saying, 'You've made such a good job of it, Mr Setchell, that I wish you had been on our firm in the Sixties.' He laughed.

I had to spend a month resting – and to get me to lie in bed unless I've got a hangover was really hard. Frank and I had been invited to do a pilot show for a detective quiz show that Johnny Vaughan was doing. The idea was that a copper and a villain or writer had to team up and solve a robbery or a murder. Frank was paired up with Brian Hilliard who'd been a copper and the editor of *Police Review*, and for a bit I was afraid Frank wouldn't talk to him; but when it came to it, they got on really well and won their heat. The show was on a boat down on the River Thames. We had to be there at 12 noon, but we were a bit late and as we got on the boat there was no one about but only empty bottles of champagne and streamers. It looked as if they had had a real drink-up. I was moaning and saying to Frank, 'I told you it was Greenwich Pier and not Tower Pier; they've finished the pre-cocktail party without us.' He told me to stop moaning, and that we had probably got the time mixed up, instead of 12 noon it was probably last night. As we were walking around somebody from the production company popped his head up and said, 'Hi, I'm Jeremy, Mr Vaughan's researcher, we are all down here.'

As we got downstairs the cameramen, make-up people and other guests were all drinking cups of coffee. We said our hellos, then Johnny Vaughan said, 'It won't be long; the set is being put up. These are your lines, Frank – and, Marilyn, you just pretend you're drinking champagne as if it's a cocktail party.' When we told him what we thought had happened everybody just laughed. Unfortunately the series never took off, though.

So you see, everybody is human and in life you have to have a sense of humour. I like that saying of Frank Sinatra's, 'Never trust a person who doesn't drink.'

A couple of years ago the 21st birthday party for Charlie Richardson and his wife Ronnie's daughter was being held on a boat at Greenwich and naturally we were invited. Steven Berkoff was there along with James Booth and John Daly, the film producer who made *The Last Emperor*, as well as Richard Harris. John Daly's Uncle George was a boxer and the Daly family all grew up in Frank's neighbourhood and were well known to each other. John had asked Frank a couple of years before that if he could do the film of his book, so we were getting really excited. John mentioned Gary Oldman as playing Frank well before Gary's career really took off. I was over the moon, seeing that Gary came from New Cross.

I was looking forward to the film being made and maybe having a small part, but we are still waiting. I suppose we should have realised. After all, when Frank was in Leicester prison all those years ago with Dad there was talk of Richard Burton playing him in a film, but nothing came of it. And poor Lennie McLean – his film was on and off for years before he died. Unfortunately this film game seems to really take time. I'm pleased to say Gary's *Nil By Mouth* did well because I could relate to that. I had seen my father hit my mother like that while under the influence of the bad cocaine habit that he once had. I'm pleased to say that he has finished with all that crap now, and after all the troubles they've been through one way and another, they are now a really devoted couple.

I too have had a bad coke habit and a crack habit too. I lost a lot of my self-respect on and off during the last 15 to 20 years. I was a powder addict more than anything else. Whilst I was in the States I was spending $1,000 a week. All I can say is this, for young girls reading this book, that I lost quite a lot of respect for myself, especially when my father was sent to prison for the second time. I drank so as to hide and cut out the grief I was feeling. For what? All this drug business does is just cause misery and pain to yourself, your children, friends and parents. If you look at where your hard-earned money is ending up, it just seems pointless. But there again it's like any legal drugs today – and by that I mean cigarettes and alcohol. They're a waste of money really.

Well, I got really carried away with Frank's two books and how well they had done. I was thrilled, when there was serious talk of the film, especially to think that I was the one who had pushed him to write the books in the first place. I knew our money problem with the bankruptcy would be solved. But we're still waiting. It has taken me all this time to understand that motto, 'Don't count your chickens until they are hatched.' The other thing I never realised was that certain people would be so jealous of a man who had done over 40 years in prison.

Frank and I experienced this not only with complete strangers but also our own people. We would understand it from these do-gooders of our so-called society – the ones who take home their office stationery and use the company's telephone to phone their Aunt Elsie who lives in Canada, or cheat their expenses by £10 per week – but to take being completely left out in the cold by his own has been hard.

Time and time again Frank has said to the media and people who've asked him, 'I went down the road I chose to. Now I've paid my debt to society.' Surely you have to shake his hand for being so honest. Yet recently there have been at least seven gangster films in the making. So it's OK for your greedy film-makers to feed off the likes of Frank Fraser, Ronnie and Reg Kray, the Train Robbers and the Richardsons and their stories, but it's not all right for them to earn some legit money to stay out of trouble. And what about Jonathan Aitken? He involves his own daughter in perjury, and five minutes after he comes out of prison the media are all over him. It's all double standards.

When Frank's first book, *Mad Frank*, was selling very well, I begged him to go on holiday to Cancun. He's not a great traveller but finally he agreed. Once we arrived people at the airport were taking photos of him. I think we were also having our photographs taken by some of the Mexican or English police. This guy was following us everywhere, a typical undercover. He had a wife with him, but you only saw her every so often during the course of the day, unless she was teaching an aeroplane-load of Japanese tourists scuba diving. Señor 'El Gringo' was his nickname. We kept waving to him and laughing until one day I turned round to him and said, 'Next time, tell your superiors that you really do need to take more money on a vacation and get some more new shirts.' With his typical football shirts on he tried to act like a guy from South London, but you could smell him out from a mile. Maybe I wouldn't have sussed him if it had been on the Costa Del Sol in Marbella or Puerto Banus, but 3,000 miles away in Mexico, he just didn't look part of the élite set of Cancun.

One day in 1999 Frank got a telephone call from a young lady, Claire, from an advertising company. She wanted to speak to me, to ask me if I would like to open at The Kabaret. Claire told me that was a spot off Regent Street; in fact it was where that old night-club Murray's had been. I managed to get Alan Berry – a piano player, who had accompanied Frank and me when we did a show over in Dublin at the Andrews Lane Theatre – for the Monday night. It was a rushed opportunity, but we managed to get our act together. In fact the paint was still wet when I got to the venue on that first opening night. As I approached the club, I knew Alan would have a hard job finding it as they had told me it was in Beak Street but, in actual fact, the entrance was in Upper John Street.

It was a cold evening and there I was standing in my fur coat waiting for him; like me, other people were looking for the entrance. So after I found it and as I was standing there I was pointing out the entrance to anyone who asked and a couple thanked me; it was Camilla Parker-Bowles' brother-in-law. Then I thought a blonde girl I saw was a friend of mine from

Islington; in fact I thought it was a barmaid who had worked with us at the horse-racing.

'Oh, hello,' I said, but the girl looked at me as if I was a ghost and then I realised I had got the wrong person. It was Meg Matthews who was with her close friend Fran Cutler. She was ever so nice and didn't mug me off when I realised my mistake.

I then knew that it was going to be quite an opening night, and this was when my nerves started. Alan pulled up and got his electric piano out with the help of the doormen. They strapped it to a pulley on wheels, with the piano in a large container. As Alan and the doormen were lifting it downstairs I said to him, 'You've left this poor guy's arms and legs sticking out.'

The stars were arriving. There were no dressing-rooms at all and I went into the ladies' room to change. As I say, the paint was still wet and half my fur coat stuck to the wall. My friend Michael Jennings had come to give me some support as Frank had to do a show up North that night, and I was glad of his company. I'd met Michael when he came on one of Frank's gangland tours.

The sound system wasn't good at all. By the time I went on stage Noël Gallagher had turned up and there was Goldie, Natasha (Michael Caine's daughter), Tom Parker-Bowles and James, Jimmy Tarbuck's son, who were all nice and friendly. When I began I said, 'If I had known all of you lot were coming, I would have asked Count Basie to have accompanied me. I honestly didn't know till the last minute.'

Noël Gallagher and Meg Matthews were really hospitable and made me feel like one of the family. It was a great evening. When we left at 2 a.m. I went out of that place floating and the rest of that week went well. Frank came on the Thursday night. Camilla's sister was there unbeknown to us, and this time the crowd was an older one. In fact it was the best crowd to sing to. People that could appreciate the old Cole Porter numbers and Rogers and Hammerstein. I was hoping to meet Prince William and Prince Harry, as a whisper went round that Prince William was going to pop in, so I could sing that song 'I've Got a Crush on You, Sweety-Pie', a Frank Sinatra number, but he did not come down. Yes, that week was full of interesting showbiz, Piers Adams introduced me to Guy Ritchie, the screen writer and producer of *Lock, Stock and Two Smoking Barrels*. They were all a good crowd and made me feel welcome. I have to say that in all the week I was down there I never saw anyone taking any drugs. In fact later on when the media had a go at Tom Parker-Bowles, I said, 'I didn't see anything like that, they were all enjoying the champagne and dancing.'

One night Chris – a friend of Mark Laurenson, the old Liverpool footballer – came to hear me sing. Later we went down to the K-Bar in Wardour Street. This particular night my feet were very hot, we were drinking champagne and I said, 'I'm sorry but I have to sit down.' 'What's the problem?' I explained and said, 'I feel like putting my feet in that ice bucket.' So Chris said, 'Go on then.' He took the champagne out of the ice bucket and I put my feet in one at a time. It was heaven. Everybody laughed when Debbie, who owns Kudos Productions, told me who he was friendly with and I said, 'Oh, don't worry, we are all humans.' My medical problems were soon solved.

I'd always wanted to meet Ronnie Biggs. His wife Charmaine had been one of my Mum's friends and he was the only one of the Train Robbers I'd never seen. Of course I'd read a lot about him and Frank had been on the radio with him to congratulate him after the Brazilian government refused to extradite him back to England. So when I sold my flat in 1998 and paid off the debts and had a few quid over, I got on a plane and went to see him. Well, actually, American Express had kindly given me and Frank a Gold Card, so I put it on that. I asked Frank if he wanted to come, but he said he wasn't much for travelling; then I asked a friend, Pat, but she wasn't well. So in the end I went on my own.

Ronnie knew I was coming but he didn't have room to put me up. I was booked in the Copacabana, but when I saw how skint Ronnie was I decided to stay somewhere cheaper and treat him. I'd leave my three-star and walk over and use the Copacabana's pool and things. If you put on a face, no one challenges you. It was just like that time in Fort Lauderdale all those years ago.

That was when I nearly got mugged by a cute little blond boy who came up to me, begging. He had such an angelic face that I opened my bag and was about to give him three dollars or so when his face changed and he pulled out a Stanley knife. I had the bag on my shoulder and I swung it at him saying, 'You fucking little bastard! I'll tell your mother' – same as I'd do to a kid here who tried it on. There was an old Brazilian guy who waved the kid away, but when I walked on to some traffic lights there's the kid following me again. This time I was really angry and when I saw two police patrolmen I yelled, '*Policia, policia!*' But in a way it was more to warn him off than to get their attention. I didn't want him arrested. They shoot street kids there, don't they? But I was really shaken up.

I was in Rio for three weeks and I saw Ronnie nearly every day. He took me to see pre-Carnival samba competitions and one day we was walking through one of the markets and he found a crystal glass train engine. He bought it for me, saying

I must have it as Charmaine had one exactly like it. I've got it at home on the television.

Just before I left I took Ronnie out for dinner and we had a terrific evening. I sang with the band and American Express bought us loads of Crystal champagne. I was telling him he should come back, but he wouldn't have any of it. I said, 'You're not in top health. Now, you wouldn't even do seven years.' But he wouldn't listen. Two weeks later he had that first stroke. I rang him and said I hoped it wasn't all the champagne and he really should think about home, but he only laughed.

Poor Ronnie, I've heard that now he's had another stroke and can't really speak. When it comes to it, the Train's done no good for any of them.

I have travelled all over the world, Asia, South America, the Caribbean, all magnificent in their own uniqueness, but for me there are only two countries that have pure beauty and character and they are Scotland and Ireland. Even the people reflect the beauty of their countryside, so us English have a lot to really answer for. Over centuries you are what your Government are.

Frank and I got invited to the Fraser clan gathering which has been held for the last twenty years in Scotland. To be honest, we didn't go because Frank really thought that the Lovats and Frasers lived in this most beautiful castle and wouldn't want the bad publicity. Plus, I have to admit we were a bit skint. Then, on 18 May 1999, we were invited up to Edinburgh for radio interviews. It was then, half as a joke, I said to Frank, tell them you're up to visit your clan, the Frasers. These friends of ours said that if we wanted to go they would take us, as it was 40 minutes to Castle Fraser. Well, we couldn't believe the weather which was glorious, the first bit of sunshine we had seen in Scotland on that visit. We stopped for lunch at a lovely little hotel and then drove to Castle Fraser. It took my breath away. As Frank was walking towards the castle with his friend Colin, I was looking up at the mighty tower and shouting, 'Frank! Frank! You've locked me out!' as if I'd left my keys. The funny part was that back when Frank did a show at the Old Red Lion Hotel in Border country, the owners had given both Frank and me lovely woollen Fraser clan scarves, and I was wearing mine. Although the sun was shining there was still a slight crisp cold wind, so I was delighted I could wear this tartan scarf with pride. As we entered the tour reception I felt so happy to be able to tell the kind lady (Merlyn her name was) that Frank was a Fraser. She looked at him with a slightly inquisitive look, and then when she frowned I said, 'It's OK, he's not only the bad one of them. He's also mad.' When they asked Frank to write something in the book he put down, 'It's better here than in Broadmoor.' And he was right.

Sometimes I think my family would prefer me to be with someone more my own age, but since I'm so complicated maybe Frank's the only one who'll put up with me. Certainly he's been the longest-lasting of all my men. It's a shame we can't turn the clock back and wave a magic wand so as to be nearer in age. Then if he'd met me he wouldn't have gone through all that. If he'd had just one good tickle and I'd been with him I'd have put it to some good use in a business, but as they say better late than never.

People say to me, 'What are you going to do when Frank goes?' It's a reasonable question. After all, he is thirty years older than I am. But I think he's indestructible. He'll be shovelling the dirt over me rather than the other way around.

A lot of the others have gone – Danny Magano who helped me so much in Palm Springs, and Arturo, Frank Sinatra's valet.

Once when Frank Sinatra was coming through London he said he wanted to meet me. Arturo rang up and said could I get to Heathrow, but I'd promised Jonathan and half a dozen of his friends to take them to Parliament Fields Lido to swim. And you can't disappoint young kids. Arturo told me later that I'd been paged to go to the VIP lounge, but you can't hear things like that if you're on Hampstead Heath and there weren't mobile phones then. At least I got to meet Frank later with Mum and Dad. Rina is still alive. Of course, she's not that old but she's retired and is living in San Francisco. I still see Jenny from Palm Springs days; she's living in Kent. I've lost touch with Gill Hussey and also with June Edwards. Buster's family still has the flower stall at Waterloo though.

I don't really know what happened to Kelly. We did sort of kiss and make up before I left America. It's funny though. When Frank was down in Southend signing his paperback *Mad Frank and Friends*, in which I did a short chapter, a woman was leafing through it and she told him she was English and she knew Kelly from Palm Springs.

Jenny came back to England before me. She'd split up with her boyfriend and she was really miserable. On the flight she'd treated herself to business class and there was a smart executive sitting next to her. They got chatting and when they arrived in London, he said he'd carry her bag for her. Next thing they'd both been nicked by the Customs and are being searched for drugs. They kept them for about six hours before they let them go. 'Poor bloke,' said Jenny. 'All he does is try to help me and he ends up over a table with a finger up his arse.' I don't think she ever saw him again.

Danny the dog's gone as well. He got really ill back at the end of 1998, and he was getting so old. Frank and me took him to the vet at the Blue Cross in Victoria, and when we handed him over he must have had this intuition about what was happening to him and he started struggling. He fought like a little tiger to get away. It half-way broke my heart.

He was another member of the family who'd done a bit of bird. When Mum and Dad gave up the Traf they took a motel in Palm Springs. They thought they were going to stay for ever and so they had Danny over with them. He was a game little thing. Their motel was at the edge of the desert and he used to trot off all by himself: he'd go miles. Then one day their friend Fat Willie asked where Danny was and when Mum told him he'd gone out for his toilet, Willie said he shouldn't be allowed to roam because of the coyotes. Fat Willie had one of the same breed called Pebbles. He'd had a little diamond-studded collar and the coyotes had got him. All they found was the collar and bits of fur stuck to the cactuses. After that Mum wouldn't let Danny out of her sight.

Mum didn't like it over there and so she came back. Tom wanted to stay, but she said it was the motel or her so Dad sold up and Danny came back into quarantine. The place reminded me of High Down. Danny was in 'B' wing; I'd go and visit him in the kennels every weekend. He couldn't bear to let me out at the end of the visit and one day he squeezed through my legs and was off. It caused a great deal of trouble because the other dogs started throwing themselves against their cages and one big dog managed to get out and began fighting with Danny. I called out for one of the kennelmaids and she broke them up. She was terrified someone would find out and she'd lose her job. I'm glad quarantine's being scrapped.

Reggie Kray was the only person I'd go and see in prison. Strangely, I never met Ronnie Kray, but I often spoke to him on the phone when he rang Frank and he would always acknowledge me in his short and sweet letters. He even sent me a beautiful flower arrangement when I was in Homerton Hospital having my hysterectomy. Charlie was a very sweet gentleman with a lovely smile. Poor Charlie died in April 2000. A few days before Charlie died Frank and I had been down to see Reggie in Parkhurst, and we'd meant to go and see Charlie who was in hospital on the Island but by then he was too weak. I'll never believe he was involved in dealing in cocaine. I remember when Rina was over and we went to a do for Reggie at a night-club in Homerton, she wanted some cocaine. I mentioned it to Charlie and he flew at me; he jumped down my throat as if I'd robbed a bank.

It was funny when we were at Portsmouth that day waiting for the ferry. Frank said this place had one of his happiest memories. I thought he must be talking about his youngest son who was a professional footballer, but no, or even because of the day we'd first gone out together. What he meant was that this was where he brought his football team, the Soho Rangers, when they came to play the inmates at Parkhurst.

Of course we went to Charlie's funeral. Frank said it was bigger even than Ronnie's. We were in the fifth car of seventeen and Frank sat at the front of the church with Reggie. He also called for three cheers for Reggie as he come out of the church, and again at the grave, and both times he got a big response. Reggie made sure Frank and me were near him the whole time. We kept getting separated in the crowd and he'd be calling out, 'Frank, Frank'. I threw a red rose into the open grave. Charlie Richardson came, which was a nice gesture seeing how they was meant to have been deadly enemies.

My godfather, Freddie Foreman, was at the undertaker's but I wouldn't shake his hand – not after he appeared on a television programme with that grass Albert Donoghue who actually gave evidence against him at the Mitchell trial. I just can't understand how Fred of all the stand-up people could go on telly with Donoghue and admit he'd been right all those years. Fred asked why I wouldn't shake his hand and I said I was ashamed of him. Fred didn't have any shame, though; he just went and hugged Reggie as though nothing had happened.

I'll never forget when we visited Reggie one day in Maidstone and he said we could expect a little present the next week. We had to go over to Dublin to do shows at the Andrew Lane Theatre and as we weren't being paid until the end of the week we were skint. All sorts of people were at the shows, including the man they called 'The General', Martin Cahill, and a lot of celebrities such as Dermot Morgan who played Father Ted. We were invited out to after-show dinners and we were worried that we wouldn't be able to pay our share or afford to invite them out the next night. Then one morning there was a registered envelope and when Frank opened it there were sixteen £50 notes that Reggie had sent us. We both had big grins and chorused, 'God Bless Reggie!' To his dying day he never knew how much we needed the money – £200 would have been enough.

I didn't go and see Reggie after he came out of prison and he was dying up in Norfolk but Frank did. He went up unexpected and the moment he arrived Reggie's friend Bradley Allardyce was actually on the phone asking if Frank could visit. Reggie was asking for me to come and sing him the Sinatra and Tony Bennett songs he loved but, by then, it was too late.

As he was the last of the brothers the funeral was much more subdued, but there were still a lot of friends and faces there, including Joey Pyle and Roy Shaw as well as my friends Brian Emmett and Arthur Sutty. The service was lovely with

'Morning Has Broken' and 'Fight the Good Fight' as the hymns. It seems so strange and sad now they're all gone.

Funnily enough my boy Jonathan is courting Victoria, Michael Corbett's niece. Victoria was the first baby to be born in Holloway Prison. She made history. I am thrilled to say that I am also a grandmother-to-be.

My cousin Johnny eventually married Michael's sister Megan and they had two daughters. Life's full of coincidences. 'Blind' Tom Corbett went to St Patrick's School, the same one where Frank went. That family came out of Ethlan Street at the back of The Cut, which in the 1920s was one of what Frank calls 'Kill 'em and eat 'em streets'. It was known as Effing and Blinding Street amongst the locals.

Why do women stay with men who are in and out of prison, and why do they go out with them in the first place? I think they like the excitement. Also they like men who are at home and not out every day on a 9–5 boring job. It's also having a bundle of money to spend. It's different, a different way of life. Then there's the freedom. You'll be skint for nine months and the man can more or less guarantee one touch a year and that'll take care of everything.

Looking back when things are analysed, however, the money they get from the robberies only averages about £300 a month. If they looked at it like that maybe they'd change their minds, but they never think they're going to get caught and there's always going to be that one big hit. Basically it's just a waste of time for the amount of bird they get. You've got to do one big job and take a chance – that's what I'd have done if I'd been a man. You've got to aim for that pot of gold.

I would not have wanted my child to go through with the criminal life and having a parent in and out of prison all the time. For all of you young people, think twice, and if you're a man who is thinking of taking the road to crime, please do not have children or get married. Full stop. It is not fair to your children to grow up and visit their father in those terrible places called prisons, and it's not fair to your wife, girlfriend or mother. At the end of the day it's not just you that suffers. Everyone does.

But when I was writing this book I asked my father if, in retrospect, he'd have wanted to be married at the age of 22 and have a family, and spend 20 years of his life in prison. Tom looked at me with his lovely blue eyes and made no comment.

Index

Index

Index

Index

251

Index